THE
SCOTTISH
QUIZ
BOOK

THE
SCOTTISH
QUIZ
BOOK

GEDDES & GROSSET

First published 2002 by Geddes & Grosset

© 2002 Geddes & Grosset,
David Dale House, New Lanark, ML11 9DJ, Scotland

ISBN 1 84205 098 2

Printed and bound in Europe

Contents

QUESTIONS

General Knowledge 1

1 Where is the Queen's View?
2 How many Scottish members sat in Parliament after the Act of Union in 1707?
3 In which century did Balmoral Castle come into the possession of the Royal Family?
4 Which ruined Scottish castle is said to have inspired Bram Stoker?
5 Where is the Scottish Lead Mining museum?
6 What was the profession of John Kibble, who erected the Kibble Palace in Glasgow?
7 With which Scottish island is the name of the author Gavin Maxwell associated?
8 Where is the Angus Folk Museum?
9 Some people believe that Pontius Pilate was born in Scotland. Where is he said to have been born?
10 Where are the Falls of Braan?
11 In which city is the Rosemount Viaduct?
12 What is the name of the steam railway that operates out of Aviemore?
13 Why does the earth move in the village of Comrie?
14 What is the Larthorn of the North?
15 Near which village on the north coast is Smoo Cave?
16 Where is Flora MacDonald buried?
17 Name the musician who was voted Scotswoman of the Decade in 1990.
18 Which building in Haddington is known as 'the Lamp of the Lothians'?
19 What was the name of the medieval murder-mystery film in which Sean Connery starred in 1986?
20 What was the name of the world's first paddle-steamer, built on the Clyde in 1812?
21 Which famous Scottish painter lived in Howden House in Livingston?
22 Near which town in Dumfries and Galloway is The Motte of Ur?
23 Which famous Scottish writer is buried at Dryburgh Abbey?
24 In which Scottish castle did Madonna and guy Ritchie tie the knot?
25 By which name was Port Glasgow once known?

Answers: p174

1 What was Scotland's most important export in the mid-eighteenth century?
2 Which two Scottish cities were centres of the whaling industry in Scotland?
3 Which city was once the biggest tobacco trading port in Great Britain?
4 What was the dominant textile industry in the first half of the nineteenth century in Scotland?
5 Where on mainland Scotland is the centre of the whisky distilling industry?
6 What part of Scotland is famous for its commercial soft fruit growing?
7 Where did whisky blender Johnny Walker first set up shop?
8 In which town in Scotland was George Sandeman (of Sandeman's Port) born?
9 Which two names in whisky are associated with Perth?
10 What was the name of the Scottish grocer who made his name and fortune in the tea trade in the nineteenth century?
11 In which village in Scotland was the Bonawe iron furnace?
12 Which company pioneered the brewing of lager in Scotland?
13 What was produced at the Dens works?
14 Where is the Baxters foods company based?
15 What was the Camperdown Works?
16 Where was the Singer sewing machine factory based in Scotland?
17 In which year did the Ravenscraig Steelworks open?
18 Where was the Seafield Colliery?
19 Which two industries were based at Prestonpans?
20 Where in central Scotland was the shale-oil industry based?
21 When was Ravenscraig finally closed down?
22 When did the Linwood car plant open?
23 Which company bought over Bell's Whisky in the 1980s?
24 What were the St Rollox works?
25 In which city was the Timex factory?

Answers: p174

Sport 1

1 Which swimmer won an Olympic gold medal for the 200 metres breaststroke in 1976?
2 Name the Scottish racing driver who was world champion in 1971.
3 Which Scottish runner became the oldest winner of the 100 metre sprint in the Olympic Games in 1980?
4 In which year was Bill McLaren awarded the Freedom of Scottish Rugby?
5 Name the Scottish racing driver and former world champion who was born in 1936.
6 With which sport is the name of Willie Auchterlonie associated?
7 Where was the Millennium British Open golf championship held?
8 With which sport is the name of Benny Lynch associated?
9 In which month of the year is the Ben Nevis race traditionally held?
10 Which world-class Scottish snooker player was born in Edinburgh in 1969?
11 Who was the first Scot to become World Rally Champion?
12 Which sport do the Scottish Claymores play?
13 Which Scottish golfer won the British Open in 1985?
14 Which Scottish jockey won the Derby in 1979 on Troy?
15 Which Scot won the 1999 British Open?
16 Name the gold medal-winning Scots yachtswoman of the 2000 Olympics.
17 Who made the fastest female marathon debut in the New York Marathon in 1991?
18 In which athletics event did Alan Wells compete before he took up sprinting?
19 With which Edinburgh swimming club did David Wilkie train?
20 When was Stewart Grand Prix sold to Ford?
21 Which Scottish rugby international broke the record held by Andy Irvine for point scoring for Scotland in international matches?
22 Who became the youngest-ever winner of the Embassy World Snooker Championship in 1990?
23 Where did Alex Ferguson begin his career as a football manager?
24 What is Olympic pentathlon champion Stephanie Cook's connection with Scotland?
25 In which year was Kenny Dalglish asked to manage Liverpool?

Answers: p175

1   What is the name of the real village which is the location for 'Glendarroch' in *High Road*, and where is it?

2   Which television comedy show spawned the catchphrase 'Gonnae no dae that?'?

3   Which Scottish chef and television personality had a Wild Harvest?

4   Name the Scotsman who starred in *One Foot in the Grave*.

5   What was the name of the lugubrious minister played by Rikki Fulton on television?

6   On which channel did Rab C. Nesbitt appear?

7   Name the Scottish comedian and footballer who co-hosted a series of chat shows with Fred Macaulay.

8   Which Scottish presenter fronted *Left Right and Centre*?

9   Name the Scot who moved from *Blue Peter* to *Wheel of Fortune*.

10 Who presented *Scottish Women*?

11 With which news programme is Jackie Bird associated?

12 Which young television presenter made a show of herself on the houses of Westminster?

13 With which kind of television programme is Hazel Irvine associated?

14 Name the presenter of *The White Heather Club*.

15 In which Scottish village was the TV series *Hamish MacBeth* filmed?

16 Where was Ronnie Corbett born?

17 Who played the lead role in *Cracker*?

18 In which TV comedy series did Fulton Mackay co-star with Ronnie Barker?

19 Who presented *Cartoon Cavalcade*?

20 Who sang the the theme tune for *Hazell*?

21 Which Scot presented *Red Alert*, the National Lottery Show?

22 Which character in the second series of *Dr Finlay* was played by Ian Bannen?

23 Who wrote *Tutti Frutti*?

24 Which young Scot moved from the *High Road* to the *Crow Road*?

25 Which actor starred in the 1970s series *Callan* as Lonely?

Answers: p175

General Knowledge 2

1   Who founded Sweetheart Abbey?
2   Who became Colonel-in-Chief of the Queen's Own Cameron Highlanders in 1953?
3   What hobby might you pursue at Barns Ness, near Dunbar?
4   Who painted *The Village Politicians* in 1806?
5   A memorial to the writer Gavin Maxwell stands in Monreith Bay near Port William. What form does this memorial take?
6   In which village in Strathclyde are four of the daughters of Robert Burns buried?
7   Name the industrialist and philanthropist who wrote *The Gospel of Wealth*.
8   What television comedy part is Gregor Fisher best known for?
9   Where did John Dewar first set up shop?
10 In which Angus seaside town is there a bell called Big Peter?
11 Where is the Merrymass fair held?
12 Where is the oldest example of a mercat cross still in its original site?
13 Beneath which hills are King Arthur and his knights said to rest?
14 Name the loch by which stands Tibbie Shiel's Inn.
15 Which family of industrialists is associated with the town of Paisley?
16 Where in Lothian was a children's village created by Mrs Stirling Boyd?
17 Which cathedral in Strathclyde claims to be the smallest cathedral in Europe?
18 In which decade did drilling for oil begin in the North Sea?
19 What do the initials SSPCK stand for?
20 Who was the last Scottish king to speak Gaelic?
21 Where were the Churchill Barriers erected during the Second World War?
22 In which region are the Sands of Forvie?
23 To the nearest five miles, how long is the West Highland Way?
24 What do Crieff, Dunblane and Peebles have in common?
25 Who, in the seventeenth century, is said to have predicted the building of the Caledonian Canal?

Answers: p176

1 Who wrote *The Brus*?

2 Name the Scottish poet who wrote 'The Thrissil and the Rois' while serving as a courtier to James IV.

3 Where was Edwin Morgan born?

4 Which Scottish poet was also a skilled translator and collaborated with his wife on a translation of the works of Franz Kafka?

5 Which Scots poet published a collection of work entitled *Loaves and Fishes*?

6 Which poet and playwright published *True Confessions and New Clichés*?

7 What was the title of Kilmarnock edition of Robert Burns's poetry?

8 What was the major work of Blind Harry?

9 Which Scottish poet died at Penzance in 1909?

10 Which Gaelic poet received the Queen's Gold Medal for Poetry in 1990?

11 Which eighteenth-century Edinburgh poet wrote 'Auld Reekie'?

12 Who collaborated with Sorley Maclean to produce *Seventeen Poems for Sixpence* in 1940?

13 Which famous noble soldier wrote the following lines?
'He either fears his fate too much
Or his deserts are small
Who dares not put it to the touch
To win or lose it all.'

14 Who published *A Kist o' Whistles* in 1947?

15 Who was Robert Burns's 'Clarinda'?

16 Who published *Lays of the Scottish Cavaliers* and *Poland, Homer and Other Poems*?

17 Where was Norman MacCaig born?

18 Who wrote *The Kingis Quair* ?

19 Who wrote the children's poem 'The Land of Counterpane'?

20 Which Scottish poet worked as an exciseman?

21 Where was James Hogg born?

22 Who wrote 'The Ballad of the D-Day Landings'?

23 Which poet wrote three *Hymns to Lenin*?

24 Which poet published collections entitled *A Man In My Position* and *The Equal Skies*?

25 What was the title of Edwin Morgan's first published collection of poetry?

Answers: p176

Wildlife 1

1   What is the Latin name for the Spear Thistle, emblem of Scotland?

2   What does the name 'capercaillie' mean?

3   What is the main food of grouse?

4   Which small animal, farmed for over twenty years in Scotland, has escaped into the wild in great numbers over time and now poses a significant threat to many species of wildlife?

5   What is Scotland's largest wild animal?

6   What kind of tree can be seen flourishing particularly well in Rothiemurchus Forest?

7   What kind of bird overwinters on Islay, causing disputes between conservationists and islanders?

8   What is machair?

9   Where do the Sika deer in Scotland originate from?

10 Where did the ospreys return to in Scotland?

11 In which decade were reindeer reintroduced to Scotland?

12 Which species of squirrel is larger, the native red or the import from America, the grey?

13 Which two main rivers in Scotland are sources of freshwater mussels that contain pearls?

14 Why is the blue hare so called?

15 Where is the Scottish wildcat most commonly found?

16 What is a Scotch Argus?

17 Which one of Scotland's lochs has the largest number of fish species?

18 Which Scottish nature reserve was the first nature reserve to be established in Britain?

19 What was the first tree to become established in Scotland after the Ice Age?

20 What is the botanical name for Scots Pine?

21 In which century did wolves finally disappear from Scotland?

22 Where was the last great auk killed?

23 Name the only bird that is unique to Scotland.

24 Where on Scotland's coastline can bottle-nosed dolphins still be seen?

25 Which relative of the weasel was exterminated in Scotland by the end of the nineteenth century?

Answers: p177

The Life & Works of Sir Walter Scott

QUESTIONS

1   Which school in Edinburgh did Sir Walter Scott attend?

2   What ailment struck Scott when he was a young child?

3   When was the *Minstrelsy* first published in a three-volume edition?

4   What were the names of Scott's four brothers?

5   Which literary figure did Scott meet at Adam Ferguson's house when he was 15?

6   What is the name of the female character who faces execution in *Heart of Midlothian*?

7   What is the name of the place where Scott spent much of his early childhood with his parents?

8   How old was Scott when he first went to university?

9   To whom did Scott dedicate the poem *The Field of Waterloo*?

10   In which century is *Kenilworth* set?

11   Where did Scott move to from Lasswade in 1804?

12   In which year was *Guy Mannering* first published?

13   By which name was Robert Paterson known?

14   Which important event did Scott attend in July 1821?

15   Name the hero of *The Antiquary*.

16   After the visit of George IV to Scotland, what moveable feature of Edinburgh Castle, removed to the Tower of London in 1745, was returned at Scott's request?

17   In which work does the character of John Mowbray feature?

18   When did Scott marry?

19   What was the name of Scott's wife?

20   What is the name of the play by Goethe translated by Scott and published in 1799?

21   What was the title of the work (unpublished) that Scott was working on in his final months?

22   In which novel do Torquil of the Oak and Oliver Proudfute appear?

23   Whom did Scott's son Walter marry?

24   How many (surviving) sons did Scott have?

25   With which two brothers did Scott set up a publishing firm?

Answers: p177

General Knowledge 3

1   Who became head of the House of Stuart after the death of Bonnie Prince Charlie?
2   How is the Signal Tower in Arbroath used nowadays?
3   Which saint came to Scotland before St Columba and established churches on Iona, Mull and Tiree?
4   When was the first printing press established in Edinburgh?
5   The chief of which clan was given the title Buichaille nan Eileanan (Shepherd of the Isles)?
6   Who was the master of Greyfriars Bobby?
7   Who was the first detective in Chicago?
8   Which art gallery in Edinburgh houses the Paolozzi Collection?
9   Where and when was the Revised Book of Common Prayer for Scotland read in public for the first time?
10 What was the name of James VI's scholarly but brutal tutor?
11 Where was the first British Open Golf Championship held?
12 What was the fate of the architect who designed the Scott monument in Edinburgh?
13 In which trade did the artist Sir Henry Raeburn originally train?
14 What was the name given to the area which included Argyll, Kintyre and nearby islands when Kenneth McAlpin came to the throne?
15 Where was Captain Kidd born?
16 Who led the troops who burnt the Campbell stronghold of Inveraray to the ground in 1644?
17 Who founded the Advocate's Library in Edinburgh?
18 Where is the oldest working mill in Scotland?
19 In which borders village is Tibbie Shiel buried?
20 Where are 'The Twa Brigs'?
21 Where was Scottish racing driver Jim Clark born?
22 Which Scottish city once had the fourth largest cable tram system in the world?
23 In which Scottish city is 'Little France'?
24 What do the letters SQA stand for?
25 Which Lord Provost headed the 'Glasgow's Miles Better' campaign?

Answers: p178

1   Where is the Lost Valley?

2   What is the most easterly point on the Scottish mainland?

3   In which city will you find The Howff?

4   What is the largest granite-built church in the British Isles?

5   Where is Stac an Armin?

6   Where will you find Magnus, Clair, Columba, Dunlin and Piper?

7   Where would you go to visit the Clickhimin Broch?

8   What is the name of the commando training centre near Spean Bridge?

9   Where is the King's Knot?

10   Near which town in Perthshire would you find the Dunfallandy Stone?

11   Where did Edinburgh's Royal Observatory move to in 1896?

12   Where is Argyll's Lodging?

13   What is the Grey Mare's Tail, near Moffat?

14   Where is the site of the sunken Spanish galleon, *Florida*?

15   Where can you see the Loch Faskally Dam?

16   Where is the former home of David Dale?

17   Where is Hugh Miller's cottage?

18   Where in Peebleshire is said to be the grave of the wizard Merlin?

19   In which city are the McManus Galleries?

20   Where is Inchmahome Priory?

21   Where is the Scottish Rugby Union Museum?

22   In a church in Strathcarron can be seen, scratched on the windows, the names of people evicted from their homes in Glencalvie during the clearances of 1845. What is the name of the church?

23   Where in Scotland are the Open Gold Panning Championships held annually?

24   In which region of Scotland are the Cairnholy chambered cairns?

25   Where is Black Mount?

Answers: p178

Music 1

1   Which group had a chart hit with 'Don't Leave Me This Way'?

2   What was the instrumental hit of the Average White Band in 1975?

3   Who sang 'Darlin''?

4   In which country did the Bay City Rollers split up?

5   Which band produced an album called 'Street Fighting Years' in 1989?

6   With which kind of music were the Rezillos associated?

7   Where do Del Amitri hail from?

8   Which Scottish rock star was married to Patsy Kensit?

9   Which Glasgow-born artist had a hit in 1956 with 'Rock Island Line'?

10 Who had a hit with the 'Boat That I Row'?

11 Where did the Beatles make their first appearance in Scotland?

12 Which Scottish group produced an album called *The Man Who . . .*?

13 Which Glasgow band brought out a record called *Now We're Thru* in 1964?

14 Who was the lead singer in the Tourists?

15 On the soundtrack of which film can you hear '(I'm Gonna Be) 500 Miles' by the Proclaimers?

16 Name the Scot who had a hit with *Personality* in 1974?

17 What was the title of the football song with which Andy Cameron had a hit in 1978?

18 Which street did Gerry Rafferty sing about?

19 Which artist sang the theme tune to *Taggart*?

20 Where did Texas see in the Millennium?

21 Which band had a hit with 'The Boston Tea Party'?

22 Which band did Midge Ure play in?

23 Who had a hit with 'I Should have Known Better'?

24 What was the name of the lead singer in Marillion?

25 In which year did Pilot have a hit with 'January'?

Answers: p179

QUESTIONS

1 Who brought Benedictine monks to Dunfermline?
2 What is the other name by which St Kentigern is known?
3 From which century does Dryburgh Abbey date?
4 Which disciple of St Columba went to Lindisfarne to convert Northumbria?
5 Where is John Knox buried?
6 When is St Andrew's day?
7 Who became minister of St Giles in Edinburgh in 1560?
8 Which football club is named after a saint?
9 In which part of Scotland did St Regulus carry out his mission?
10 Where is The Apprentice Pillar?
11 Where is St Mungo's Chapel?
12 In which Cathedral were James V and Mary of Guise married?
13 Where is Scotland's Buddhist Temple?
14 Who founded the Free Church in Scotland?
15 Which Scottish King founded the abbeys of Holyrood, Kelso and Jedburgh, among others?
16 Orkney has an annual festival in honour of which saint?
17 Which order of monks lived at Deer Abbey?
18 Who was responsible for the founding of the first university in Scotland?
19 On which island are ancient kings of Scotland and Norway buried?
20 With which part of Scotland is St Cuthbert associated?
21 What is the name of the Catholic martyr who became Scotland's first post-reformation saint?
22 Which cathedral in Scotland survived the Reformation relatively unscathed?
23 From which century do the ruins of Elgin Cathedral date?
24 In which abbey is James III buried?
25 Where did St Baldred live?

Answers: p179

1 Which university medical school became the first to admit a woman, in 1869?

2 Which Scottish poet wrote a Scots translation of *Cyrano de Bergerac*?

3 Who became secretary of the newly formed Scottish Miners' Federation in 1886?

4 When was the hydro-electric power station opened at Ben Cruachan?
a) 1965 b) 1948 c) 1971

5 Which title was forfeited by James IV in 1491 in retaliation for a rebellion led by Alexander of Lochalsh?

6 Who raised the standard for James Francis Edward Stewart at Castletown in Braemar, proclaiming him King James VIII of Scotland?

7 Which political party was inaugurated at Stirling in 1928?

8 When was the Highlands and Islands Development Board created?
a) 1956 b) 1959 c) 1969

9 Which Scot became Northern Ireland Secretary in 2001?

10 What was the fiery cross used for?

11 When did the wearing of tartan clothing become illegal in Scotland?

12 What was the name of the ship in which Bonnie Prince Charlie sailed from France to Scotland?

13 What did Margaret Chalmers, Maria Riddell, Elizabeth Paton, Jenny Clow, Anna Park, Agnes Maclehose, Jean Armour and Mary Campbell have in common?

14 When was the Anatomy Act passed, giving teachers of anatomy access to a legal supply of bodies for dissection? a) 1747 b) 1838 c) 1832

15 Which Scottish Island was once owned by Keith Schellenberg?

16 In what year was Glasgow's University of Strathclyde established?

17 Near which Highland village is Smoo Cave?

18 What is Scotland's rarest mammal?

19 Where is the Strait of Corryvreckan?

20 During which king's reign was the religious centre of Scotland moved from Iona to Dunkeld?

21 In which year did William Wallace become an outlaw?

22 What sport is played by Kyles Athletic?

23 What is the name of the female character whose life story is told in *A Scot's Quair*?

24 Which three Williams' names are associated with the history of publishing in Scotland?

25 Which famous Scottish socialist politician and activist died in 1923?

Answers: p180

QUESTIONS

1   In which year was the Declaration of Arbroath made?
2   When was the Stone of Destiny stolen from Westminster Abbey?
3   Where did Bonnie Prince Charlie raise his standard in 1745, to rally the support of the Highland chiefs?
4   In which year was Mary, Queen of Scots forced to abdicate the throne of Scotland?
5   Which entire Roman legion was lost in an attempt to subdue the rebellious Scots?
6   In the reign of which king did the 'Bloody Assizes' take place?
7   In which year did Bonnie Prince Charlie die?
8   In which year did James II lay seige to Roxburgh Castle?
9   Upon whose death did Malcolm Canmore succeed to the throne?
10 Who succeeded Malcolm II to the throne?
11 Who killed Duncan I?
12 In which year was John Balliol forced to surrender his crown to Edward I?
13 Where was Charles I held prisoner prior to his trial at Westminster?
14 Who became the only Scottish royal saint more than two centuries after her death?
15 Where was Mary, Queen of Scots held prisoner in the period leading up to her trial and execution?
16 Against whose forces were the Covenanters successful in the Battle of Drumclog?
17 In which year did the Battle of Solway Moss take place?
18 In which century did Orkney come under Scottish rule?
19 In which year was the Treaty of Northampton signed?
20 Whose forces defeated the army of Edward I at Stirling Bridge?
21 In which year did the first expedition to Darien set out?
22 What was the name of the great warship built as pride of the navy of James IV?
23 What was the name of the man who captured William Wallace and took him to London where he was executed?
24 Whom did Andrew Melville refer to as 'God's sillie vassal'?
25 How many Scottish representatives were allowed to sit in Parliament at Westminster while Cromwell was in power?

Answers: p180

Literature 1

1 What is the name of the Clyde puffer in *Para Handy*?

2 Who wrote *Whisky Galore?*

3 Which nineteenth-century Scottish churchman and writer founded *The Bookman* and *Woman at Home* and was editor of *The British Weekly*?

4 What is the name of the famous fictional character created by Sir Arthur Conan Doyle?

5 Which Scots writer wrote a *History of The French Revolution*?

6 Which Scottish novelist lived at Abbotsford?

7 Which modern Scottish novelist won the 1993 Booker Prize?

8 What was the title of the book that won the Booker Prize in 1993?

9 What are the names of the three autobiographical books written by Eric Linklater?

10 Who wrote *The Blue Fairy Book*?

11 What is the title of Cliff Hanley's autobiographical account of life in Glasgow?

12 Under which name did Sir Walter Scott originally publish his novels?

13 Name the contemporary novelist who wrote *The Crow Road* and *The Wasp Factory*.

14 Which nineteenth-century Scottish writer wrote *The House with the Green Shutters*?

15 Name the book written by Irvine Welsh that was made into a box-office success at the cinema.

16 Who wrote *Lanark*?

17 *A Treatise on Human Nature* was one of the most important pieces of philosophical writing in the eighteenth century. Who wrote it?

18 In which century did the Scots historian Thomas Carlyle live?

19 Name the author of *Cloud Cuckoo Land* and *Black Sparta*.

20 What was the famous trilogy of novels written by Lewis Grassic Gibbon?

21 Who wrote *The Thirty-Nine Steps*?

22 Inspector Rebus is the central character in several books by which crime writer?

23 Who wrote *The Trick Is To Keep Breathing*?

24 What was the name of the first book published by Robin Jenkins?

25 What was the name given to a school of Scottish fiction in the nineteenth century characterized by romanticism and sentimentality?

Answers: p181

QUESTIONS

1 Which tree is believed to protect against evil spirits?

2 What is the name of the monster of Loch Morar?

3 What is a kelpie?

4 What is the name of the hill near Inverness where fiddlers played at a fairy ball?

5 Who prophesied the fall of the Mackenzies of Seaforth?

6 What should be placed in the hand of a newborn child?

7 What was the name of the black magician, calling himself 'the wickedest man on earth', who had a house on the shores of Loch Ness?

8 What was the purpose of a lykewake?

9 Where is the lighthouse whose keepers mysteriously disappeared?

10 What was the name of the seer who is said to have foretold the death of Alexander III?

11 Why should the shells of boiled eggs be turned upside down and smashed once empty?

12 Who is Domhnull Dubh?

13 Where is the community where scientists were baffled by the ability of the people to grow marvellous crops in barren and inhospitable conditions?

14 Which Scottish leader was reputed to have been in league with the Devil and to have been killed by a silver bullet when he fell in battle?

15 What powers did the waters of the Fiddler's Well in Cromarty supposedly have?

16 Which prominent Scot of the seventeenth century was said to have beaten the Devil in a card game, which led to the Devil throwing a table into a pond?

17 To which holy man did a water monster, now thought to be Nessie, appear on Loch Ness in the sixth century AD?

18 What is the unusual ghost that is said to haunt Drumlanrig Castle?

19 Which playing card is known as 'the Curse of Scotland'?

20 What is the colour of the spiritual creature known as a glastaig?

21 What was the name of the female seer from Perthshire who is supposed to have predicted the Clearances and the Tay Bridge disaster?

22 What powers could a selkie have?

23 What are the magical powers of the fairy flag in Dunvegan Castle?

24 On which island do the ghostly shapes of Viking invaders appear from time to time?

25 What are brunaidh?

Answers: p181

General Knowledge 5

1   Name the head of Unique Scotland, organizers of Edinburgh's Millennium celebrations.
2   Which Scottish news programme did Mary Marquis present?
3   Who was the founder and director of the Celtic Film Festival?
4   Which film star did a voice-over for an SNP party political broadcast in 1991?
5   When was the Edinburgh Festival launched?
6   When was the village of Forteviot rebuilt?
     a) the 1690s b) the 1920s c) the 1860s
7   In which year did entertainer Jimmy Logan die?
8   What was the fictional name for the setting of the television series *Hamish MacBeth*?
9   Which powerful position was George Robertson appointed to in 1999?
10   Which city has a Camera Obscura?
11   In which country did the trial take place of the Lockerbie Bombing suspects?
12   What were the titles of the three books in *A Scots Quair*?
13   Where are the headquarters of Radio Scotland?
14   Which Scottish businessman bought the controlling share in Rangers Football Club in 1988?
15   With which political party is the name of Donald Gorrie associated?
16   In which decade was the Special Unit set up in Barlinnie Prison?
17   Where was the poet William Soutar born?
18   Who was lead singer of The Communards?
19   When was the 'Rough Wooing'?
20   Which Scots-born sailor fought against the British in the ship *Bonhomme Richard*?
21   When was the Poll Tax introduced in Scotland?
22   Who printed the first *Encyclopaedia Brittanica*?
23   Which Scottish Field Marshall founded the British Legion?
24   Who took on the role of acting First Minister in the Scottish Parliament while Donald Dewar was recovering from heart surgery in 2000?
25   Which Scottish author spent much of his childhood at Sandyknowe in the Borders?

Answers: p182

QUESTIONS

1   What was the occupation of John Buchan's father?
2   What was the name of his younger sister who died when she was a young child?
3   From where did the family move to Glasgow?
4   What serious injury did John Buchan suffer as a child?
5   What school did John Buchan attend in Glasgow?
6   To whom did John Buchan dedicate *Scholar Gipsies*?
7   In which publication was *John Burnet of Barnes* serialized before being published as a novel?
8   Under whom did John Buchan take up his first post abroad?
9   In which magazine was *The Power House* serialized?
10 Which novel was originally given the title *The Black Stone*?
11 The *Nelson History of the War* was published in how many parts?
12 In which novel did Dickson McCunn first appear?
13 In which year did John Buchan accept the post of Governor-General of Canada?
14 In which two books do we encounter Richard Hannay?
15 What is the name of Buchan's autobiography, published in 1941?
16 How many children did John Buchan and his wife have?
17 In which book does the character of John Laputa feature?
18 What is the title of the last novel written by John Buchan?
19 Who made the first film of *The Thirty-Nine Steps*?
20 What is the title of the poem for which Buchan won the Newdigate Prize for Poetry?
21 What was John Buchan's chosen title as a peer?
22 What was the name of Buchan's first novel, published in 1895?
23 In which year did Buchan join the Intelligence Corps?
24 What was the name of Buchan's wife?
25 In which year was John Buchan first elected to Parliament?

Answers: p182

Aberdeen 1

1   Aberdeen once had an opera house, which then became the Tivoli. What was its name?
2   Where is the statue of Prince Albert?
3   In which year did the last hanging take place at Craiginches prison?
4   Name the architect who designed the façade of St Nicholas's Church in Union Street?
5   Aberdeen is known as The Granite City. What is the name of the great hole in the ground from which granite was once quarried?
6   Name the three hills upon which Aberdeen was built.
7   When was Marischal College founded?
8   Who founded King's College?
9   In which year in the 1980s did Aberdeen Football Club win the European Cup-Winners Cup?
10 Which poet is commemorated with a statue outside the Grammar School?
11 What is the name of Aberdeen's cathedral?
12 Which flower was depicted on the coat of arms of Old Aberdeen?
13 In which century was the Town House built?
14 Which newspaper was founded in 1748?
15 Which museum is housed at St Luke's house?
16 Where does the Mercat Cross now stand?
17 What is the city's railway station called?
18 Which Queen moved from St Nicholas Street to Queen's Cross?
19 What is the motto of Aberdeen?
20 Which historian wrote *The Silver City by the Grey North Sea*?
21 Where is the statue in memory of the men who lost their lives in the Piper Alpha disaster?
22 Who wrote *A Thousand Years of Aberdeen*?
23 Which theatre in Aberdeen was opened in 1906?
24 Who was The Laird of Inversnecky?
25 What is the oldest street in the city?

Answers: p183

Heroes & Villains 1

1   Which Scot was responsible for founding America's National Parks?

2   In which year was William Wallace executed?

3   Where did Black Agnes fight off the English?

4   How did 'Bluidy Clavers' meet his death?

5   Name the Scottish founder of the SAS.

6   How and where did William Kidd die?

7   Who founded the Ragged Schools?

8   Name the Scots born mass-murderer whose crimes were discovered when the bodies of his victims blocked the drains of his London home.

9   Which football manager became president of Manchester United football club in 1980?

10 Name the head of a family of cannibals who terrorized south-west Scotland for many years in the seventeenth century.

11 What is the name of the Scottish industrialist who founded the mill-town at New Lanark?

12 Which Scots hero was excommunicated in 1306?

13 Who was 'the Wizard of the West Bow'?

14 What was William Quarrier's outstanding achievement?

15 Name the serial murderer hanged in Glasgow in 1958.

16 Name the Edinburgh surgeon who was supplied with bodies by Burke and Hare.

17 Which Scots woman, accused of murdering her sweetheart, caused scandal when her letters were read out in court?

18 An extremely learned man of the thirteenth century, his name came not only to be associated with scholarly pusuits but with wizardry. He is believed to be buried in Melrose Abbey. Some say he haunts there. Who was he?

19 Who was the Scottish miner who founded the Scottish Labour Party?

20 How did Dr Pritchard kill his wife and his mother-in-law?

21 Which city did the courageous missionary, Mary Slessor, come from?

22 Name the Olympic athlete and missionary who refused to run on the Sabbath.

23 Hopes were pinned on this man to become Labour Prime Minister of Great Britain, but he died suddenly in 1994. What was his name?

24 What was the name of the laird of Buckholme Tower who slaughtered two Covenanters awaiting trial in the cellars of his home?

25 Name the Scots woman who took ambulances and medical help to troops in Serbia in the First World War.

Answers: p183

General Knowledge 6

1   Where is McCaig's Folly?
2   What are the names of the three lochs in the Caledonian Canal?
3   Where is the largest model railway in Britain?
4   When did David Dale begin work on his project at New Lanark?
5   Who was the wife of John Balliol?
6   Where is the Logan Botanic Garden?
7   Where is the National Trust for Scotland's Tenement House?
8   What is the name of the highest village in Scotland?
9   Who played the part of Janet in *Dr Finlay's Casebook*?
10 In which city was footballer Graeme Souness born?
11 When was the Bank of Scotland founded?
    a) the 1570s b) the 1690s c) the 1820s
12 Which Scot discovered the Victoria Falls?
13 Which Scottish town was crowned 'Scotland's most dismal' in the
    Carbuncle Awards 2001, run by Scottish business magazine, Unlimited?
14 Which Scots actress was 'Supergran'?
15 Which historic event took place on July 1, 1999?
16 Who was captain of the 1974 Scottish World Cup Squad?
17 Where is the Fife Folk Museum?
18 Which Scottish Explorer discovered the source of the Blue Nile?
19 Who painted the portrait of Robert Burns which hangs in the Scottish
    National Portrait Gallery?
20 Which future king of Scotland married Anne Hyde when he was Duke of
    York?
21 The daughters of which sixteenth-century Earl were known as the Seven
    Pearls of Loch Leven?
22 Where, near Edinburgh, can you view the wonders of the deep all around
    you from a transparent tunnel?
23 Where is John Duns Scotus said to have been born?
24 What was the profession of Sir William Burrell?
25 What strange occurrence was reported in *The Inverness Courier* in 1933?

Answers: p184

Feasts, Festivals & Fun

1   Where in Fife is the Links Market held every year?

2   In which month are the 'Honest Toun' celebrations held?

3   What is set alight during the Shetland festival of Up-Helly-Aa?

4   What is the name of the fair held annually in St Andrews?

5   In which month does the Edinburgh Festival begin every year?

6   What is celebrated on January 25?

7   When do you dook for apples?

8   Which town hosts Great Glen Sheepdog trials each year?

9   In which month is the Braemar Highland Gathering held each year?

10 In which town is the Beltane festival held?

11 In which area of Scotland are the Common Ridings held?

12 Which university stages the annual Kate Kennedy procession?

13 On which day of the year is the Burning of the Clavie ceremony held?

14 Which date is still sometimes called Gowkie Day?

15 When is Handsel Monday?

16 In which Scottish town is Whuppity Stourie celebrated?

17 In which city do the world pipe band competitions take place each summer?

18 Which saint is remembered on June 9?

19 How do the energetic celebrate May 1 in Edinburgh?

20 When is St Andrew's Day?

21 What was Shrove Tuesday once known as in Scotland?

22 Which festival is Britain's second largest arts festival?

23 Where does the Boys Ploughing Match take place annually?

24 Which town in Fife has a New Year torch procession?

25 Where would you see 'The Burry Man'?

Answers: p184

Great Scots 1

1   What was the name of the Scottish educationist who founded Summerhill School?
2   Where did Mary Slessor work as a missionary?
3   In which country did Samuel Greig achieve fame?
4   In which century was John Duns Scotus born?
5   Who wrote *Sketchbook of Popular Geology*?
6   In honour of whom were the villages of North Queensferry and South Queensferry named?
7   Which philosopher wrote a five-volume *History of England*?
8   Which great Scot was sentenced to the galleys in 1547?
9   Name the famous Scottish artist who started his career by painting miniatures.
10 Who died in the Palazzo Muti in Rome in 1788?
11 Which famous Scot was married to John George Stewart-Murray, Marquess of Tullibardine in 1899?
12 Of which university did Adam Smith become Lord Rector in 1787?
13 What was the name of Flora Macdonald's husband?
14 Which Scots writer published a collection of translations of the work of several writers entitled *Rites of Passage*?
15 Who was stabbed to death by Robert the Bruce?
16 Which Scottish writer was Governor-General of Canada in the 1930s?
17 Which great Scottish inventor founded the journal *Science*?
18 Who wrote a twenty-volume history of Scotland entitled *Rerum Scoticarum Historia*?
19 Which king introduced the order of the Knights Templar to Scotland?
20 Who established the second law of thermodynamics?
21 What was the title held by James Burnett, judge and anthropologist of the eighteenth century?
22 Which well-known Scottish writer published a biography of Mungo Park?
23 What was the Christian name of the 1st Earl Haig of Bemersyde?
24 Who was the geologist who published *A Theory of the Earth* in the eighteenth century?
25 Which early twentieth-century Scots political activist campaigned for a Scottish Workers' Republic?

Answers: p185

QUESTIONS

1   What is the main ingredient of cullen skink?
2   What is crowdie?
3   What is traditionally used as the casing for haggis?
4   What food product is Arbroath famous for?
5   Which Scottish town is famous for its bridies?
6   What is traditionally eaten with haggis on Burns Night?
7   What other ingredient is put in Scotch broth apart from vegetables and stock?
8   What kind of meat is used for making potted haugh?
9   What is a Selkirk bannock?
10 When is black bun traditionally served?
11 What beverage is produced at Traquair?
12 What is thought to give malt whisky its distinctive flavour?
13 What was a mutchkin?
14 What gives the Fountainbridge area in Edinburgh its distinctive smell?
15 What are 'silver darlings'?
16 What are the ingredients of Atholl brose?
17 What is gundy?
18 What does *uisge-beatha* mean?
19 What is a Jethart Snail?
20 What are stovies?
21 What is the main ingredient of partan bree?
22 What dish is made with oatmeal, cream and raspberries?
23 From which part of Scotland does Dunlop cheese originate?
24 Which breed of cattle has given Scottish beef an international reputation for quality?
25 What is traditionally sprinkled on porridge before it is eaten?

Answers: p185

General Knowledge 7

1 Name the village that is home to Skibo Castle, made famous by Madonna and Guy Ritchie's wedding there in 2000.

2 What was the name of the Kirkcudbright fishing boat that sank off the Isle of Man in January 2000?

3 What is the name of the man who composed the fanfare for the opening of the Scottish Parliament?

4 What is the name of the woman who has become known as 'the Cashmere Queen'?

5 What large chunk of Scottish property was bought by tycoon Mukhtar Sandhu in 2000?

6 Who took over from Sam Galbraith as Scottish Education Minister?

7 From whom did Edinburgh Council buy Calton Hill in 1725?

8 Where was a proposal for a £70 million superquarry finally rejected after a 10-year battle?

9 What was moved from Calton Hill to Blackford Hill in Edinburgh in 1896?

10 How old was James IV when he took part in the Battle of Sauchieburn?

11 When was the last woman executed for witchcraft in Scotland? a) 1678 b) 1727 c) 1809

12 In which century did the crime of witchcraft first appear in the statute book in Scotland?

13 Which former Scottish rugby international player joined Scotland's bid to host the Ryder Cup?

14 Name the Scottish singer who rose to fame after taking part in *The Big Time* in 1980.

15 Which Scottish writer was inspired to write his best-loved book by childhood visits to Moat Brae House in Dumfries?

16 Whom did politician Gordon Brown marry in 2000?

17 What is the name of the brother of TV chef Nick Nairn?

18 Which TV personality published *Scotland: Story of a Nation*?

19 In which year was Donald Dewar born?

20 What is the name of the island that was used for BBC Television's *Castaway*?

21 What was the name of the TV serial in which actor Dougie Henshall played a manic depressive doctor working in a psychiatric hospital?

22 It was decided in 2000 to build a new gallery to house The Queen's Royal Collection of art. In which building?

23 What was the last lighthouse in Scotland to be automated?

24 With which health scare was John Barr's shop in Wishaw associated?

25 Which Scots-born singer was voted best male artist at the Brit Awards in 1998?

Answers: p186

1 What was 'hamesucken'?

2 What is the verdict unique to Scots Law?

3 When was capital punishment abolished in Scotland?

4 What is the name of the supreme court in Scotland for civil matters?

5 When was the first female judge appointed in Scotland?

6 What are the two most commonly reported crimes in Scotland?

7 What is the maximum sentence handed out by the sheriff courts?

8 What is the name for the hearings system which deals with children under the age of 16 in Scotland?

9 Who was the last person to be hanged in Scotland?

10 What was the name of the young lady who caused a great scandal in Victorian times when she was accused of poisoning her lover with arsenic?

11 What is the name of Edinburgh's prison?

12 What was 'stouthrief'?

13 For what crime was Eugene Chantrelle hanged?

14 Who heads the High Court of Justiciary?

15 What was the most common means of execution of witches in the sixteenth century?

16 Where is Scotland's hospital for the criminally insane?

17 What is the Scottish equivalent of a barrister?

18 Which Scottish university has the largest law school?

19 What is the name of the largest prison in Scotland?

20 What difference between Scots and English Law brought people running across the border to Gretna Green pre-1969?

21 Where is Scotland's first privately run prison?

22 Which Scottish judge was referred to as 'the Jeffreys of Scotland'?

23 Name the eighteenth-century Scottish judge who is remembered for his eccentricity and interest in anthropology as much as for his abilities as a judge.

24 Which Scottish university was the first to appoint a woman as a professor of law?

25 What is the title of the president of the Faculty of Advocates?

Answers: p186

Scotland & the Media 1

1   Who became editor-in-chief of Scotsman Publications Ltd in 1986?
2   Name the company which publishes *The Sunday Post*.
3   By which name was *The Herald* previously known?
4   The paper which was once called *The North British Daily Mail* is now known as what?
5   In which decade did the *Scottish Daily News* make a brief appearance?
6   What is the name of Magnus Magnusson's TV presenter daughter?
7   What is the name of Scotland's oldest-surviving journal?
8   Which Scottish daily newspaper moved its offices to a new site in the year 2000?
9   In which century was the *Scots Magazine* first published?
10 Name the Scot who was director-general of the BBC from 1927 to 1938.
11 Of which paper was Alastair Dunnett editor before he became editor of *The Scotsman*?
12 Which newspaper did John Gordon edit from 1928 to 1952?
13 With which Scottish newspaper is Oor Wullie associated?
14 In which century was the *Edinburgh Evening Courant* first published?
15 What is the English name for *Comadaidh Craolaidh Gàidhlig*?
16 What was the name of the company formed by John Logie Baird in 1925?
17 In which decade was Scotland first enabled to receive television broadcasts?
18 Where are the headquarters of BBC Scotland?
19 With which city is the *Evening Times* associated?
20 With which city is the *Press and Journal* associated?
21 What is the name of the television production company co-founded by Kirsty Wark?
22 Name the Scotswoman who co-presented BBC's coverage of the 1996 and 2000 Olympics.
23 Which female TV presenter was chosen to front the Channel 4 programme *dotcomedy*?
24 Suzie McGuire made her name as a presenter with which radio station?
25 When did Grampian Television come into being?

Answers: p187

QUESTIONS

1   Which former Scottish rugby international player was known as 'the White Shark'?

2   The first Rugby World Cup Sevens took place in Scotland. In which year?

3   How many times did Scotland win the Grand Slam between 1925 and 1990?

4   Who was captain of the Scottish rugby team when Scotland won the Grand Slam in 1990?

5   In what year did the first rugby international take place between England and Scotland?

6   When was the first Calcutta Cup match?

7   When was Murrayfield Stadium first opened by the SRU?

8   For which FP team did former Scotland captain, Andy Irvine, play?

9   Who were the 'Three Bears'?

10 In 1997 one rugby club won the League Championship, the Tennents Cup, the Border League and the Melrose sevens tournament. Which club was it?

11 How many players were in each team for the first ever rugby international?

12 Which team won the Scottish championship for the first five seasons between 1974 and 1978?

13 When did Gavin Hastings retire as captain of the Scottish team?

14 What was the name of the captain of the Scottish team for the first Scottish Grand Slam victory?

15 Where were international matches played in Scotland between 1899 and 1925?

16 What record did Scott Hastings achieve during his years as a Scottish international player?

17 Which club plays at The Greenyards?

18 In which year was the first ever seven-a-side tournament held in Melrose?

19 Between 1883 and 1998, which was the only team to win fewer Grand Slams than Scotland?

20 How many times did Scotland win the Triple Crown between 1883 and 1998?

21 Who became head coach of the Scottish international rugby squad in 1998?

22 How many divisions are there in the BT Premiership?

23 How many times was Scott Hastings capped for Scotland?

24 What illness prevented commentator Bill McLaren from pursuing his career as a player?

25 Who took over as Scottish captain after Gavin Hastings?

Answers: p187

General Knowledge 8

1 Who retired as Bishop of Edinburgh in 2000?
2 What is the name of the children's entertainment group composed of Nicky, Spatz and Mr P?
3 Which legal ghost is said to haunt Edinburgh's Greyfriars Kirkyard?
4 Who was appointed Minister of Finance and Local Government in the Scottish Cabinet in Autumn 2000?
5 Bill Millin became known as the Mad Piper during World War II. Why?
6 Which eminent Scottish doctor was obstetrician to Queen Charlotte Sophia?
7 Where in Fife is Fife Animal Park?
8 Which mountain by Loch Broom was sold in 2000?
9 New evidence came to light in October 2000 about a case that has mystified the Glasgow police for more than thirty years. What case was it?
10 Which football team did Frank McAvennie play for?
11 The flight between which two Scottish islands achieved recognition as the shortest scheduled flight in the world?
12 The Macallan Short Story award is run in conjunction with which Scottish newspaper?
13 Where is Rob Roy's house?
14 Numbers of snow buntings and ptarmigans have decreased sharply in Scotland in recent years. What is believed to be the reason for this?
15 Gillian Glover has become a very well-known jounalist and restaurant critic. In which paper?
16 When was the nuclear processing plant at Dounreay built?
17 Which TV series was inspired by the work of Ian Stephen, Peterhead-born psychologist?
18 What is the name of the architect of the Scottish Parliament who died in July 2000?
19 Which city hosts the Scottish Storytelling Festival?
20 Which bird, extinct after the late nineteenth century in Scotland, has been reintroduced to the country since the 1990s?
21 Which Scottish island was declared unsafe by the Ministry of Defence between 1945 and 1990?
22 Who founded Loretto School in Musselburgh?
23 With which famous Scottish musician does accordionist Phil Cunningham perform and record?
24 Which former member of Runrig has become a politician?
25 Name the engineer responsible for the construction of the Forth Railway Bridge.

Answers: p188

1   Which architect designed the Glasgow School of Art?

2   Who designed the Observatory on Edinburgh's Calton Hill in 1818?

3   Who designed the Edinburgh Academy Building?

4   Where is the Winter Gardens Pavilion designed by Alex Stephen?

5   Who submitted the winning design for the Burrell Gallery in Glasgow?

6   Who designed the National Wallace Monument in Stirling?

7   What is a black house?

8   For whom did Charles Rennie Mackintosh design Hill House in Helensburgh?

9   What is a broch?

10 Who designed Fettes College, the Bank of Scotland headquarters on the Mound and the Royal Infirmary in Edinburgh?

11 What were the names of William Adam's two most famous architect sons?

12 Which Scottish architect designed Coventry Cathedral?

13 Which young architect was responsible for the design of Edinburgh's New Town?

14 What is the name of the school close to the west end of the city of Edinburgh designed by William Henry Playfair?

15 What was the name of the architect who designed the famous Templeton's Carpet Factory in Glasgow?

16 What was the name of the school in Glasgow, now a museum of education, designed by Charles Rennie Mackintosh?

17 What is a 'but and ben'?

18 What was the name of the architect who designed the original building of Hopetoun House?

19 Who designed the Scottish National War Memorial?

20 Which castle in Ayrshire is regarded as one of Robert Adam's finest achievements?

21 What is the name of the only church designed by Charles Rennie Mackintosh?

22 Which Scottish architect designed Blackfriars Bridge in London?

23 Who designed Moray Place in Edinburgh?

24 What was the name of the architect who designed theRoyal High School building on Edinburgh's Regent Road?

25 Who designed the Chatelherault Hunting Lodge?

Answers: p188

Politics 1

1 Who became Presiding Officer of the Scottish Parliament after it was opened in 1999?

2 Where will you find a Gaelic Bible in the House of Commons?

3 In which year did Alex Salmond step down as leader of the SNP?

4 Who was the leader of the Scottish Conservative Party at the time of the Conservative Party Conference in September 2000?

5 Which Euro MP was dubbed 'Madame Ecosse'?

6 Who was Education Minister at the time of the furore over the SQA exam results confusion in 2000?

7 How many Scottish representatives sat in Westminster after the Scottish Reform Bill of 1832?

8 What were the names of the two men who founded the Scottish Labour Party in 1888?

9 In which year were the headquarters of the Secretary of State for Scotland moved from Westminster to St Andrew's House?

10 In which year in the twentieth century was a Scottish Covenant drawn up, calling for a Scottish Parliament within the UK?

11 In March 1979, what percentage of the whole Scottish electorate voted in favour of a Scottish Assembly? (Answer to the nearest per cent)

12 Before his death, what position did Donald Dewar hold in the Scottish Parliament?

13 Who was voted National Chairman of the Young Communist League in 1952?

14 During which years was Arthur Balfour Prime Minister of Great Britain?

15 Name the Scottish peer who was Prime Minister from 1963 to 1964.

16 Who replaced Sir Alec Douglas-Home as leader of the Conservative Party?

17 Who was elected as leader of the SNP following the resignation of Alex Salmond?

18 Who was Chief Executive of the SNP from 1994 to 1999?

19 Where is former Labour leader John Smith buried?

20 What cabinet position was Sarah Boyack appointed to in the new Scottish Parliament of 1999?

21 Who was made Prime Minister on the resignation of Lord Derby, in 1852?

22 Which nationalist thinker published *Account of a Conversation concerning a Right Regulation of Governments for the Common Good of Mankind* anonymously in 1704?

23 Who led a work-in at Upper Clyde Shipbuilders in 1971?

24 Which former leader of Red Clydeside died in 1923?

25 Who were the two contenders for leadership of the Labour Party in Scotland after the death of Donald Dewar?   Answers: p189

39

QUESTIONS

1 Which theatre company is based in Tay Square?

2 Which famous missionary's life is commemorated in stained glass in the City Museum?

3 Who designed the Morgan Tower?

4 What is the name of the city's largest park?

5 In which street did William McGonagall live?

6 What was 'The Fifie'?

7 When did Dundee become a royal burgh?

8 Who designed the first Tay Bridge?

9 Whose statue stands in front of the Albert Institute?

10 What was the name of the whaling vessel from Dundee which was used by Sir Ernest Shackleton in his polar voyage?

11 What is the name of the oldest British warship afloat, which is anchored in the city's docks?

12 What is the name of Dundee's observatory?

13 In which month does the Dundee City Festival take place?

14 Which famous women's long-distance runner was born in Dundee?

15 Which famous rock band of the 1970s came from Dundee?

16 Which king granted Dundee its royal charter?

17 What is the nickname for Dundee United?

18 When was the University of Dundee founded?

19 Which character in horror fiction was created in Dundee?

20 When was Dundee stormed and plundered by the forces of General Monck?

21 In which decade was the Dundee and Newtyle Railway opened?

22 Which family owned the Dens Mills?

23 Which family owned the Camperdown Works?

24 What is the proper name of the Coffin Mill?

25 Who was provost of Dundee from 1788 to 1819?

Answers: p189

General Knowledge 9

1   In which year did the Ibrox Stadium disaster take place?

2   At which Scottish prison did riots take place in 1979?

3   In which city was Jim Watt, the boxer, born?

4   Name the former newspaper editor who became a leading light in Scotland's oil industry.

5   Which publisher became Queen's Printer for Scotland in 1862?

6   What activity is associated with the letters RSCDS? What do the letters stand for?

7   Where was the first radio broadcast of an opera in Britain transmitted from?

8   What profession was followed by Robert Louis Stevenson's famous grandfather?

9   Which engineer was responsible for the building of the Menai Suspension Bridge?

10   In which century did Thomas the Rhymer live?

11   In which industry did the Thomson family of Dundee make their fortune before branching out into the newspaper industry?

12   Who introduced 'the Maiden' to Scotland in the sixteenth century?

13   When did the *Comet* make her first trip?

14   What does SCWS stand for?

15   What kind of plant are the gardens of Achamore House on Gigha famed for?

16   What is the former Advocate's Library in Edinburgh now known as?

17   Who founded St Andrew's University?

18   Who invented the adhesive postage stamp?

19   Who wrote *A Letter of Adieu to the Scotch*?

20   Where was the National Covenant of 1683 subscribed?

21   In which decade was a public postal system installed in Scotland?

22   Who became director of the Edinburgh Festival in 1979?

23   Which port was merged with the city of Edinburgh in 1920?

24   In which city is the Dolphin Arts Centre?

25   How many education authorities are there in Scotland?

Answers: p190

1   Name the Scottish woman golfer who led Europe to victory in the Solheim Cup in 2000.

2   Which Scottish golfer won the British Open with a set of clubs which he had made himself?

3   In which year was the British Open held for the last time at Musselburgh?

4   Where was Old Tom Morris born?

5   Where was the first 18-hole golf course made in Scotland?

6   Where did the qualifying matches for the British Open of 2000 take place?

7   What is the name of the championship course at Gullane?

8   In which year did the first British Open take place?

9   What is the name of the first golf club to be founded in Scotland?

10   Which Scottish king banned the playing of golf?

11   Which self-proclaimed Scot won the British Open in 1985?

12   Where is the Scottish Golf Union based?

13   Who won the first British Open?

14   In which year did Tom Watson win the British Open at Turnberry?

15   Which is the Road Hole on the Old Course at St Andrews?

16   Where is 'home' to the Honourable Company of Edinburgh Golfers?

17   On which Scottish course was the Solheim Cup played in 1992?

18   How many Scottish courses have hosted the British Open since it began?

19   Which course hosts the Scottish Open on the European Tour?

20   Which Scot won the championship belt of the British Open for the third time in a row in 1870?

21   Who scored the first hole-in-one recorded in the British Open?

22   In which year did Sandy Lyle become the first Briton to win the US Masters?

23   When did Carnoustie first host the British Open?

24   What is the name of the main course at Gleneagles?

25   How many holes were there at St Andrews before it was made into an 18-hole course in 1764?

Answers: p190

Films & Film Stars 1

1   With which actress did Scottish actor Tom Conti star in *Heavenly Pursuits*?

2   Name the Scots star of *Sliding Doors*.

3   How many films of Rob Roy have been made?

4   Who played the object of Gregory's desire in *Gregory's Girl*?

5   Who directed *Shallow Grave*?

6   Where was *Venus Peter* filmed?

7   Which film, based on a book by Alastair Maclean, was filmed on the island of Mull?

8   In which Bill Forsyth film did actor Bill Paterson find himself caught up in ice-cream wars?

9   Where was *Ring of Bright Water* filmed?

10 Which bridge features in the film of *The Thirty-Nine Steps*?

11 Where is the setting for *Small Faces*?

12 Who directed *That Sinking Feeling*?

13 Who starred in the film of Jessie Kesson's book *Another Time, Another Place*?

14 What real event provided the inspiration for *Whisky Galore*?

15 What role did Robert Carlyle play in *Trainspotting*?

16 Which fondly remembered Scottish actor appeared in *The Great Escape*, *Whisky Galore*, *The Prime of Miss Jean Brodie* and *Mutiny on the Bounty*?

17 Name the young Scots actor who starred in *Star Wars: The Phantom Menace*.

18 Who wrote the book upon which the film *The Big Man* is based?

19 Which Scots actor won an Academy Award for his part in *The Untouchables*?

20 Which Scottish hero was played in film by Liam Neeson?

21 Which Scots actor was chosen to play the part of Hagrid in the film version of *Harry Potter and the Philosopher's Stone*?

22 Who wrote the book upon which the film *Ring of Bright Water* is based?

23 Who played Gregory in *Gregory's Girl*?

24 Which fictional Edinburgh schoolteacher was played by Maggie Smith in an Academy Award winning film?

25 Which book by Compton Mackenzie was made into a film?

Answers: p191

QUESTIONS

1 Which famous publishing family is associated with Peebles?
2 Who founded Melrose Abbey?
3 Which two architects were involved in the design of Floors Castle?
4 Where are Priorwood Gardens?
5 On which two rivers is the town of Kelso situated?
6 In which Borders castle did Malcolm IV die?
7 Which castle was used in the filming of *Greystoke*?
8 In which park are the Jedburgh Border Games held each year?
9 In which town is the Cornice Museum of Ornamental Plasterwork?
10 In which month is the Hawick Common Riding held?
11 What is housed in Gala House?
12 Which Borders fishing port suffered terrible losses to its fishing fleet in a storm in 1881?
13 Which Borders town celebrates The Braw Lads Gathering every year?
14 Which famous Scottish poet was born in Ettrick?
15 Which wizard is said to have split the Eildon Hills from one hill into three?
16 Which famous racing driver grew up in the village of Duns?
17 In which century was the original priory at Coldingham founded?
18 Near which Borders town are Kailzie Gardens?
19 How many arches are there in the bridge over the Tweed at Kelso?
20 Near which Borders Town is Ferniehurst Castle?
21 Which abbey was the largest of those built in the Borders?
22 On the roof of which Borders abbey can a pig be seen be seen playing the bagpipes?
23 Where is St Ronan's Well?
24 Which Borders abbey was founded by Hugo de Morville?
25 Where are the ruins of Tinnis Castle?

Answers: p191

General Knowledge 10

1   In which decade was education for all children between the ages of 5 and 13 made compulsory in Scotland?
2   What crisis hit Scotland in 1622-3, particularly in the Highlands?
3   During which king's reign was Mons Meg brought to Britain?
4   What disease spread through Scotland around 1350?
5   For what purpose was the Kelvingrove Museum and Art Gallery first built?
6   In which century were potatoes first grown in Scotland?
7   Where did George IV first wear a kilt?
8   What is the EICC?
9   What anniversary of Scottish history fell in April 1996?
10 What was the name of the first lighthouse built in Scotland?
11 Which Scottish nobleman was sued unsuccessfully by Oscar Wilde?
12 What is the name of the man whose execution sparked off the Porteous Riot?
13 Name Glasgow's second university which was established through the amalgamation of the Royal College of Science and Technology and the Scottish College of Commerce.
14 Name the Scots husband of Amy Johnson who crossed the Atlantic with her in 1933.
15 George MacLeod is remembered as the founder of the Iona Community. In which sphere of political action was he also very much involved?
16 Where is the Scottish home of Paul McCartney?
17 What profession did poet Norman McCaig follow?
18 Where was Eric Liddell born?
19 Where is David Livingstone buried?
20 How many times did John Knox marry?
21 Who published memoirs entitled *Roamin' in the Gloamin'*?
22 What is the name of the dancer who married Ludovic Kennedy?
23 The first known film footage made in Scotland featured whom, and where?
24 What is the name of the artist who used to own the Island of Eigg?
25 For what purpose was the site on which the Dounreay nuclear power plant was built formerly used?

Answers: p192

1   What brought hopes of wealth and prosperity to the Cononish Estate near Tyndrum for a while in the 1990s?

2   What industry is the biggest private employer in Orkney?

3   In which year did a sodium-cooled fast reactor go on fire at Dounreay?

4   Name the Scot who was first director-general of the Concorde project.

5   What kind of industry was established by Thomas Nelson in Edinburgh in the late nineteenth century?

6   In which century was the booksellers John Smith founded?

7   Where was the first Chamber of Commerce in Britain founded?

8   Where was the oldest coal mine in Scotland?

9   What used to be mined on the island of Luing?

10 Who founded the New Lanark Twist Company?

11 When was the Clydesdale Banking Company founded?

12 When was the STUC formed?

13 Where did Scotland's worst pit disaster take place?

14 Who wrote *A General View of the Coal Trade of Scotland* in 1808?

15 What was the season for Scottish herring fishing?

16 How were herring caught?

17 What disastrous occurrences hit Scottish farming in 1836 and 1846?

18 What kind of decorative product is associated with Caithness?

19 When were the post offices of England and Scotland united?

20 When was The Highlands and Islands Development Board set up?

21 In which industry was Alexander McDonald a leader of the workers in the nineteenth century?

22 In which decade was the Institute of Bankers of Scotland formed?

23 Which bank was formed in 1695?

24 Where did J. & P. Coats base their business in Scotland?

25 Where was the SCWS formed?

Answers: p192

1 Which member of the present Royal Family holds the title of Lord of the Isles?
2 Who was David II's father?
3 In what year was Charles I executed?
4 Who was the mother of Mary, Queen of Scots?
5 To whom was the Maid of Norway betrothed?
6 In what year was James III born?
7 Where did James V die?
8 Which Scottish king was killed at the battle of Flodden?
9 Who was the last Stewart on the throne?
10 Which king was the grandson of David I?
11 In what year did the young Mary, Queen of Scots arrive back in Scotland from France?
12 How did James II die?
13 Who was the mother of James V?
14 Which king boasted that he ruled Scotland with his pen?
15 What was the name of Macbeth's wife?
16 In what year did James VI become king of both Scotland and England?
17 Which King was crowned at Holyrood in 1633?
18 When did James VII ascend the throne?
19 What relation was William of Orange to James VII?
20 Who acted as regent in James V's minority?
21 How old was James IV when he became king?
22 Whom did James VI marry?
23 Which Scottish monarch was killed when his horse threw him over a cliff?
24 Where was Bonnie Prince Charlie born?
25 Which Scottish king was murdered in 1437?

QUESTIONS

Answers: p193

QUESTIONS

1   In which museum in Fort William is there a 'secret portrait' of Bonnie Prince Charlie?

2   How many locks are there in Neptune's Staircase?

3   Where is St Conan's Kirk?

4   Where are the remains of Rob Roy MacGregor buried?

5   Which loch is crossed by the Corran ferry?

6   Which town was demolished and rebuilt to make way for a castle?

7   Name the famous Scottish fiddler/composer who was born in Banchory.

8   Where is the seat of the Duke of Sutherland?

9   On which loch is the town of Lairg situated?

10 What drew people to Strathpeffer in Victorian times?

11 On the outskirts of which town is the Glengarioch Distillery?

12 On which loch is Castle Tioram situated?

13 Where is the terminus of the West Highland Railway?

14 Where does the Caledonian Canal join Loch Ness?

15 Where is the start of the Devil's Staircase?

16 Where is Cape Oreas, referrered to by Greek historian Diodorus Siculus in his writing?

17 Which Highland town, site of a major distillery, was once also a centre of the aluminium industry?

18 What is the name of the nature reserve that is situated to the south-east of Loch Maree?

19 What is the name of the man who established the gardens at Inverewe?

20 What is the name of the Benedictine abbey situated a few miles to the south-west of Elgin?

21 In which century was the town of Grantown-on-Spey founded?

22 Which castle in Grampian has towers called Preston, Meldrum, Seton, Gordon and Leith?

23 After which king is Fort William so called?

24 Where was the Brahan Seer put to death?

25 In which loch is Macphee's Island?

Answers: p193

Football 1

1   When was the Scottish First Division championship superseded by the Premier Division championship?
2   Which football club has won the First/Premier Division championship the most times since 1891?
3   Which team won the European Cup in 1967?
4   Who was the celebrated Scottish manager of Manchester United for over 20 years?
5   How many caps did Kenny Dalglish win for Scotland?
6   For what reason was the FA Cup withdrawn in 1909?
7   In which season did Third Lanark win the First Division championship?
8   How many times did Rangers win the First Division between 1900 and 1950?
9   In what year was the FA Cup renamed the Tennants Cup?
10 With which English team is the name of former Scottish footballer Dennis Law associated?
11 Which football team is known as 'the Jags'?
12 Which football team plays at Easter Road?
13 With whom does Dennis Law share his record of most goals scored for his country?
14 In which year was Dundee United founded?
15 Who was the manager of the Lisbon Lions?
16 Who are 'the Bankies'?
17 Which Scottish player scored the winning goal for Liverpool in the European Cup Final of 1978?
18 Which team won the Scottish cup final in May, 2001?
19 Name the famous football manager who was born in Govan in 1941.
20 What are the colours of the Kilmarnock football team?
21 Which team beat Rangers in a replay in the final of the 1905 FA Cup?
22 During which two decades did East Fife win the League Cup a total of three times?
23 During which World War was Scottish Football League competition suspended?
24 Which team is affectionately known as 'the Jam Tarts'?
25 Which team plays at Brockville?

Answers: p194

QUESTIONS

1   What is the name of the RSPB nature reserve on the shores of Loch Leven?
2   What is the name by which the vast areas of woodland which once covered much of Scotland are known?
3   What is an SSSSI?
4   Which two Scottish islands were joined by causeway in 2000?
5   Where is Scotland's only *natural* World Heritage Site?
6   Who/what were Megan and Morag?
7   Where is the east end of the Southern Upland Way?
8   Why have the villages of East Wemyss and West Wemyss needed Government funding for their own protection?
9   What is Scotland's only native breed of hunting dog?
10 Which Scottish female singer was awarded an OBE for her services to music in 2000?
11 In which year did the Dunblane tragedy, in which 16 children and their teacher were killed by a gunman, occur?
12 Edinburgh-born man, Richard Tait, invented the fastest-selling board game in history. What is it called?
13 Where is Scotland's first 'Booktown'?
14 Which king introduced the feudal system to Scotland?
15 For how many years was Mary, Queen of Scots, kept in captivity by Elizabeth I of England?
16 With which football club is the name of Ebbe Skovdahl associated?
17 Name the politician who published a book entitled *Imagine*.
18 How did actor Richard Wilson 'die a death' in November 2000?
19 Who sponsors the 'Spirit of Scotland' awards?
20 In which decade did soldier, diplomat and historian Fitzroy Maclean die?
21 What was the trade of Kirkpatrick Macmillan?
22 Which famous criminal case featured in Ludovic Kennedy's *A Presumption of Innocence*?
23 Which well-known firm of Edinburgh booksellers was founded in 1848?
24 Who was the brother of the Wolf of Badenoch?
25 The name of which Scottish loch is associated with kippers?

Answers: p194

Art 1

1 Which artist painted many beautiful scenes of the coast at Catterline?
2 With which type of painting is Sir Henry Raeburn associated?
3 What relation was Allan Ramsay, painter, to the poet of the same name?
4 Name the contemporary Scottish painter who produced a series of pictures while in hospital recovering from a liver transplant.
5 Which Scottish sculptor is associated with the question mark?
6 What was the name by which Fergusson, Cadell, Peploe and Hunter were known collectively?
7 Which Scottish artist and writer transformed his home into 'Little Sparta'?
8 In which city is the Scottish National Portrait Gallery?
9 Which Scottish artist was appointed Britain's war artist in Bosnia?
10 Who painted *The Porteous Mob* in 1855?
11 Where did William Gillies study art?
12 With which group of painters is the name of James Guthrie associated?
13 Who became head of Glasgow School of Art in 1885?
14 What was the name of Charles Rennie Mackintosh's artist wife?
15 Who painted *The Indian Rug*?
16 Which contemporary artist painted a series of murals for The People's Palace in Glasgow?
17 He was a painter working at the end of the nineteenth century, who produced energetic and powerful seascapes, such as *The Storm*. Who was he?
18 Which painter succeeded Raeburn as the king's official artist?
19 Name the Italo-Scottish sculptor and printmaker who was a pioneer of Pop Art.
20 Where are the Phoebe Anna Traquair murals to be found?
21 With which group of artists were Margaret Macdonald, Frances Macdonald, Jessie Newbery and Jessie King associated?
22 Which Scots artist was known for his paintings of fairies?
23 Where are the McManus Galleries?
24 Broughton House, Kirkcudbright was once the home of which artist?
25 Which famous Scottish cartoonist and caricaturist died in 1997?

Answers: p195

QUESTIONS

1 Near which town is the castle of Drumlanrig?
2 Where did Robert the Bruce stab the Red Comyn?
3 Which town is the smallest royal burgh in Scotland?
4 In which year did the Lockerbie air disaster occur?
5 What stands on the Colvin fountain in Moffat?
6 Near which town is the Craigleuch Explorers' Museum?
7 What is the name of the artist E.A. Hornel's former home in Kirkcudbright?
8 In which century was Glenluce Abbey founded?
9 Which textile industry once flourished in Gatehouse of Fleet?
10 On the estuary of which river is Kippford situated?
11 In which abbey (now ruined) in Dumfries and Galloway did Mary, Queenof Scots spend her last night in Scotland?
12 On which river is St John's Town of Dalry situated?
13 In which village were Covenanting declarations made in 1680 and 1685?
14 In which century was the castle of St John in Stranraer built?
15 Where is the Monreith Cross?
16 How many Wigtown Martyrs were there?
17 Where was Kirkpatrick Macmillan, inventor of the bicycle, born?
18 Where is the Stewartry Museum?
19 In which churchyard is Robert Burns buried?
20 Which castle near Castle Douglas was a stronghold of the Douglas family?
21 In which village was William Paterson, founder of the Bank of England, born?
22 Where is the second-oldest subscription library in Great Britain?
23 What is the White Coomb?
24 Near which town is Craigcaffie Castle situated?
25 In which village was Thomas Carlyle born?

Answers: p195

Plays & Theatres 1

1 Who wrote the play *Mary Queen of Scots Got Her Head Chopped Off*?
2 Which theatre company toured with *The Cheviot, the Stag and the Black, Black Oil*?
3 Where is the Byre Theatre?
4 Who wrote *The Slab Boys*?
5 Where does Scotland's largest repertory company have its base?
6 Where is the Citizen's Theatre?
7 What was the real name of music-hall star Harry Lauder?
8 What is the name of the largest theatre in Aberdeen?
9 Who wrote *Ane Satyre of the Three Estaitis*?
10 Who were Francie and Josie?
11 Name the stage and television actor who married actress Una MacLean.
12 Who wrote *The Sash*?
13 In which town is The MacRobert Arts Centre?
14 Who wrote *The Gentle Shepherd*?
15 Who wrote *The Steamie*?
16 What is the name of the smallest theatre in Scotland?
17 Which leading Scots actor has provided the television commentary for many royal occasions?
18 Which Scottish music-hall performer is remembered for the song *I Belong to Glasgow*?
19 Who wrote *The Hard Man* and *Animals*?
20 Where is the Traverse Theatre?
21 Which Scottish actor and comedian starred in a Scottish translation of *Le Bourgeois Gentilhomme*?
22 Where was Scots stage and film star Alastair Sim born?
23 What is the name of the theatre company set up by Robert Carlyle in 1991?
24 Name the Scots choreographer of the Royal Ballet who died in 1992.
25 Who wrote *The Wallace*?

Answers: p196

General Knowledge 12

1 In which decade was the SYHA formed?

2 Where is Robert Adam buried?

3 In which decade did the first postage stamps come into use in Scotland?

4 On which foreign island did Alexander Selkirk survive alone for more than four years?

5 What was the real name of Kinmont Willie?

6 By which name was James Crichton of Eliock, the sixteenth-century scholar, also known?

7 In which century was the first Bible printed in Scotland?

8 In which century did General Wade come to Scotland?

9 What is the name of the largest teachers' union in Scotland?

10 What are the titles of the two Law Officers of the Crown?

11 In which decade were the Reith Lectures instituted?

12 What relationship did John Playfair bear to William Playfair?

13 What Nobel Prize did James Mirrlees win in 1996?

14 Name the Scot who produced the first waterproof cloth.

15 At which exhibition did Margaret Macdonald, wife of Charles Rennie Mackintosh, win a diploma of honour in 1902?

16 In which country was Scots medical pioneer, Elsie Inglis born?

17 Which one was the younger: obstetrician William Hunter, or his surgeon brother John?

18 What was the profession of David Octavius Hill, 1802–70?

19 Who was goldsmith to James VI and Anne of Denmark?

20 When did the first Edinburgh Military Tattoo take place?

21 Which mountains were put up for sale by John Macleod in 2000?

22 In which year did an explosion take place in a waste shaft at Dounreay?

23 Which agricultural event takes place at Ingliston every year in June?

24 What is the name of the construction firm started by George Balfour in 1909?

25 In which year did John Balliol make his claim to the Scottish throne?

Answers: p196

Music 2

1   With which instrument is the name of Tom Anderson associated?
2   Name the four members of The Boys of the Lough.
3   Who wrote the song 'And werena my Heart Licht I wad Dee'?
4   Who composed the music for Tyrone Guthrie's production of *Ane Satyre of the Three Estaitis* in the 1948 Edinburgh festival?
5   Who composed the opera *Confessions of a Justified Sinner?*
6   Where is the home of the Scottish Chamber Orchestra?
7   Where is the Russell Collection of keyboard instruments housed?
8   What is the popular venue for rock and pop gigs in Glasgow nowadays?
9   When was the Royal Concert Hall in Glasgow opened?
10 Who composed the *Scottish Piano Concerto*?
11 What instrument did Hector McAndrew play?
12 Where did Tom Anderson come from?
13 In which century was James Johnson's *Scots Musical Museum* compiled?
14 Where is the Royal Scottish National Orchestra based?
15 Which Scots comedian and musician played in the Humblebums?
16 Where was composer Thea Musgrave born?
17 Where did percussionist Evelyn Glennie train?
18 Who wrote Rod Stewart's hit 'Sailing'?
19 Name the McGuinness Flint hit of 1970.
20 Which instrument does Mike Marra play?
21 Who wrote 'Dirty Old Town'?
22 Which town does jazz saxophonist Tommy Smith come from?
23 Where is the music venue 'King Tut's'?
24 Which instrument is associated with jazz musician Archie Semple?
25 Who was the first Scot to represent Britain in the Eurovision Song Contest?

Answers: p197

The Islands of Scotland 1

1   What is the name given to the line of islands stretching from Barra Head to Butt of Lewis?
2   Where is Eilan Glas lighthouse?
3   Barra is the seat of which clan?
4   In what year was the island of St Kilda abandoned?
5   What is the magical heirloom kept in Dunvegan Castle?
6   On which island can you find the 'Singing Sands'?
7   What is the capital of Orkney?
8   Where on Mull does the ferry from Oban land?
9   What island inspired Mendelssohn to write *The Hebridean Overture*?
10   On which island is Prince Charlie's Cave?
11   What is the island port of North Uist?
12   What sport can you play on Arinagour on Coll?
13   Where is St Oran's chapel?
14   Where is Bowmore?
15   On which island is the Clan Donald Centre?
16   Where on Mull is the Mull Little Theatre?
17   The Thrushel Stone is the largest single stone in Scotland. Where is it?
18   What is the name of the castle in Castlebay harbour?
19   What is the name of the highest peak on South Uist?
20   What is the man-made landmark on the Butt of Lewis?
21   What is the name of the gardeners' paradise on the island of Gigha?
22   Where did George Orwell write 1984?
23   What is the name of the home of the Dukes of Hamilton on Arran?
24   What is the most northerly island of Orkney?
25   What is Scapa Flow famous for?

Answers: p197

Great Scots 2

1 Which philosopher and historian wrote an *Essay on the History of Civil Society* in 1767?

2 Which Scottish politician of the early twentieth century spent some time working as a rancher in South America?

3 Which Scottish writer and broadcaster wrote *Euthanasia: the Good Death*?

4 Name the poet and writer who published *The Brownie of Bodsbeck* in the nineteenth century.

5 Name the Scottish theologian who published *Institutes of Theology*.

6 Which anaesthetic did James Young Simpson introduce into midwifery?

7 Name the Scottish lawyer and writer who published *Jus Feudale* in 1608.

8 Name the Scottish painter and King's Limner in Scotland who was knighted in 1836.

9 What is the name of the journal founded by Scots philosopher and psychologist Alexander Bain?

10 In which occupation was Lord Reith originally trained?

11 What is the name of the Scots theologian who published his own translation of the New Testament in 1968?

12 Name the Scottish football manager who began his management career with Dunfermline Athletic.

13 Name the racing hero who received a knighthood in the Queen's Birthday Honours List in 2001.

14 What was the profession of John Boyd Dunlop?

15 Name the Scottish barrister who published *Eve Was Framed*.

16 Which famous Scot became an outlaw after being accused of embezzling money from the Duke of Montrose?

17 Which Scottish physicist wrote *An Elementary Treatise on Rational Mechanics*?

18 What is the name of the Scottish lexicographer who edited a large part of the *New English Dictionary*, which later became the *Oxford English Dictionary*?

19 With which branch of learning is James Clerk Maxwell's name associated?

20 What was the profession of Nobel Prize winner Sir William Ramsay?

21 Of which institution was Lord George Thomson of Monifieth the chairman from 1981 to 1988?

22 Name the Scottish obstetrician who became physician to the Queen in Scotland in 1847.

23 Which nationalistic poet has been called The Voice of Scotland?

24 Name the Scots scientist who, in conjunction with Lord John Kayleigh, discovered argon.

25 Which eminent Scottish bacteriologist worked as a shipping clerk before taking up medicine?

Answers: p198

1 Where is the world's largest colony of gannets to be found?

2 Who does Charlie's monument in Coldstream honour?

3 Where is the start of the Southern Upland Way?

4 How many lambs has Dolly the sheep had altogether?

5 By what name did Arthur Stanley Jefferson become famous?

6 Where is BBC Tweed based?

7 For what purpose would a bannock stane be used?

8 Which novel by Sir Walter Scott features Jinglin' Geordie?

9 In which decade was the North Bridge in Edinburgh built?

10 What would a targe be used for?

11 Which objects were sometimes given the nickname 'black breeks'?

12 What is a souter?

13 Which prime minister of Great Britain encouraged the raising of highland regiments to fight for the British government?

14 Whose murder is described in *Kidnapped*?

15 What was the *Yellow Carvel*?

16 During which king's reign did Berwick finally become an English town?

17 In which decade was the General Teaching Council of Scotland established?

18 How are the Law Officers of the Crown selected?

19 Where was the first Bible printed in Scotland?

20 In which year was Lord Darnley murdered?

21 What is Hunt the Gowk?

22 What was the name given to the mythical giant of the Eildon Hills?

23 Which sculptor created a *Straw Locomotive* and a *Paper Boat*?

24 In which century was the Boys' Brigade founded?

25 'Some people think that football is a matter of life and death. I don't like that attitude. I can assure them it is much more serious than that.' Who said this?

Answers: p198

Strathclyde 1

1. On which peninsula is the town of Dunoon situated?
2. What is the Greenock Cut?
3. What are the names of the two sets of falls in the Falls of Clyde Nature Reserve?
4. By which name is Ben Arthur also known?
5. Where are the King's Caves?
6. What is the name of the port on Loch Gilp, at the entrance of the Crinan Canal?
7. Which village on Loch Lomond has been called the prettiest in Scotland?
8. Name the famous botanic garden which is situated on the Cowal Peninsula.
9. What is the name of the naval base which is situated near Garelochhead?
10. Where are 'St Columba's Footsteps'?
11. In which coastal resort of Strathclyde was John Loudon McAdam born?
12. In which town in Strathclyde is the Purves Puppet Theatre?
13. Where is the waterfall of Corra Linn?
14. Where is the Necropolis?
15. Where is the only surviving coal-fired gasworks in Scotland?
16. Where is William Wallace believed to have been born?
17. What is the Lang Whang?
18. In which century was the Battle of Bothwell Brig fought?
19. On which island does the town of Millport stand?
20. Which two Scottish kings died in Dundonald Castle?
21. Where is the oldest subscription library in Scotland?
22. In which town was a famous edition of the poetry of Burns printed?
23. Which three rivers meet at Irvine?
24. Which town in Strathclyde was once famous for the manufacture of snuff boxes?
25. Where were Quarrier's Homes built?

Answers: p199

1 With which two famous characters in history is the song 'Over the Sea to Skye' associated?
2 Who first hit the British Top Ten with 'Shout'?
3 Which folk-singing duo made 'Flower of Scotland' popular?
4 Which pop group sang 'Shang-a-Lang'?
5 Who wrote 'Ae Fond Kiss'?
6 Who is remembered for 'Roamin' in the Gloamin'?
7 Who wrote 'Charlie is my Darling'?
8 Which Scottish entertainer asked Donald where his troosers were?
9 Which Scots lass hit the big time with '9 to 5'?
10 Who wrote 'Jerusalem the Golden'?
11 Who wrote 'Afton Water'?
12 Who had a chart hit with 'Baker Street'?
13 Who sang about his old man, the dustman?
14 Which battle is remembered by 'Hey, Johnny Cope'?
15 Which Scottish singing duo sang about 'Sunshine on Leith'?
16 Who composed 'The Bonnie Wells o' Wearie'?
17 Which items of footwear did Billy Connolly praise in song?
18 Name the band which asks 'Why does it Always Rain on Me?'
19 Who wrote 'O, my Luve's like a Red, Red Rose'?
20 Which young Scots lass sang 'Ma, He's Making Eyes at Me'?
21 What was the song that made Will Fyffe famous?
22 With which song did Lulu win the Eurovision Song Contest?
23 Who is remembered for 'The Bluebell Polka'?
24 About whom was the lament 'Will Ye No' Come Back Again?' written?
25 Who wrote 'Scots Wha Hae'?

Answers: p199

Castles 1

1 Where is Scalloway Castle?
2 Dunrobin Castle is the seat of which noble Scottish family?
3 What is special about Caerlaverock Castle?
4 Which Scottish mathematician's family once owned Lauriston Castle in Edinburgh?
5 Which family owned Hailes Castle in East Lothian in the fourteenth century?
6 Which castle near Elie in Fife is now part of an exclusive timeshare development?
7 For which family was Castle Tioram built?
8 For which purpose is Carbisdale Castle now used?
9 Where did the Black Dinner of 1440 take place?
10 To which famous Edinburgh benefactor did Lennox Castle belong?
11 In which castle did Robert III die?
12 To which castle did Mary, Queen of Scots go immediately after her escape from Loch Leven?
13 Of which castle was the Goblin Ha' a part?
14 Which family owns Roslin Castle in Lothian?
15 What kind of ghost is said to haunt Abergeldie Castle in Deeside?
16 Which family owns Cortachy Castle in Angus?
17 From which century does MacLellan's Castle in Kirkcudbright date?
18 Name the castle near North Berwick which was built in the fourteenth century by William, 1st Earl of Douglas.
19 Near which town is Castle Campbell?
20 On which island is Muness Castle?
21 Where is Kisimul Castle?
22 Who was responsible for the restoration of Duart Castle on Mull?
23 Which castle near Castle Douglas once belonged to Archibald the Grim?
24 Where is Dunvegan Castle?
25 In which century was the present Balmoral Castle built?

Answers: p200

1   What did the Physic Garden in Edinburgh eventually become?

2   What was the name of Robert II's mother?

3   Whose autobiography is entitled *Wearing Spurs*?

4   In which decade did the trams stop running in Edinburgh?

5   Which Labour politician won the Nobel Peace Prize in 1934?

6   Which eminent Scot was Deputy Chief Prosecutor at the Nuremberg Trials?

7   Name the Scot who was Chancellor of the Exchequer under John Major from 1990 to 1993.

8   Where did Charles I surrender to the English forces in 1646?

9   What relationship did Malcolm III bear to Duncan I?

10 Who was Lord High Chancellor of Great Britain from 1987 to 1997?

11 Which prize was awarded to John MacLeod in 1923?

12 What is the middle name of the author Iain Banks?

13 How did Dame Isobel Baillie become famous?

14 In which century was Arthur James Balfour, 1st Earl of Balfour, Chief Secretary for Northern Ireland?

15 What was the name of the open-air swimming pool at Macduff?

16 Whose death sparked off the Wars of Independence in Scotland?

17 Who was known as the Scottish Hogarth?

18 In which year did the last lighthouse keeper in Scotland leave his post as automation took over?

19 In which year did Chancellor Gordon Brown marry?

20 Which Scottish school did Prince Phillip, Prince Charles and Prince Andrew attend?

21 Which Scottish driver narrowly escaped death in a crash in Corsica in 2000?

22 Who was the first Scottish king to issue his own autonomous coinage?

23 In which century was the last wild boar in Scotland hunted down?

24 What title did James VII hold before he became king?

25 When was universal male suffrage granted in Scotland?

Answers: p200

Literature 2

1   Who created Dr Jekyll and Mr Hyde?

2   Who wrote *My Schools and Schoolmasters* in 1852?

3   Who wrote *A Window in Thrums*?

4   Which nineteenth-century Scottish novelist wrote *The Annals of the Parish* and *The Provost*?

5   Whose autobiography, *Brave Days*, was published in 1931?

6   Where was Scots writer Jessie Kesson born?

7   Which Scots writer was 1st Baron Tweedsmuir?

8   Name the author of *At the Back of the North Wind* and *The Princess and the Curdie*.

9   Who wrote *The Big Man*?

10   Name the author of *Tunes of Glory*.

11   Which contemporary Scottish writer won the Macallan Golden Dagger for Fiction for his novel *Black and Blue*?

12   Who wrote *Tales of a Grandfather*?

13   Who published the first collection of the Waverley novels?

14   Fanny, the wife of Robert Louis Stevenson, burned the first draft of one of his books because she did not think it would be a success. Which book was it?

15   What is the Ashestiel Manuscript?

16   In which year was the New Testament first published in Gaelic?

17   Who wrote *The Grey Coast*?

18   Which Scottish literary magazine was started in 1817?

19   In which decade was *Chambers's Journal* started?

20   Laura Jackson is a successful and respected biographer of celebrities such as Brian Jones and Ewan McGregor. Where in Scotland does she live?

21   What is the name of the man who writes under the pseudonym of Ian Hay?

22   In which trade did novelist James Kelman originally train?

23   Who wrote *Letters to dead Authors* in 1886?

24   Who wrote a *History of Scottish Literature* in 1977?

25   Which novel by George Orwell was largely written on the Isle of Jura?

Answers: p201

Politics 2

1 Which Scottish constituency did Malcolm Rifkind lose in the 1997 election?

2 Who fell out with the Labour Party and stood as an independent in the 1997 General Election, winning Falkirk West?

3 What is the name of the Scot who followed in Betty Boothroyd's footsteps as Speaker in the House of Commons?

4 From whom did Donald Dewar win Aberdeen South in 1966?

5 Which Scot was the last leader of the Liberal Party?

6 Who was National Convenor of the SNP from 1979 to1990?

7 What position was held by William Whitelaw from 1972 to1973?

8 Where was Labour politician George Robertson born?

9 In which year was Alex Salmond first returned to the house of Commons as an MP?

10 Which Scot became Prime Minister after Gladstone?

11 Name the Socialist MSP who was imprisoned for refusing to pay Poll Tax.

12 When was the construction of the new Scottish Parliament buildings originally supposed to be completed?

13 Which Scottish politician was made Chief Secretary for Ireland in 1887?

14 Name the Scot who was Prime Minister from 1922 to1923.

15 After local government reform in Scotland in 1975, how many mainland regional councils were there?

16 In which year was the document *A Claim of Right for Scotland* drawn up?

17 How many MPs did Glasgow have in 1831?

18 What did the Scottish Unionist Party change its name to in 1965?

19 What was the name of the report produced in 1973, recommending an elected Scottish Assembly?

20 How many MEPs does Scotland have?

21 In which year was the Second Claim of Right made, stating that the Church of Scotland was to be free of state interference?

22 In which year was the Scottish Constitutional Convention established?

23 Following the approval of the Local Government (Scotland) Bill of 1994, how many local authorities were established in Scotland?

24 In which year was the Scottish Home Rule Association founded?

25 What do the letters SWRC stand for?

Answers: p201

Around and About in Scotland 2

1   By which Moray town can you see Sueno's Stone?
2   Where is James III buried?
3   Where is Barra Castle?
4   Where is the Branklyn Garden?
5   In which city is Lady Stair's House?
6   Where can you visit the Dynamic Earth Exhibition?
7   Where can you see a royal tennis court?
8   Near which village in East Lothian is Hailes Castle?
9   Where is the best-preserved broch in Scotland and what is its name?
10   Where is Loch Brittle?
11   In which Scottish burgh is Madras College?
12   Where are the falls of Lora?
13   For which town was the Stanely reservoir created?
14   What is Neptune's Staircase, and where is it?
15   Where is the Innerpeffray Library?
16   Where is the Devil's Beeftub?
17   Near which town is the Glenmorangie Distillery?
18   Where in Scotland can you walk along the Khyber Pass?
19   Which Scottish island was host to *Bacillus anthracis* from 1942 to 1987?
20   Where is the Scottish Fisheries Museum?
21   In which group of islands is the island of Fetlar?
22   Where can you visit the David Livingstone Centre?
23   Where are the Falls of Glomach?
24   What is the Pineapple and where is it?
25   Where is the Devil's Staircase?

Answers: p202

QUESTIONS

1   In which king's reign did Somerled, Lord of Argyll attack Glasgow?
2   Where was *The Great Michael* built?
3   After which battle in 1644 did Montrose take Perth?
4   What does HIA stand for in politics?
5   Which Scot was made chairman and chief executive of British Telecom in 1985?
6   Which Scottish prison faced closure in 2000?
7   Which Scottish Soap features Mrs Mac?
8   Which Edinburgh publisher had two books short-listed for the Whitbread Awards in November 2000?
9   In which century was the Scottish Fisheries Commission established?
10 Who announced that he would step down as chairman of the Scottish Tourist Board in 2001?
11 Where was Cardinal Thomas Winning born?
12 Where was the first purpose-built mosque in Scotland built?
13 Where did Jim Watt become World Champion?
14 In the 1970s 'I found it at Bruce's' was the slogan for what kind of business?
15 In which decade did Scottish miners finally become free men?
16 In the nineteenth century, which Scottish University had the largest number of students?
17 Who went on strike throughout Scotland in 1812?
18 Who wrote *Journals and Memorials of His Time*?
19 Which political activist was tried for sedition in 1918?
20 With which author is the character of 'Wee Jakie' associated?
21 Which serial killer famously conducted his own defence at his murder trial in 1958?
22 With which island is the name of St Molaise associated?
23 What is the name of the Trust established in 1984, to acquire wild land in Great Britain?
24 Whom did Thomas Reid succeed as Professor of Moral Philosophy at Glasgow University in 1764?
25 In which year did the Porteous Riot take place?

Answers: p202

Bonnie Prince Charlie

1 What was the exact date of Prince Charles Edward Stewart's birth?

2 In which year was Charles's brother Henry born?

3 In which year did his mother die?

4 Charles went on tour in the year 1737. To which part of Europe did his travels take him?

5 In which year did Charles see his father for the last time?

6 Who led the French fleet into the Channel in the attempt to invade England in 1744?

7 Who were the 'Seven Men of Glenmoriston'?

8 Where was Flora Macdonald taken to for imprisonment after her arrest?

9 Who led the troops against the Jacobite forces at the battle of Falkirk?

10 What was the name of the Englishman among the Seven Men of Moidart?

11 What was the first battle victory for the Jacobite cause?

12 Which part of Edinburgh remained in the possession of the Government troops after Charles's entry to Edinburgh?

13 In which month was Carlisle captured?

14 In which month was the decision taken to retreat from England?

15 After which event in the '45 did Charles lose the support of Lord George Murray for a while?

16 In which year did Charles meet Clementina Walkinshaw?

17 Where had the Jacobite forces reached when the decision was made to turn back?

18 How many months did Charles remain in Scotland after Culloden?

19 When Charles revisited London in 1750, how long did he stay?

20 In which year was Charles's daughter born?

21 In which year did Charles convert to the Protestant faith?

22 Who was the last man to be executed for his part in the '45 rebellion?

23 In which year did Clementina Walkinshaw leave Charles?

24 Whom did Charles marry in 1772?

25 What was the name of the man for whom Charles's wife left him in 1780?

Answers: p203

QUESTIONS

1 In which century was the East Neuk town of Crail granted status as a royal burgh?

2 Whose remains were discovered and then re-interred in Dunfermline Abbey in the early nineteenth century?

3 In which Fife seaside town is the Lady's Tower?

4 At the foot of which hills does the town of Falkland stand?

5 Name the airforce base in Fife which hosts a major air show.

6 Which village is situated beneath the north end of the Forth Railway Bridge?

7 Where is St Fillan's Cave?

8 In which Fife town is St Rule's tower?

9 Which two industries, apart from fishing, were once associated with St Monans?

10 In which Fife town is St Mungo's Chapel?

11 Name Fife's new town and centre of light industry.

12 In which town is Pittencrieff Park?

13 With which industry is Mossmorran associated?

14 From which century does the castle at Aberdour date?

15 What is housed in St Ayles' Land, in Anstruther?

16 Where is the nearest railway station to St Andrews?

17 Which textile industry once flourished in the town of Dunfermline?

18 In which town in Fife did James V die?

19 Near which town in Fife is Scotland's 'Secret Bunker'?

20 In which town in Fife might you take a walk along The Lade Braes?

21 In days when corporal punishment was still permitted in schools, to which town in Fife might a teacher go to buy a new tawse?

22 Which fishing town in Fife has a windmill?

23 Which Scottish monarch was thrown from his horse at Kinghorn?

24 In which historic Fife town is Stinking Wynd?

25 By which Fife burgh is Kincraig Point?

Answers: p203

Films & Film Stars 2

1   Which famous Scot played James Bond?

2   Which city hosts an International Film Festival?

3   Name the Scots actor who bared his all in the film *The Full Monty*.

4   Which Scots actor and comedian starred in *Nuns on the Run*?

5   In which box-office sell-out did Scottish actor John Hannah recite a poem by W.H. Auden?

6   Which village in the north-east was used as a backdrop for the film *Local Hero*?

7   Who played the prison officer in the television comedy *Porridge* and also had a major role in the film *Local Hero*?

8   Which Scottish actor co-starred with Pauline Collins in *Shirley Valentine*?

9   Where was *Trainspotting* set?

10 Name the Scots comedian who co-starred with Judi Dench in *Mrs Brown*.

11 Where is the beach that features in the opening sequence of *Chariots of Fire*?

12 What is the name of the film that is based on the life of Jimmy Boyle?

13 Which Scots film actor, who died in 1976, played a leading role in *The Belles of St Trinian's*?

14 Which Scots actor co-starred with Dirk Bogarde in the *Doctor* films?

15 Who was the Scottish director of *Trainspotting*?

16 When was *Tunes of Glory* made?

17 Who played the Scots missionary Eric Liddell in *Chariots of Fire*?

18 Who was the Scots star of *A Life Less Ordinary*?

19 Name the Scots comedian who played a serious role in the film *Gorky Park*.

20 Which Scots entertainer had a role in *Elstree Calling* in 1930?

21 In which year did Deborah Kerr star in *The King and I*?

22 Name the Scots comedian, entertainer and actor who made his first film appearance in *Geordie* in 1956?

23 Who made a film entitled *Comrades*?

24 Which famous part did Robert Powell, Robert Donat and Kenneth More play in separate film versions of a popular thriller?

25 Name the Scots-born documentary maker who made *Drifters* and *Housing Problems* and who set up the National Film Board of Canada.

Answers: p204

1   To which prominent Scot was Mary Somerville married?
2   Who designed the equestrian statue of the Duke of Wellington in Edinburgh?
3   What should you do with guga?
4   What is the name for the feral sheep which live on St Kilda?
5   Whom did Jane Beaufort marry?
6   Where is the Centre for Contemporary Art?
7   What do we know the festival of Samhain as?
8   In which year did the Scottish football team first win a game in the World Cup?
9   In which century did the General Assembly of the Church of Scotland, as we know it today, first meet?
10 What was the name of the bill, passed in 1689, which limited the powers of the monarchy and stated that the monarch must be Protestant?
11 Who issued the first Declaration of Indulgence?
12 For how many years did the Stone of Destiny remain at Westminster?
13 Which conflict ended with the Pacification of Berwick?
14 What was the proper title of Black Agnes?
15 Of which king was it recorded that he 'happinit to be slane'?
16 Which King James of Scotland lived the longest?
17 Where are the highest cliffs in Great Britain?
18 Where would you go to visit the Crannog Centre?
19 Which football club was founded in 1877?
20 Who was accused of murdering Pierre Emile l'Angelier?
21 In which year were the heritable jurisdictions of the clan chiefs abolished?
22 Which by-election did Jim Sillars win in 1988?
23 In which battle in 1545 was Lord Dacre victorious over the Scots?
24 Of which other literary Robert was Robert Burns an admirer?
25 In which year did James IV declare war on Henry VIII of England?

Answers: p204

Sport 2

1   Which Borders team did John Jeffrey play for?

2   What is Gavin Hastings's first name?

3   In which year did Stephen Hendry become the youngest-ever snooker player to win the Rothman's Grand Prix?

4   Which football player and manager was known as 'Caesar'?

5   When did Jackie Stewart retire as a motor racing driver?

6   In which sport did Willie Wood win a Commonwealth Games gold medal?

7   What is the name of the newest course at Turnberry?

8   How many Scots were in the British 2000 Paralympics squad?

9   Which Edinburgh school did Andy Irvine attend?

10   What position did David Sole play?

11   Which part of Scotland does Sam Torrance come from?

12   How old was Alan Wells when he won his Olympic gold?

13   Where did swimmer David Wilkie spend his early childhood?

14   In which year did David Sole retire from international rugby?

15   Name the Scottish football manager who used to play for Preston North End.

16   When was the Caledonian Curling Club formed?

17   Who scored the winning goal in the European Cup in 1967?

18   When did the Wembley Wizards beat England?

19   How many Scots won gold medals in the 1912 Olympics in Stockholm? a) 5 b) 15 c) 12

20   From where to where did the Claymores move in 2000?

21   Which Scottish runner won silver in the 400 metre relay in Munich in 1972?

22   Which motor racing team is distinguished by a tartan strip on its cars?

23   In which event did Scottish sportsman Craig MacLean win a silver medal at the 2000 Sydney Olympics?

24   With which local club is rugby international Craig Chalmers associated?

25   In which year did Benny Lynch win his world title?

Answers: p205

QUESTIONS

1   Which famous conservationist was born in Dunbar?
2   Where did the last Scottish Parliament for over 350 years meet in 1646?
3   In which Lothian town is the Knox Academy?
4   Where is the Phantassie Doocote?
5   Which river flows through the village of Pencaitland?
6   Where is the Museum of Flight?
7   Where is the site of St Colm's Abbey?
8   Who founded Roslin Castle?
9   Where is the Lady Victoria Colliery?
10 Where is the home of Edinburgh Crystal?
11 Where in East Lothian did a notorious witch trial and burning take place in 1591?
12 In which century was Newbattle Abbey founded?
13 Where in West Lothian did John Knox lead his first Protestant communion?
14 Where is the Lizzie Bryce roundabout?
15 What is the name of the nature reserve beside Dunbar?
16 In which town in Lothian was King Alexander II born?
17 In which castle did Mary, Queen of Scots and Bothwell take refuge after they were married?
18 Where is 'Little France'?
19 Which famous writer lived for a number of years in Lasswade Cottage?
20 Which industry has left its mark on the landscape around Mid Calder?
21 What is the name of the military barracks at Penicuik?
22 Near which village is Hopetoun House?
23 Which river flows through Bonnyrigg?
24 Where is Pinkie House?
25 Which monarch's name is associated with Carberry Hill?

Answers: p205

Language

1   What is a puddock?

2   What is a corbie?

3   What would you do with a bodle in times gone by?

4   What is your thrapple?

5   'Weel done, Cutty Sark!' cried Tam o' Shanter in the famous poem by Robert Burns. What does Cutty Sark mean?

6   'Sic-like' means 'unwell'. True or false?

7   What does the phrase 'Dinna fash yersel' mean?

8   When you flit from one place to another, are you airborne?

9   What time of day is 'the gloamin'?

10   What does 'clishmaclaver' mean?

11   What is 'glaur'?

12   What are your 'hurdies'?

13   What would you do with 'parritch'?

14   What is a 'whang o' kebbuck'?

15   A 'bummie's bike' is a means of transport. True or false?

16   What are 'quears' and 'loons'?

17   If someone said you had a 'muckle gab', would you be flattered? Why/why not?

18   What is a 'moudiwart'?

19   What kind of artisan would use a 'lapstane'?

20   Would you like to be described as 'couthie'? Why/why not?

21   'There was a cloker, dabbit at a man,
He dee'd for fear, he dee'd for fear . . .'
What is a cloker?

22   'As I gaed up the Canongate, and through the Netherbow,
Four-and-twenty wabsters were swingin' in a tow . . .'
What is a wabster and what is a tow?

23   What does 'wi' a tyauve' mean?

24   What was a doit?

25   What is the name for the dialect of the area around Aberdeen?

Answers: p206

Poetry 2

1 Which Scottish poet's mother was called Margaret Laidlaw?
2 By which other name was Gaelic poet Robert Mackay also known?
3 Who wrote *A Chronicle of Scottish Poetry* in 1802?
4 'Home is the sailor, home from the sea,
And the hunter home from the hill.'
Who wrote these lines?
5 'The King sits in Dunfermline town
Drinking the blude red wine . . .'
Which Scottish poem begins with these lines?
6 Who wrote *Rokeby*?
7 Which eighteenth-century Scottish poet died in an asylum for the insane?
8 Which Scots poet was a favourite at the court of James IV and Margaret Tudor?
9 Which twentieth-century poet wrote *Elegies*, after the death of his wife?
10 In which century did the poet John Barbour live?
11 Name the heroine of the Border ballad 'Tamlane' or 'Tam Lin'?
12 In 'The Twa Corbies', what are the two birds talking about?
13 Who wrote 'So We'll Go No More a Roving'?
14 From which historical poetical work is the following taken?
'A! Freedom is a noble thing!
Freedom mays man to haiff liking;
Freedom all solace to man giffis;
He levys at es that frely levys.'
15 Name the twentieth-century poet who wrote the sonnet 'At Robert Fergusson's Grave'.
16 Name the contemporary author of *Six Glasgow Poems*.
17 Where is the Scottish Poetry Library?
18 In 'The Ballad of True Thomas', how long is Thomas told that he must live in Elfland?
19 Which Scottish poet wrote 'Culloden and After'?
20 From which well-known ballad is the following taken?
'Why weep ye by the tide, ladie,
Why weep ye by the tide?'
21 Which Scots poet published a collection called *The Flying Corset*?
22 Name the novelist and poet who wrote the poem 'A Mile an' a Bittock'.
23 Who wrote the poem 'Lock the Door Lariston'?
24 Which sixteenth-century poet wrote 'Upone Tabacco'?
25 From which poem is the following taken?
'The pawky auld carle cam ower the lea
Wi' mony good-e'ens and days to me,
Saying "Gudewife, for your courtesie,
Will you lodge a silly poor man?"'

Answers: p206

1   In which century was Barlinnie Prison built?

2   In which century was the Andersonian Institute founded in Glasgow?

3   Who founded the Ben Nevis Observatory?

4   Where were the four quarters of William Wallace sent?

5   What was the name of James Watt's English partner in business?

6   Which Scot found the source of the Blue Nile?

7   In politics, what did the initials SHRA stand for?

8   Which military unit was founded by Sir Archibald David Stirling?

9   Whom did Graeme Souness succeed as manager of Liverpool in 1991?

10 What were the names of the two clans of the Picts?

11 Which sporting organization was formed in 1873?

12 Which Scottish regiment was raised by the Earl of Leven?

13 Under which monarch was the College of Justice instituted in Scotland?

14 Which town in Berwickshire is associated with the Glasgow School of painters?

15 What title was General Wade given when he came to Scotland?

16 In which century were mail coaches introduced between London and Edinburgh?

17 What is the only English team in the Scottish football league?

18 Where is the Brig o' Doon?

19 What does 'carse' mean?

20 In which part of Scotland was the real Admirable Crichton born?

21 In which year was the Flodden Wall built?

22 What are the names of the characters played which brought fame to Forbes Masson and Alan Cumming?

23 At which Scottish University did Prince William choose to study?

24 Which female Scots TV presenter fronted a series about the Munros?

25 What are the names of Glasgow's two main railway stations?

Answers: p207

QUESTIONS

1   Which river flows through Dunblane?

2   Which loch provides most of Glasgow's water?

3   Which school was founded by John McNabb?

4   Which mountain is 'the fairy mountain of the Caledonians'?

5   In which Tayside town did the dispute take place which led ultimately to the Disruption?

6   Blairgowrie is now known for the soft fruit that is grown in the region, but what industry did the town build its wealth on in the nineteenth century?

7   In which year did William Wallace take Stirling Castle?

8   Is Ben Ledi, by Callander, a Munro?

9   Which two rivers flow through Doune?

10   In which house near Fettercairn can visitors see a collection of Gladstone memorabilia?

11   What song was written by Robert Burns about the countryside around Aberfeldy?

12   Which organization manages the site of Bannockburn?

13   What is the name of the hill by Scone Palace where kings of Scotland were once crowned?

14   From which river was Loch Faskally created?

15   What tragedy is said to have struck the village of Balfron three centuries ago?

16   Where was 'Perkin's Mauve' famously used?

17   What is the highest mountain in Perthshire?

18   Which saint is believed to be buried in Balquhidder?

19   From which century does the tower of the ruined Muthill church date?

20   In which Perthshire town can be found the Little Houses?

21   Which educational institution is situated in the Airthrey estate?

22   Near which loch is Ardvorlich House?

23   Which architect designed Kinross House?

24   In which century was the library at Innerpeffray opened?

25   Through which hills does Gleneagles run?

Answers: p207

The Life & Career of Sean Connery

1 In which year was Sean Connery born?
2 What was the name of his father?
3 What was the maiden name of his mother?
4 What was the name Sean Connery's parents gave him?
5 Why did Sean Connery leave the navy?
6 In what year did he recieve an honorary degree from Heriot-Watt University?
7 What is the name of Sean Connery's son?
8 Who co-starred with Connery in *Family Business*?
9 In which year was *The Hill* released?
10 What is the name of Sean Connery's second wife?
11 Which film, set in the depths of the jungle, did Connery star in in 1992?
12 What role did Sean Connery play in *Robin Hood, Prince of Thieves*?
13 What is the name of Sean Connery's stepson?
14 What was the second Bond film in which Sean Connery starred?
15 What was the first stage musical in which Sean Connery secured a small part?
16 What was the name of the first film in which he appeared?
17 What sport does Sean Connery play and watch for relaxation?
18 In which year did he appear in *Dr No*?
19 What was the name of the 1965 film in which fellow Scot Ian Bannen starred with Connery?
20 Whom did Sean Connery marry in 1962?
21 What part did Sean Connery play in *The Untouchables*?
22 In which film did Connery appear as Colonel Arbuthnot?
23 What year was *Never Say Never Again* released?
24 In which film did Sean Connery co-star with Harrison Ford in 1989?
25 How old was Sean Connery when his younger brother Neil was born?

Answers: p208

1   Name the Liberal politician who founded the Territorial Army.

2   What was the main reason why Keir Hardie lost his parliamentary seat in 1915?

3   Name the Scottish general who handed Charles I over to Parliament in 1646.

4   Who were the parents of Mary II?

5   In which year was James Maxton expelled from the House of Commons?

6   In which year was the Second Book of Discipline drawn up?

7   Agnes Sampson was tortured and put to death at North Berwick for witchcraft. What other charge was laid against her?

8   Who was consecrated Archbishop of St Andrews in 1660?

9   In whose reign did the Union of the Parliaments of Scotland and England take place?

10 When was the Glorious Revolution?

11 Who was the mother of the Old Pretender?

12 What was the last battle won by Bonnie Prince Charlie before his defeat at Culloden?

13 In which year did James VI sign the Confession of Faith?

14 When did the Gowrie Conspiracy take place?

15 In which year did the evacuation of St Kilda take place?

16 When did the pupils of Edinburgh High School riot?

17 When was the Caledonian Canal opened?

18 Who was responsible for the burning of Elgin Cathedral?

19 Which Highland town was founded in 1776?

20 In which year did the Old Pretender leave Scotland for good?

21 What were the two warring factions in the Battle of the Braes?

22 In which year did Mary, Queen of Scots marry Bothwell?

23 In which year was Elgin Cathedral burned?

24 Where did John Balliol abdicate?

25 In which year did James IV marry?

Answers: p208

1   Name two former inmates of the Special Unit at Barlinnie Prison who, while they were there, discovered they had considerable artistic ability, particularly in sculpting.

2   Who is the author of the 'Katie Morag' books?

3   What are the colours of Partick Thistle Football Club?

4   How was Skara Brae discovered?

5   Which position was taken up by Lord Gordon of Strathblane in 1998?

6   In which decade was Scottish Ballet formed?

7   What is the name of the company owned by wealthy Scottish businessman Brian Soutar?

8   Which king banned golf and football in 1457?

9   What was a leister and what was it used for?

10   What is the Scottish Blackface?

11   Name the Scot who made the first ascent of the southwest face of Everest.

12   What is the name of the town which features in *The House with the Green Shutters*?

13   Which two Scottish brewing firms merged in 1931 to form Scottish Brewers?

14   In which decade was the Bilingualism Project launched in some primary schools in the Outer Isles?

15   In which Scottish industry was the Egyptian Wheel once used?

16   Why was one Scottish locomotive nicknamed 'The Diver'?

17   Which Scottish footballer distinguished himself by being sent off during his first game as player/manager?

18   In which area of the world of music has Ian Hamilton made his name?

19   Who collected a *Tea-Table Miscellany*?

20   In which decade was the Scottish Law Comission established?

21   Which famous Scottish artist painted *The Vegetable Stall*?

22   Who designed the bridge at Dunkeld?

23   Where is the 369 Gallery?

24   What relationship did James VII bear to William of Orange?

25   In which year were Glasgow and Edinburgh first linked by rail?

Answers: p209

1   When was the Battle of Bannockburn fought?
2   Who emerged as victors in the Battle of Pinkie?
3   Who led the English troops in the Battle of Prestonpans?
4   When was the Battle of Stirling Bridge fought?
5   Who led the English troops at the battle of Culloden?
6   What was the date of the battle of Culloden?
7   Who led the Scottish troops in the Battle of Dunbar?
8   Which battle, fought in 1679, was a significant defeat for the Covenanters?
9   Against whom were the Covenanters victorious in the Battle of Philiphaugh in 1645?
10   At which battle did John Claverhouse lose his life?
11   Which battle was fought in 1513?
12   Where was Mary, Queen of Scots defeated by Moray in 1568?
13   What battle was fought between the Saxons and the Picts in 1685?
14   At what battle was Malcolm III killed in 1093?
15   Who commanded the Scots at the battle of Stirling Bridge?
16   In which battle, in 1388, did the Earl of Douglas defeat the English under the command of Henry Percy?
17   Who commanded the Jacobite forces that were defeated at the Battle of Sheriffmuir?
18   When was the Battle of Largs?
19   Which side won the Battle of Ancrum: Scots or English?
20   Which king was killed after the Battle of Sauchieburn?
21   When did the battle of Kilsyth take place?
22   In which battle in 1679 was Viscount Dundee beaten by the Covenanters?
23   When was the Battle of Falkirk?
24   When was the Battle of Dunkeld?
25   Where was Dalyell's victory over the covenanters in 1666?

Answers: p209

Edinburgh 1

1 What is the name of Edinburgh's extinct volcano?
2 In which century was the Abbey of Holyrood founded?
3 Which hotel stands at the corner of Lothian Road and Princes Street?
4 Name the street that stretches from Edinburgh Castle to Holyrood Palace.
5 Name the wall that was built to add to the city's defences in the early sixteenth century.
6 Where is the Scott Monument?
7 Who was murdered in Holyrood Palace in 1566?
8 Name the hidden street that lies below the City Chambers in Edinburgh.
9 By which signal can the citizens of Edinburgh set their clocks each day?
10 What draws hundreds of spectators to the castle esplanade in August every year?
11 Where is the Heart of Midlothian?
12 Which famous animal has a statue in his memory on George IV Bridge?
13 From which century does Edinburgh's New Town date?
14 Which seaside resort, named after a town in Panama, was the first to have bathing machines?
15 Where was the Nor' Loch?
16 What was a Luckenbooth?
17 Which two galleries stand at the foot of the Mound?
18 How frequently does the Edinburgh Book Festival take place?
19 Meadowbank Stadium was built for which games?
20 What is the name of the 'unofficial' arm of the Edinburgh Festival?
21 What is the name of the famous cannon at Edinburgh Castle?
22 Where is the Witches Well?
23 With what cry did the citizens of Edinburgh's Old Town dispose of their waste matter out of their windows at ten o'clock every night?
24 Who designed the buildings on the north side of Charlotte Square?
25 What is the name of the bridge designed by Telford that spans the Water of Leith at the west end of town?

Answers: p210

Politics 3

1   Where was Tony Blair born?

2   Who was leader of the Labour Party from 1992 to 1994?

3   When was the Scottish Nationalist Party founded?

4   Who became Scotland's First Minister in November 2000?

5   When was the first seat in Westminster won by an SNP candidate?

6   Which position did Malcolm Rifkind hold in the Cabinet immediately before the election of 1997?

7   In which industry did Keir Hardie begin his working life?

8   Who was the first Conservative woman minister?

9   Where is the site of the new Scottish Parliament building?

10 Which Prime Minister was forced to resign in 1855 over the Crimean War?

11 Who became leader of the Scottish National Party in 1990?

12 How many seats did the Labour Party win in Scotland in the 1997 election?

13 How many Scottish Prime Ministers of Britain have there been, including Tony Blair?

14 Whom did Tony Blair appoint as Chancellor of the Exchequer in 1997?

15 For how many years did Malcolm Rifkind hold the same seat in Parliament?

16 In which year did Katharine, Duchess of Atholl, resign her seat in Parliament?

17 Which political party does Gavin Strang represent?

18 Where are the headquarters of the Scottish National Party?

19 How many MPs does Scotland have in the House of Commons?

20 In which election was the Conservative party defeated in every constituency in Scotland?

21 In what year did Sir Henry Campbell-Bannerman become Prime Minister?

22 What was the name of the committed Marxist who became the first Soviet Consul in Scotland?

23 Name the socialist leader, born in Scotland of Irish parents, who was executed for his part in the Easter Rising in 1916.

24 Which Scottish literary figure became MP for the Scottish Universities in 1927?

25 Who was appointed the first president of the Scottish Labour Party in 1888?

Answers: p210

1   Which well-known author assisted in the appeal against the conviction of Oscar Slater for murder?

2   Which song do the following lines come from?
    'It's the call of sea and shore,
    It's the tang of bog and peat,
    And the scent of brier and myrtle
    That puts magic in our feet.'

3   Name the daughter of Malcolm Canmore who married Henry I.

4   What invention by James Dewar has brought warmth to many a cold outing in Scotland and elsewhere?

5   Where did the philosopher Adam Ferguson go to university?

6   What was the middle name of Scots journalist Alastair Dunnett?

7   Which Scottish medical pioneer was knighted in 1944 and won a Nobel Prize in 1945?

8   In which country did nineteenth-century industrialist James Finlayson establish the textile factory of Oy Finlayson Ab?

9   How many King Jameses died a natural death?

10 Who was the only surviving direct descendent in the House of Canmore after the death of Alexander III?

11 Name the Scottish author of *Ice Station Zebra*.

12 Through which mountain range does the Lairig Ghru run?

13 Which Scots pop group urged their fans to 'Keep on Dancin''?

14 Which football club did rock singer Jim Kerr try to buy?

15 With which two industries is the name of Sir Ian Kinloch McGregor associated?

16 Which university has taken over the former Thomas Clouston Clinic at Craiglockhart in Edinburgh?

17 With which city is architect Archibald Simpson most associated?

18 When was the Tay Road Bridge opened?

19 With which four teams did Gordon Strachan play during his professional footballing career?

20 Where in the west of Scotland was the Nobel explosives plant built?

21 Name the biologist and sociologist who wrote *The Evolution of Sex* in 1889 and *Cities in Evolution* in 1915.

22 Where was the politician Michael Forsyth born?

23 After which Scottish botanist is *Gentiana forrestii* named?

24 With which branch of learning is the name of James Ferrier associated?

25 Who was the royal husband of the daughter of the 14th Earl of Strathmore?

Answers: p211

1   Where is the Horse Shoe Bar?

2   When was Glasgow Cathedral consecrated?

3   In what year did fire wreak havoc in Glasgow, destroying almost one third of the town?

4   What is the motto of Glasgow?

5   Which station is the terminus for the Glasgow–Edinburgh railway?

6   Where is the Burrell Collection?

7   Where was the original Paddy's Market?

8   When was Glasgow University founded?

9   Which two American artists topped the bill at the Gig on the Green at Glasgow Green in 2001?

10 Where are Glasgow's City Chambers?

11 When was the People's Palace built?

12 Where would you see a fish, a ring, a tree, a bird and a bell?

13 What is the name of Glasgow's famous weekend market?

14 What would you find in the Kibble Palace?

15 Which company owned a particularly exotic factory building in Glasgow?

16 What is the name of the oldest house in Glasgow?

17 Where does Sir Walter Scott stand on high in the city?

18 Where can you see a penny farthing?

19 In what year did Glasgow play host to the Garden Festival?

20 What are the names of the three main docks constructed on the Clyde between 1864 and 1897?

21 Where in Glasgow is Provand's Lordship?

22 In which century was Glasgow Academy founded?

23 Where is the Fossil Grove?

24 In what year was Glasgow proclaimed European City of Culture?

25 What is the name of the theatre in Gorbals Street?

Answers: p211

Literature 3

1   Where is Alastair MacLean's *When Eight Bells Toll* set?
2   What is the subject matter of *The Silver Bough*, by F. Marian McNeill?
3   Who was the father of Naomi Mitchison?
4   Which nineteenth-century writer used the pen-name Fiona MacLeod?
5   Which historical event featured in *Consider the Lilies*?
6   Who wrote *The Adventures of an Atom*?
7   Where did Muriel Spark live for some years after she was married?
8   Which book by Robert Louis Stevenson describes his own travels in France?
9   Who wrote under the pseudonym of Christopher North?
10   Who wrote *The Lymond Saga*?
11   For whom was *The Wind in the Willows* written?
12   Who wrote *The Steps to the Empty Throne*?
13   To which group of writers did Mrs Margaret Oliphant belong?
14   Who wrote a *Life of Byron* in 1830?
15   What is the profession of the central character in *Mr Alfred MA* by George Friel?
16   What were the first names of two Scots novelists and sisters, the Findlaters?
17   Who wrote a *History of the Five Jameses* in the early seventeenth century?
18   Who wrote *The Rodney Stone*?
19   What was the name of the first novel published by J. Leslie Mitchell?
20   In which part of Scotland was contemporary Scots writer Duncan McLean born?
21   Which famous children's book begins with the words 'The Mole had been working hard all the morning, spring-cleaning his little home'?
22   What is the name of the central character in Robin Jenkins's *Happy for the Child*?
23   Which Scottish novelist was judged Best of Young British Writers in 1993?
24   Which Scott novel was adapted for television in the 1990s?
25   Which Scottish writer published a collection of stories called *Where You Find It* in 1997?

Answers: p212

Rivers, Lochs & Falls

1 Which two rivers flow into the sea at Aberdeen?

2 Which three lochs form part of the Caledonian canal between Loch Linnhe and Loch Ness?

3 In which century did work first begin on the Clyde to make its waters deeper between Glasgow and Port Glasgow?

4 What is the name of the deepest loch in Scotland?

5 What is the name of the largest loch in Scotland?

6 What is the name of the sea loch which cuts into the west coast at Tarbert?

7 Which river passes through Dumfries before joining the Solway Firth?

8 Where is the source of The Water of Leith?

9 What are the names of the two lochs at either end of the Trossachs?

10 Which river joins the Forth at Cramond, in the north-west of Edinburgh?

11 Near the head of which loch is Dalwhinnie?

12 What is the highest waterfall in Britain?

13 On which loch was Mary, Queen of Scots held against her will?

14 What is the name of the river that flows through the Pass of Killiecrankie?

15 What is the name of the river that is spanned by Rumbling Bridge?

16 Which waterfall is known as 'the Gloomy Falls'?

17 Where does the Scottish River Tyne meet the sea?

18 When was the Forth Road Bridge opened?

19 What is the name of Scotland's second longest river?

20 'And me and my true love will never meet again . . .' Where?

21 What is the name of the source of the River Tweed?

22 Where is the source of the River Clyde?

23 To the nearest five miles, how long is the River Forth?

24 What is the name of the longest river in Scotland?

25 What is the name of the biggest tributary of the River Spey?

Answers: p212

General Knowledge 20

1   Where is Dyce Airport?
2   Where is McCulloch's tree and what is it?
3   Who sang 'I Love a Lassie'?
4   In which part of Scotland did the Levellers Revolt of 1724 take place?
5   Where was Allan Pinkerton born?
6   Which Scottish king married Euphemia Ross?
7   Where is Dunderave Castle?
8   What is the name of the freshwater herring found in the waters of Loch Lomond?
9   What treasures were found on Traprain Law in East Lothian?
10 Where would you go to visit Lady Stair's House?
11 Which Scottish publishing firm had its origins in the printing and publishing of educational and temperance texts?
12 Name the Scottish industrialist who worked for the Pennsylvania Railroad Company in the 1860s.
13 Where is the headquarters of the Scottish Forestry Commission?
14 Name the Scots poet who was made Professor of English at St Andrews University in 1991.
15 Which story by Arthur Conan Doyle was the first featuring Sherlock Holmes?
16 Which team did Sir Alex Ferguson manage before he moved to Aberdeen?
17 Which famous Scottish patriot was made MP for Haddingtonshire in the 1670s?
18 What is the name of the hospital for disabled ex-servicemen in Renfrewshire?
19 Which tragedy in nineteenth-century Scotland was caused by *phytophthora infestans*?
20 What is Wemyss Ware and where was it produced?
21 In which year were the Magnox reactors at Hunterston 'A' closed down?
22 Which famous Scots musician was born in Inver?
23 Which fishing port in the north-east is known as 'the Broch'?
24 Where was explorer John Rae born?
25 Who/what was Peaty Sandy?

Answers: p213

Great Scots 3

1 Name the philosopher who was keeper of the Advocates Library in Edinburgh in the 1750s.

2 In which continent did Mungo Park meet his death?

3 Name the Scots author of *The Divided Self*.

4 Which Scottish saint is said to have founded the abbey of Durrow in Ireland?

5 Which Scottish philosopher is commemorated with a monument on Calton Hill?

6 What tree is named after David Douglas, the famous botanist?

7 Who won the Nobel Prize for Chemistry in 1957?

8 Who was sent to France to escape the dangers of the 'Rough Wooing'?

9 Which Scottish theologian was nicknamed 'the Blast'?

10 In which decade was Charles Rennie Mackintosh born?

11 Which twentieth-century minister translated the New Testament from Greek into Scots?

12 How was the 'Red Fox' killed?

13 Which great Scots mathematician was born in Merchiston Castle, Edinburgh?

14 Which Scottish engineer entered into a manufacturing business partnership with Matthew Boulton?

15 In which country did Thomas Glover make his name and his fortune?

16 Name the famous Scottish sports commentator who began his working life as a teacher of PE.

17 Name the Scottish architect who succeeded his brother Robert as Architect of the King's Works in 1769.

18 Which famous Scottish Quaker was non-resident Governor of East New Jersey in the late seventeenth century?

19 In what profession did John Smith, former leader of the Labour Party, train?

20 Which future king of Scotland went into battle against his own father?

21 In which year did Anne, daughter of James VII, become Queen of Great Britain and Ireland?

22 Who was the Scottish economist who wrote *Inquiry into the Nature and Causes of the Wealth of Nations*?

23 When was the philosopher David Hume born?

24 Who was the geologist and writer who wrote *Scenes and Legends of the North of Scotland*?

25 Which Scottish criminologist wrote accounts of the trials of William Pritchard, Madeleine Smith and Oscar Slater, among others?

Answers: p213

Perth

1   Where did John Knox preach in 1559?
2   Who was The Fair Maid of Perth?
3   What is the name of the oldest established hotel in Scotland?
4   Where is the Regimental Headquarters and Museum of the Black Watch?
5   Which famous figure was moved from the High Street to King Street?
6   Who owns the Branklyn Garden?
7   Which Perth family's business interests moved from umbrellas, to dye, to dry cleaning?
8   When was the worst recorded flood in the history of Perth?
9   Who moved from Muirton Park to the Crieff Road?
10 When was the Fergusson Gallery opened?
11 What was swept away in the flood of 1621?
12 Which building makes a connection between whisky and curling?
13 Where will you find Ave Maria, Johannes Baptiste and Agnus Dei?
14 In which century was the King James VI Golf Club founded?
15 In which year were the four monasteries around Perth devastated by Reformers?
16 When was the Perth Civic Trust founded?
17 What event took place on the North Inch in 1397?
18 Who designed Perth Bridge?
19 How many bells are there in St John's Kirk?
20 When was Perth City Hall built?
21 Which two men were responsible for the land purchase, plans and building of Perth's New Town in the eighteenth century?
22 Where is the Perth Museum and Art Gallery?
23 In which year were three women put to death for witchcraft on the North Inch?
24 Where was Little Willie found?
25 Where did Arthur Bell begin his career in whisky blending and retailing?

Answers: p214

1 What is a clarsach?
2 What was the name of the first chart hit for the Scottish band Texas?
3 What is the difference between Highland pipes and Northumbrian pipes?
4 Which French composer wrote *Chanson Ecossaise*?
5 What is the name for the characteristic rhythmic figure found in Strathspey music?
6 Who wrote the Scottish anthem, 'Flower of Scotland'?
7 Of which musical duo was the composer of 'Flower of Scotland' one half?
8 What is mouth music?
9 Jimmy Shand is known worldwide for his music. What instrument does he play?
10 What do the Proclaimers have in common with Jimmy Shand?
11 Who was the Scot responsible along with Bob Geldof, for the launch of Live Aid in 1985?
12 How many drones do Scottish bagpipes have?
13 What is the time signature of reel music?
14 Which band had a hit with 'Thorn in my Side'?
15 Which musical organization was founded by Sir Alexander Gibson?
16 What kind of music did John Riddell compose?
17 Who wrote *The Art of Touching the Keyboard*?
18 Niel Gow's skills as a fiddle player and songwriter are still recognized nearly two hundred years after his death. Where was he born?
19 Which popular Scottish tenor was born in 1927?
20 What instrument did Helen Hopekirk play?
21 Name the Scottish pop group whose version of 'Love is All Around' featured in the film *Four Weddings and a Funeral*.
22 Which Scottish singer sang 'A Scottish Soldier'?
23 Which German composer wrote *The Scottish Symphony*, inspired by a visit to Holyrood?
24 Name the concerto written by Max Bruch, based on Scottish tunes.
25 What instrument does Shetland musician Aly Bain play?

Answers: p214

General Knowledge 21

1. After the deaths of Alexander III and the Maid of Norway, who were the two main contenders for the Scottish throne?
2. How many kings of Scotland were called Malcolm?
3. Which Dundee team plays in orange strips?
4. In which part of the United States is the SS *Queen Mary* now berthed?
5. Of which river is the Beltie Burn a tributary?
6. What was the profession of Sir Arthur Conan Doyle?
7. Which football team plays at Muirton Park?
8. In which century was the Duke of Atholl granted the right to keep a 'private' army?
9. Before St Andrews Cathedral was built, what was the most important cathedral in Scotland?
10. What was the CWC, formed in 1915?
11. Name the Scot who starred in the man from U.N.C.L.E.
12. To the nearest five metres, how high is the village of Tomintoul?
13. Who was Scotland's Footballer of the Year in 1980?
14. Who founded the Society of Antiquaries of Scotland?
15. Who wrote 'Scotland the Brave'?
16. Which mountain is known as The Cobbler?
17. For which occasion was the Edinburgh Tartan designed and manufactured?
18. With which town is the name of Dewar most associated?
19. What name became inextricably linked with cartography in Edinburgh?
20. Whom did Elizabeth Bowes-Lyon marry?
21. Where is Cannonball House?
22. What is the motto of Glasgow University?
23. On which island is the village of Ardminish?
24. Who provided the money to build what is now known as the Central Library in Edinburgh?
25. Where is the eastern terminal of the Forth-Clyde canal?

Answers: p215

Mary, Queen of Scots

1   In which year did the Babington Conspiracy take place?
2   How many men altogether acted as Regent in the troubled period after Mary's abdication?
3   Who was the first Regent after Mary's abdication?
4   Who held out Edinburgh Castle for Mary following her imprisonment?
5   What relationship did Mary bear to Henry VII of England?
6   What were the surnames of the Four Marys?
7   Whom did Mary declare an outlaw within a week of her wedding to Darnley?
8   Who was presiding clergyman at the infant James's baptism?
9   In which church did Mary marry the Dauphin?
10 In which year did the Dauphin die?
11 In which year was the child Mary sent to France?
12 What two titles were conferred upon Lord Darnley by Mary, just before his marriage to her?
13 Where did Darnley fall ill?
14 What title was given to Bothwell by Mary just before he married her?
15 Who owned the castle at Loch Leven where Mary was kept prisoner?
16 What was the name of Bothwell's first wife?
17 Before he married Mary, Bothwell had to obtain an annulment of his first marriage. Who granted the annulment?
18 Who was the last Regent before King James VI assumed power?
19 Where did Bothwell and Mary see each other for the last time?
20 Where was Mary taken immediately after her surrender at Carberry?
21 Where were Mary's forces defeated after her escape from Loch Leven Castle?
22 What happened to Archbishop Hamilton after Dumbarton Castle was taken?
23 When was Regent Moray assassinated?
24 When was the Pacification of Perth?
25 Who followed Moray as Regent?

Answers: p215

Stirling

1. Who convened a parliament in Cambuskenneth Abbey in 1326?
2. With which Scots leader is Stirling Bridge associated?
3. What is sited on the Abbey Craig?
4. Where was Prince Henry, son of James VI, christened in 1594?
5. In which year was Stirling University founded?
6. In which decade was St Ninian's Church built?
7. From which century does Stirling Old Bridge date?
8. Where is Mar's Wark?
9. Who designed the Tolbooth?
10. Where is the Mercat Cross?
11. What is the 'puggy'?
12. Who commissioned the building of Argyll's Lodging?
13. Where is the Beheading Stone?
14. Which entertainment venue in the burgh was built in the seventeenth century as a charitable institution for merchants fallen on hard times?
15. Who was crowned at the Church of the Holy Rude in 1567?
16. From which century does Logie Old Kirk date?
17. What is Erskine Marykirk now used as?
18. Which Stewart monarch is buried with his wife at Cambuskenneth Abbey?
19. What is the oldest surviving part of Cambuskenneth Abbey?
20. Where is the Ladies' Rock?
21. In which century was the town wall built?
22. From which century has the site of Stirling Castle been fortified in some way?
23. Which building in the town was funded by a legacy from Thomas Stuart Smith?
24. What famous landmark can be found in Albert Place?
25. Where is Bruce of Auchenbowie's House?

Answers: p216

QUESTIONS

1   What is the name of the founder of the Iona Community?
2   Where was the missionary and explorer David Livingstone born?
3   Where is St Columba's Cave?
4   Which ecclesiastical landmark in Glasgow was designed by Alexander 'Greek' Thompson?
5   Where was Patrick Hamilton burned at the stake?
6   In which century did St Serf live?
7   When did St John Ogilvie die?
8   Who is the patron saint of Paisley?
9   On which island was St Donan killed?
10 Who is the patron saint of Bute?
11 With which other country apart from Scotland is St Andrews associated?
12 To which saint is Candida Casa dedicated?
13 Who was the first Scot to become Archbishop of Canterbury?
14 Who was the mother of St Kentigern?
15 Which prominent Edinburgh clergyman announced his retiral in 2000?
16 Which Scottish saint became bishop of Lindisfarne?
17 Who is the patron saint of Fife?
18 Which Scottish architect designed the new Coventry Cathedral in the 1950s?
19 Who wrote a biography of St Columba in the seventh century?
20 What is the name of the Scotswoman who became the first female chaplain to the Queen in 1991?
21 From which century does St Rule's Tower in St Andrews date?
22 Which cathedral was founded by St Gilbert of Moray, Bishop of Caithness?
23 In which century did St Fillan live?
24 Where did St Cuthbert die?
25 In which decade was the Central Mosque in Glasgow completed?

Answers: p216

Golf 2

1   In which year was the Ryder Cup last held in Scotland?
2   Where was the 1999 British Open held?
3   Who captained the 2000 Ryder Cup team?
4   Which course is the site for the World Invitational?
5   In which year did Scotland beat England for the first time in the Dunhill Cup?
6   Which Scottish golfer earned the reputation as 'the best player never to win a Major'?
7   Name the American owner of the Loch Lomond Course.
8   How many players competed in the first British Open?
9   Where was 1931 British Open champion Tommy Armour born?
10 When was Turnberry Golf Club founded?
11 What is the name of the championship course at Troon?
12 In which decade did Bernard Gallacher turn professional?
13 In which year did Sam Torrance win the Spanish Open?
14 Which is claimed to be the oldest golf course in use in Scotland?
15 Where is the Edinburgh Burgess Society based?
16 What is the permanent trophy of the British Open Championship?
17 What is the name of the burn at the first green at St Andrews?
18 Who won the 1984 British Open at St Andrews?
19 Where did Willie Park Senior come from?
20 Name the Scottish golfer who uses a 48-inch putter.
21 Which British Open winner had the same name as a Scottish explorer?
22 Which Scottish golf course has a hole called the Graves?
23 How many golf courses are there at Troon?
24 What is the name of the oldest golf club in Scotland?
25 What were the first golf balls made of?

Answers: p217

1   Where is most of the work on the Book of Kells thought to have been done?
2   Which nineteenth-century judge made his home at Craigcrook Castle in Edinburgh?
3   What was the name of the Norwegian king involved in the Battle of Largs?
4   What were manufactured at Cowlairs in Springburn?
5   Which treaty secured the release of James I from captivity?
6   Which clan became known as 'the clan without a name'?
7   In which century were the counties of Ross and Cromarty amalgamated?
8   Which company built the *Discovery*?
9   Which loch is the third longest in Scotland?
10 'Round and round the radical road, the radical rascal ran . . .' Where is the radical road?
11 In which decade was the land for the present Hampden Park Stadium acquired?
12 How many Orkney islands are there?
    a) 36 b) 75 c) 67
13 Which industry was associated with the River North Esk and Penicuick until the 1970s?
14 With what kind of business is the name of Daniel Macmillan associated?
15 Which town was nicknamed 'the Charing Cross of the Highlands'?
16 Where is the St Fergus oil terminal?
17 What was the name of Rob Roy MacGregor's wife?
18 Where is the Forge shopping centre?
19 What is the name of the important archaeological site on Mainland Shetland, near Sumburgh?
20 When did the Pentland Rising take place?
21 Which prominent thinker was elected Lord Rector of Edinburgh University in 1866?
22 In which decade did the Eyemouth fishing disaster take place?
23 By what name is *colicoides impunctatus*, scourge of the Highland summer, more commonly known?
24 In which two branches of the services did the author known as Lewis Grassic Gibbon serve?
25 How many items are in the Scottish Regalia?

Answers: p217

Industry 3

1   Which Scottish city was known as the centre of 'Jam, Jute and Journalism'?
2   Where is the Edinburgh Crystal factory?
3   What cottage industry is Fair Isle famous for?
4   What was manufactured at the Hydepark Works in Springburn?
5   For which industry were the mills built in New Lanark?
6   What industry is associated with Inveresk?
7   In which century was tobacco trading in Scotland at its peak?
8   Which ironworks used to make carronnades for the British army?
9   Which industry once gave the town of Kirkcaldy a distinctive smell?
10 What brought about the revival of the shipbuilding industry on the Clyde after the gloom of the Great Depression?
11 Which city is the finance centre of Scotland?
12 Which city is the centre of the oil industry?
13 Which industry is centred round the border towns of Scotland?
14 Which Scot invented a monorail system, called a railplane, in Glasgow in 1930?
15 The name of the town of Lochgelly once struck terror into schoolchildren's hearts. What was traditionally made there?
16 In which century was Collins the publishers founded?
17 What is the name of the nuclear power station near Dunbar in East Lothian?
18 When was Hunterston Nuclear Generating Station opened?
19 Where was the centre of the steel industry in Scotland?
20 In which year did the Gartcosh Steelworks close?
21 Which company makes Irn Bru?
22 Which industry is centred in Grangemouth?
23 What is the main industry on the island of Islay?
24 In which part of Scotland was the industrialist David Dale born?
25 What colourful fashion accessory did the town of Paisley give its name to?

Answers: p218

1 Which town was developed in the seventeenth century by William Stewart?
2 Where is the Mote of Mark?
3 Which museum puts on a glittering display in Creetown?
4 Which town is the capital of Stewarty?
5 What is the name of the malt whisky distillery south of Wigtown?
6 In which town is the Stewarty Agricultural Show held each year?
7 Where can you see palm trees growing outside?
8 Where is the oldest post office in Britain?
9 Who planned the town of Gatehouse-of-Fleet?
10 Where can you see a statue of Robert Paterson?
11 Which road is called The Queen's Way?
12 Where can you see sheepdog handling demonstrations?
13 Which author remembered his childhood in the region with a book called *The House of Elrig*?
14 Which organization manages the Wood of Cree Reserve?
15 Where is Bruce's Stone?
16 On which loch is the Galloway Sailing Centre?
17 Which port was the main point of departure and arrival for travellers to and from Ireland before Stranraer?
18 Which order of monks were established at Sweetheart Abbey when it was built?
19 What do Birrens, Durisdeer and Glenlochar have in common?
20 What was the name of the man whose cruel treatment of covenanters in the area earned him a fearsome reputation?
21 Which organization owns Threave Garden?
22 What is the name of the island in the bay by Auchencairn?
23 What is the name of the stone circle near New Bridge?
24 From which century does Dundrennan Abbey date?
25 Whose name is associated with Maxwelton?

Answers: p218

Architecture 2

1   Who designed the George IV Bridge in Edinburgh?
2   Which Scottish architect was known as 'Greek'?
3   Which part of St Giles was designed by Sir Robert Lorimer?
4   When was Hill House in Helensburgh built?
5   Who led the design team for the Glasgow Empire Exhibition of 1938?
6   In which genre of painting did John Watson Gordon specialize?
7   Where did William Crozier train?
8   How many architect brothers were in the Adam family?
9   With what was a motte and bailey castle generally built?
10 Which city was the centre for classical revival in architecture in the nineteenth century?
11 Which architectural style predominates in St Andrews House in Edinburgh?
12 Which city in Scotland has the largest number of high-rise blocks of flats?
13 In which century did the influence of Dutch architecture become evident in several Scottish burghs?
14 Which architect designed Regent Terrace in Edinburgh?
15 Which unfinished piece of architecture is known as 'Edinburgh's Disgrace'?
16 What was 'Edinburgh's Disgrace' supposed to be when it was finished?
17 In which year was Glasgow School of Art finally completed?
18 Who designed the Hunterian Gallery in Glasgow?
19 Who designed the Law Courts in Parliament Square in Edinburgh in 1803?
20 Who founded the Institute of Architects in Scotland?
21 With whom did architect David Bryce work in partnership?
22 Where is the House for an Art Lover?
23 With which city is the name of architect Archibald Simpson associated?
24 In which Edinburgh cemetery is the grave of William Playfair?
25 With which city is the name of architect John Smith associated?

Answers: p219

General Knowledge 23

1 Where is the Royal Dick School of Veterinary Studies?
2 Which English poet was mistakenly arrested as a spy at Fort Augustus during a visit to Scotland?
3 In which country did explorer Hugh Clapperton die?
4 What sport were crampits once used for?
5 Which two saints are said to have met at the Molendinar Burn?
6 Around which industry did the town of Lerwick grow up?
7 In which part of Scotland is Loch Quoich?
8 Who was Scottish philosopher James Mill's famous son?
9 Name the eminent politician who was born in Holytown in 1856.
10 What are Scotland's two native conifers?
11 On which of the Flannan Isles is the chapel of St Flannan?
12 Who was defeated at the Battle of Dalry?
13 In which decade was the Gaelic Books Council set up?
14 Who donated money to Iona to establish a library?
15 In which century was the first National Mod held?
16 What was the name of Harry Lauder's wife?
17 Where is the island of Inchkenneth?
18 In which century was the Scottish Grand Lodge of Freemasons formed?
19 What was the name of Charles I's older brother?
20 Which port near Edinburgh is a centre for chemical refining?
21 Where is Kinnoull Hill?
22 Where was the first teacher training institution in Scotland (and Britain)?
23 In which century was the Monkland Canal opened?
24 In which of Scotland's new towns will you find the Kingdom shopping centre?
25 Who lived at 9 Brechin Road, Kirriemuir?

Answers: p219

Myth & Mystery, Magic & Superstition 2

1   Which castle in Scotland is supposed to have a secret chamber, where the ghost of an ancient lord plays cards with the Devil for eternity?

2   What sort of ghostly phenomenon haunted a family in Rerrick in the eighteenth century?

3   What was customarily laid on the chest of a dead body awaiting burial, with the intent of keeping evil spirits away?

4   What could a cabbage plucked on Hallowe'en tell a young woman about her future husband?

5   Why was it believed unlucky to cut a baby's nails with scissors?

6   Why should new shoes never be placed on the table?

7   With which seer was the Queen of the Fairies said to have fallen in love?

8   Where is the ghost of Bluidy Mackenzie said to haunt?

9   What was the name of the mythological giant of Ben Ledi?

10 Complete the following couplet of weather lore: 'Ne'er cast a cloot . . .'

11 In times gone by, why might a suspected murderer be made to touch the corpse of the victim?

12 What is the 'holy ghost' that haunts St Rule's Tower in St Andrews?

13 Complete the following proverb: 'The Deil's bairns hae aye . . .'

14 In some parts of Scotland it was believed to be a bad omen to hear a dog howling in the night. What did it mean?

15 What was a 'Devil's Claw'?

16 Which historical event is said to have been prophesied by Thomas the Rhymer with the following lines?
    'Between Seton and the sea
     Mony a man that day shall dee.'

17 In which century did the fear of witchcraft grow to such an extent that it became a capital offence?

18 What are the Mermaid's Tears of Iona, said to have been shed by a mermaid who had fallen in love with a saint?

19 Why would windows and doors be opened in a house where a death had recently taken place?

20 Why was rocking an empty cradle believed to be unlucky?

21 Which royal figure is said to haunt Linlithgow Palace?

22 Which Scottish mountain is haunted by a 'Big Grey Man'?

23 Which hidden close in Edinburgh is believed to be haunted by a child victim of the plague?

24 What kind of ghost is said to haunt Sandwood Bay in Sutherland?

25 Which famous Scottish castle is supposed to be haunted by a woman with no tongue?

Answers: p220

QUESTIONS

1   Where are the Falls of Foyers?
2   Which act of Parliament has been called 'the Magna Carta of the West Highlands'?
3   In which century was the Speymouth Railway Viaduct built?
4   From which century does the Bishops' Palace at Spynie date?
5   Which industry is associated with Kinlochleven?
6   Which famous photographer was based at St Swithin's, Aberdeen?
7   Where are the Seatown viaducts?
8   Where was Cluny's Cage, hiding place of Bonnie Prince Charlie? (Not to be confused with Cluny's Cave.)
9   Where is Cluny's Cave?
10 Why is the Clootie Well at Culloden so called?
11 From which town did the first regular air mail in Britain run?
12 Where is the Mullardoch Dam?
13 Which main road connects Fort William and Inverness?
14 Dornoch hosted the celebrity wedding of the year in December 2000. What were the names of the bride and bridegroom?
15 What is Duff House now used for?
16 With which industry did Kishorn become linked in the 1970s?
17 Where can you visit the Boath Dovecot?
18 Which industry brought prosperity to Rosehearty in the nineteenth century?
19 What colour is Peterhead granite?
20 What kind of stone was quarried near the town of Hopeman?
21 Which organization bought Ben Nevis in the year 2000?
22 Who founded the town of Aberlour?
23 In the reign of which king was Pluscarden Abbey founded?
24 In which town in Grampian did Charles II sign the Solemn League and Covenant?
25 Which town near Aberdeen has a lavender still?

Answers: p220

The Life & Works of Robert Louis Stevenson

1   Who illustrated *A Child's Garden of Verses*?

2   Did Robert Louis Stevenson have any brothers or sisters?

3   Which book by Robert Louis Stevenson describes a journey by canoe?

4   What journey is Stevenson describing in *The Amateur Immigrant*?

5   What was the name of the historical novel for children which Stevenson wrote, published in 1888?

6   Where was Stevenson living when he wrote *The Master of Ballantrae*?

7   What did Stevenson originally go to university to study?

8   What was the second career for which Stevenson trained?

9   In which year was Robert Louis Stevenson born?

10   In which novel does Alan Breck feature?

11   With whom did Robert Louis Stevenson collaborate in playwriting?

12   What place is the subject of *Ille Terrarum*?

13   From what illness did Stevenson suffer for much of his life?

14   What ultimately caused Stevenson's death?

15   What was the name of the short story collection published in 1882?

16   In which year was *A Child's Garden of Verses* published?

17   In which year did Stevenson and his family finally settle in Samoa?

18   What was the name of the woman whom Stevenson married?

19   Who collaborated with Robert Louis Stevenson in writing *The Wrecker* and *The Wrong Box*?

20   In which century is *Kidnapped* set?

21   What was the Christian name of Robert Louis Stevenson's father?

22   What is the title of the sequel to *Kidnapped*?

23   What was the name of Stevenson's stepdaughter?

24   In which year did Robert Louis Stevenson die?

25   Name the learned friend of Stevenson's who provided him with valuable literary criticism, help and advice throughout his life.

Answers: p221

QUESTIONS

1   Where are the Rozelle Galleries?
2   Where is Fife Airport?
3   With which group of artists is the name of Sir John Lavery associated?
4   In which century was the Children's Village of Humbie founded?
5   How many sons did Mary of Guise bear by James V?
6   In which year was Torness power station completed?
7   From which Scottish port did the Darien Expedition set sail?
8   Where is the SCWS headquarters building?
9   What was the main cargo of the *Cutty Sark*?
10 In which decade was the recipe for the drink which was to become known as Irn Bru first developed?
11 Which agency is responsible for the upkeep of Edinburgh Castle?
12 In which city is the Fountain Brewery?
13 What is the name of the only football team from south of the border that plays in the Scottish league?
14 Which kind of monks lived at Jedburgh Abbey?
15 From which century does St Machar date?
16 From which part of Scotland did Covenanter Alexander Peden come?
17 Who designed the steamship *Rob Roy*?
18 Which town near Elie has the motto 'Mare Vivimus'?
19 How many islands are in the St Kilda group?
20 Which order of monks live in the community at Pluscarden Abbey?
21 Who was the last monarch to be born in Scotland?
22 Where is the Scottish College of Textiles?
23 Which body owns the site of the battlefield of Culloden?
24 Which king built the Palace at Stirling Castle?
25 How did the eighteenth/nineteenth-century songwriter Robert Tannahill meet his death?

Answers: p221

Sport 3

1 What are curling stones traditionally made from?
2 Which Scottish town is known as 'the Home of Golf'?
3 How many players are there in a shinty team?
4 When was the Scottish mountaineering club founded?
5 Where was the Silver Bell run?
6 What sport is played by the Fife Flyers and the Perth Panthers?
7 With which sport is Niall Mackenzie associated?
8 Who was World Champion motor racing driver in 1969?
9 Name the Scottish footballer who became a regular team leader on
   A Question of Sport.
10 In what year was racing driver Jim Clark killed?
11 Who was knocked out by Aurel Toma in 1938?
12 In which year did Ally McCoist join Rangers?
13 Which Scot won the women's 10,000 metres gold medal in the
    Commonwealth games of 1986 and 1990?
14 How many Scottish Grand National winners were there between 1960
    and 1980?
15 Which snooker player broke the record for the highest number of
    consecutive tournament wins in 1990?
16 What is the oldest rowing club in Scotland?
17 Who resigned as chairman of Dundee United in October 2000?
18 Where in Scotland is Britain's longest artificial ski-slope?
19 Where are the most famous Highland Games held each year, attended by
    the Royal Family?
20 Which Scot has won the title of Champion Jockey five times?
21 What is the Gaelic word for shinty?
22 For which team was David Coulthard driving when he won the Australian
    and Italian Grand Prix in 1997?
23 How many goals did Denis Law score for Scotland?
24 Which Scottish golf club determines the rules of the game?
25 What kind of races take place during West Highland Week?

Answers: p222

1   Which poem by Robert Burns is traditionally recited on January 25?

2   Name the Scottish poet who was known as the 'Ettrick Shepherd'.

3   *A Child's Garden of Verses* is an anthology of poetry for children. Who wrote it?

4   Where was the poet Iain Crichton Smith born?

5   Who wrote *Under the Eildon Tree*?

6   Who wrote *A Drunk Man Looks at the Thistle*?

7   This poet was born on the island of Raasay in 1911 and is acclaimed as one of the finest Gaelic poets of all time. What is his name?

8   Who wrote 'The Cottar's Saturday Night'?

9   Which part of Scotland did George Mackay Brown come from?

10   Which Scottish writer wrote *The Lay of the Last Minstrel*?

11   Where was the poet Allan Ramsay born?

12   Name the writer and poet who was also Sir Walter Scott's son-in-law.

13   In which year was the poet Edwin Morgan born?

14   *The Golden Treasury of Scottish Poetry* (1993 edition) was edited by which Scottish poet?

15   Which Glasgow poet wrote *The Pleasures of Hope* in 1799?

16   Which poet had a volume of poetry entitled *The Labyrinth* published in 1949?

17   This poet was also a naturalist and a clergyman, first in the Scottish church and then in the Church of England. Who was he?

18   Which poem by Robert Burns begins: 'When chapman billies leave the street'?

19   Which Scottish poet and playwright translated *Tartuffe* into Glaswegian?

20   Who wrote about Leerie the Lamplighter?

21   Who published poetry, supposedly by Ossian, in 1762-3?

22   What was the profession of poet Sorley Maclean?

23   Who wrote 'In Memoriam James Joyce'?

24   *The Queen's Wake* is a volume of poems by which poet?

25   Who was the author of 'Wee Willie Winkie'?

Answers: p222

Wildlife 2

1. What is the name of the only poisonous snake to be found in Scotland?
2. Which animal, now rare in Scotland, is also known as the tree weasel?
3. Which large member of the umbrella-flowered parsley family, introduced to this country as an ornamental plant, has now become a serious nuisance in many parts of Scotland, threatening other species of wildflower?
4. Which part of Scotland has its own sub-species of wren?
5. Which animal, inhabiting the most lonely and inaccessible places in Scotland, is seldom seen during the day?
6. What is the name of the bird reserve on North Uist?
7. Which island is home to the second-largest colony of gannets in the UK?
8. Where is the largest blanket bog in Europe?
9. Where in Scotland is the largest gannet colony in the world?
10. In which part of Scotland does the crested tit breed?
11. What colour are the flowers of *Primula scotica*?
12. In which part of Scotland can *Primula scotica* be found?
13. In which decade did the sea eagle become extinct in Scotland?
14. Which is larger; the golden eagle or the sea eagle?
15. By what other name is the sea eagle known?
16. What is the largest gull found in Scotland?
17. In which century is it thought that the Caledonian bear became extinct?
18. What is the most numerous auk found in Scotland?
19. What is Scotland's largest seabird?
20. Where is the Fowlsheugh RSPB reserve?
21. Where in Scotland can Britain's largest colony of fulmars be found?
22. Where in Scotland can Britain's largest population of breeding eider ducks be found?
23. What is a bonxie?
24. Which nature reserve in Scotland celebrated its fiftieth birthday in 2001?
25. What is the most numerous seal found in Scotland?

Answers: p223

QUESTIONS

1   What was known as 'crotal' and what was it used for?
2   Which kind of bird was re-introduced to Scotland in 1975?
3   Where is the Brent Oil Field?
4   What is a clachan?
5   What colour are Ayrshire cattle?
6   Who was named Scot of the Year in the Spirit of Scotland 2000 awards?
7   Which novel by Robert Louis Stevenson was set in the village of Borgue?
8   Which famous man was drowned off the coast of Orkney in June 1916 when the HMS Hampshire was sunk by a mine?
9   A town in the west of Scotland, an industrial centre on North Island, New Zealand, and the capital of Bermuda all share the same name. What is it?
10 Which is the longest sea-loch in Scotland?
11 Who was Queen Victoria's 'beloved friend'?
12 Where in Scotland did a Chinook helicopter crash, killing all crew and passengers, in 1994?
13 Name the theatre producer whose Highland retreat on the Nevis estate was gutted by fire in November 2000.
14 Which body owns Brodick Castle?
15 What was the name of the minister who wrote *The Secret Commonwealth of Fairies*?
16 In which year did Ken Buchanan become flyweight champion of the world?
17 What was the former name of Glasgow Airport?
18 How many Paps of Jura are there?
19 What was the name of Rob Roy MacGregor's outlaw son, executed in 1754?
20 Which bedtime drink manufacturer once owned Gigha?
21 Which family produced a king of Scotland and (his brother) a king of Ireland within a period of ten years?
22 In which year did Boswell and Johnson tour the Hebrides?
23 Which Scottish premier football club is Martin O'Neill associated with?
24 What is the name of the preparatory school for Gordonstoun?
25 From whom did David Dale purchase the land for his mill town at New Lanark?

Answers: p223

Scottish Towns & Villages

1 Where is the oldest university in Scotland?

2 Which island town's name means 'King's harbour?'

3 Which Highland village has a rare mineral named after it?

4 In which city was Dennis the Menace conceived?

5 What is the name of the spa town close to Balmoral?

6 Which clan has a museum in Newtonmore?

7 By which glen is the village of Fortingall?

8 By which river is the town of Crieff situated?

9 Where is the Tam o' Shanter pub?

10 Which town is known as 'the Capital of the Highlands'?

11 Which famous politician was born in Seatown of Lossiemouth?

12 Which Scottish fishing port was built on Bressay Sound?

13 A fish ladder and a festival theatre: which town?

14 What is the name of the village in Tayside familiar to Shakespeare lovers?

15 Which city was known as 'Auld Reekie'?

16 Which town in Ayrshire gets its name from the salt production industry?

17 On which firth is the village of Portknockie situated?

18 Which town stands at the southern end of the Caledonian Canal?

19 By which town, north of Aberdeen, is the Ugie Fish House situated?

20 From which seaside town can you take a boat trip round the Bass Rock?

21 In which border town is St Mungo's Well?

22 Where is the Goblin Ha'?

23 Which Highland port was the regular holiday haunt of the late Barbara Cartland?

24 Which town was formed from the villages of Inveralan and Pathfoot?

25 Name Scotland's first new town.

Answers: p224

QUESTIONS

1   In what year was James VI born?
2   What were the names of the two sons of Duncan I?
3   Which king married Catherine of Braganza?
4   Who was the father of Malcolm II?
5   Which king stabbed the 8th Earl of Douglas to death in Stirling Castle?
6   What nationality was Alexander III's mother?
7   Who was king before Alexander I?
8   Who was the mother of Charles II?
9   Who was crowned at Stirling in 1567?
10 What relation did Lulach have to Macbeth?
11 Who was the first wife of James V?
12 What was the name of James I's mother?
13 Which king married Ingibiorg of Orkney?
14 What was the relationship between Alexander I and David I?
15 Which king died at Forteviot?
16 How many times did Prince Charles Edward Stewart marry?
17 How old was James VII when he succeeded to the throne?
18 In which year did Henry, Prince of Wales, eldest son of James VI die?
19 What was the relationship between Charles II and James VII?
20 Which king was married to the Princess Henrietta Maria?
21 Where did John Balliol end his life?
22 Which king was the husband of Marie de Coucy?
23 In which century did Kenneth II reign as King of Alba?
24 Who succeeded Malcolm IV as king?
25 What was the name of William the Lion's wife?

Answers: p224

Plays & Theatres 2

1   Who started his career as a professional entertainer singing *Ye Cannae Shove Yer Granny off a Bus*?

2   Who wrote the play *Douglas* in 1754?

3   Who wrote *The Historie of Squyer Meldrum*?

4   Name the writer of *The Sleeping Clergyman*.

5   Who formed the Edinburgh Festival Chorus?

6   Who/what was *The Admirable Crichton* in the play of the same name?

7   Which major Scottish concert hall underwent a major restoration project in the 1990s?

8   How many seats are there in Scotland's smallest theatre?

9   In which town is the Netherbow Theatre?

10   Who wrote *Our American Cousin*?

11   As what did the poet and playwright Liz Lochhead originally train?

12   What was the title given to the Scots translation of *Le Bourgeois Gentilhomme* produced in 1985?

13   Which Scots comedian starred in the *Five Past Eight Shows* in the 1950s?

14   Which Scots actor was the first director of the Edinburgh Theatre Trust?

15   What is the name of the theatre club in Edinburgh co-founded by Richard Demarco?

16   Which theatre company was founded by Alfred Wareing?

17   What was the name of the theatre company on Edinburgh's Leith Walk, founded in 1953, which folded in 1965?

18   By which name was the Lyceum Theatre Company originally known when it was founded in 1965?

19   Who formed the 7:84 Theatre Company?

20   In which year was the Scottish Youth Theatre formed?

21   Which Scots actor wrote *All in Good Faith*?

22   What was the Festival Theatre in Edinburgh originally known as?

23   What was the real name of the performer known as Tommy Lorne?

24   Which Glasgow theatre, formerly called The Gaiety, closed in 1963?

25   What did Green's Playhouse in Glasgow change its name to?

Answers: p225

QUESTIONS

1 Which Scottish king outlawed Clan Gregor and forfeited their lands?

2 In order to finance which enterprise was the Company of Scotland formed in the late seventeenth century?

3 In which year was William Wallace captured and executed?

4 In which year did the SS *Politician* sink?

5 In which year did Clydebank suffer devastation from German Bombers?

6 Which Scottish explorer discovered the source of the Niger?

7 What disease caused panic in the city of Aberdeen in 1964?

8 Where was 'the Battle of the Braes' fought in 1882?

9 When did the Raid of Ruthven take place?

10 When did the last coronation take place at Scone?

11 Which Scottish king was known as 'The Red Crow'?

12 In which year did George IV make a state visit to Scotland?

13 Where was Charles I crowned?

14 When was the first Bishop's War?

15 Who led the massacre of Glencoe?

16 In which year was Robert the Bruce excommunicated?

17 Who led the troops which defeated Montrose at the battle of Philiphaugh?

18 Who was known as 'The Red Duchess'?

19 When was the Treaty of Berwick signed?

20 In which year was the Disarming Act of 1746 repealed?

21 In which year was the medical school at Edinburgh University established?
a) 1657 b) 1746 c) 1729

22 In the post-election referendum of 1997, what percentage of the voters voted in favour of a Scottish Parliament?

23 How many of the Scottish MPs returned to Parliament after the 1997 election were women?

24 In which year did the *Piper Alpha* disaster take place?

25 Which Scottish city was the most frequently bombed during the Second World War?

Answers: p225

General Knowledge 26

1   Name the Scot who founded the P&O shipping company.

2   Where is the venue for the Scottish Grand National?

3   On which day of which month does the Glasgow Fair traditionally begin?

4   The car ferry *Princess Victoria* sank in 1953. Which route was she travelling?

5   Which king brought the Stone of Destiny to Scone?

6   Near which town are the ruins of Cadzow Castle?

7   What was the name of the mother of John Balliol?

8   Who is Colonel-in-Chief of the Argyll and Sutherland Highlanders?

9   What statue stands on Haeval, overlooking Castlebay on Barra?

10 Which town on the east coast of Scotland has the motto 'Mare Ditat Rosa Decorat'?

11 What was the Bass Rock used as in the seventeenth century?

12 What is the largest National Nature Reserve in Great Britain?

13 In which year did the Bloody Friday Riot take place in Glasgow?

14 In which year were Aberdeen and London linked by rail?

15 On which island can the Kildalton Cross be found?

16 Which eighteenth-century sailor was awarded the Orders of St Vladimir and St Andrew by Catherine the Great?

17 In which decade did the Royal Botanic Garden in Edinburgh move to its present site?

18 What was the name of the woman who was the inspiration for the bride in *The Bride of Lammermoor*?

19 In which year was the King James version of the Bible published?

20 Which town changed hands between Scotland and England more than ten times in three centuries?

21 What is the nationality of Fernando Ricksen, football player for Rangers?

22 In the year 2000, near which Borders town was it proposed that a 'tele-village' to be called St Leonards might be built?

23 What is the full name of Bo'ness?

24 To the nearest ten miles, how long is the Antonine Wall?

25 What Scottish product was advertised as 'Made in Scotland from girders'?

Answers: p226

113

1   What is housed in Provost Ross's House?

2   What was the *Thermopylae*?

3   In which century were King's College and Marischal College united?

4   Which king ordered the Brig o' Balgownie to be built?

5   What shape is the base of the Mercat Cross?

6   What is the city's oldest school?

7   Where is St Andrew's Cathedral?

8   From which century does St Mary's Cathedral date?

9   Who designed the Girdleness Lighthouse?

10 Which building in Aberdeen is known as the Mids o' Mar?

11 In which year did Montrose sack Aberdeen?

12 What bequest did Charlotte Duthie make to the city?

13 In which century was the Bridge of Dee constructed?

14 In which decade was Hazlehead Park acquired for the city?

15 By which name is Benholm's Tower more commonly known?

16 What were the surnames of the two men named Alexander who made major bequests to Aberdeen Art Gallery?

17 What was the main fishing port for Aberdeen in the nineteenth century?

18 What colour are Aberdeen Angus cattle?

19 Who is the patron saint of Aberdeen?

20 Which student residence in Aberdeen was the first to accommodate students of both sexes?

21 In which century was Aberdeen Art Gallery built?

22 Where is the Crabstone?

23 Which church is known as the 'Mither Kirk'?

24 What anniversary was Elphinstone Hall built to commemorate?

25 Who built the Bridge of Don?

Answers: p226

Food & Drink 2

1   What is the Selkirk Grace?

2   What is a girdle cake?

3   What colour is a finnan haddie?

4   For which food crop is the region around Blairgowrie best known?

5   What are the three ingredients of shortbread?

6   What kind of fruit is a tayberry?

7   What is the main ingredient in a mealie puddin'?

8   What was gradan meal?

9   What was a bannock stone?

10 What was once known as a Crail capon?

11 Which Scottish chef opened a restaurant called Braeval near Aberfoyle?

12 In which Scottish Sunday newspaper has Clarissa Dickson-Wright featured with a regular column and recipe?

13 What is a Hawick Ball?

14 What is the 'other national drink' of the Scots?

15 Which international culinary award were Betty Allen and Hilary Brown the first women in Scotland to win?

16 For which bakery product is Kirriemuir well known?

17 Which food or drink-related industry is associated with Alloa?

18 In which year was low-calorie Irn-Bru introduced to the market?

19 What is the name of the oldest surviving brewery in Scotland?

20 Which brewing company supplied ale to Bonnie Prince Charlie's troops in 1745?

21 Which Scot was declared winner of the food category of the Spirit of Scotland Awards, 2000?

22 Around which food does the Edinburgh/Glasgow vinegar/sauce debate revolve?

23 What is Dunsyre Blue?

24 Which whisky name was registered by James Logan Mackie?

25 What kind of food is a Pentland Squire?

Answers: p227

The Romans in Scotland

1   Where was an exciting Roman find made in 1998 by a ferryman?

2   Which two rivers were connected by the Antonine Wall?

3   In which century was the Antonine Wall built?

4   What is the name of the Roman road that was built between Jedburgh and Dalkeith?

5   What was the Roman name for the fort now known as Newstead?

6   When did the Romans first invade the north of Scotland?

7   How many forts were built along the route of the Antonine Wall?

8   Where was the fort of Inchtuthil built?

9   Who led the Romans in the battle of Mons Graupius?

10 What was the Roman name for Scotland?

11 Which Roman emperor came to Britain in AD 208 to try to quell the troublesome people from the north?

12 Which Roman general was put in charge of the construction of the Antonine Wall?

13 In which part of Scotland is the Roman fortress of Auchinhove?

14 Where was the Roman fortress that was built near Dunblane?

15 When did Agricola return to Rome from Scotland?

16 Which Roman emperor was the last to mount an offensive against the people of Scotland?

17 Before the Antonine Wall was built, what construction marked the northern boundary of the Roman Empire, keeping out the marauding northern tribes?

18 Where can most of the relics from the fort at Newstead be seen?

19 When did the Romans return to the fort at Newstead after abandoning it around AD100?

20 Which Roman historian wrote an account of the life of Agricola, giving us an insight into the first attempts to conquer Scotland?

21 In what year did the Battle of Mons Graupius take place?

22 Where is the Roman fort of Rough Castle?

23 Which modern road follows the track of Dere Street?

24 Which Roman emperor ordered the first invasion of Scotland?

25 Who was the last Roman emperor to try to subdue the people of Scotland?

Answers: p227

General Knowledge 27

1   Name the Scot who developed the Visible Speech System. Whose father was he?

2   Which Robert Louis Stevenson character was kidnapped and taken on board the brig *Covenant*?

3   Which sculptor was the creator of the *Big Heids* on the M8?

4   In which year was Tam Dalyell first elected to Parliament?

5   Who founded the Botanic Garden in Aberdeen?

6   What is the name of Scotland's tallest tower house?

7   For what is Sir John Sholto Douglas, 8th Marquis of Queensberry remembered?

8   From which wood are shinty sticks traditionally made?

9   In which decade was Prestwick Airport opened?

10 What were made at the Hydepark, Atlas and Queen's Park Works?

11 What is the name of the oldest house in Alloway?

12 Where is Alexander II buried?

13 Which Scottish honour was given to Princess Anne on her fiftieth birthday by the Queen?

14 Where was the *Scotsman* Debating Championship held in November 2000?

15 Which Scottish novelist won the Saltire Society Book of the Year award in 2000?

16 Which Scottish king married Anne of Denmark?

17 At what weight did Jackie Paterson win his boxing World title in 1943?

18 In which year did Scots actor Ian Bannen die?

19 Who was named winner in the writing category in the 2000 Spirit of Scotland awards?

20 Which Edinburgh character inspired *The Strange Case of Dr Jekyll and Mr Hyde*?

21 What was the name of the rock band formed by Alan Gordy?

22 With which Scottish stone is Queen Victoria's Mausoleum built?

23 What noble title belonged to Johnny Dumfries, racing driver?

24 What is the name of the Scot who founded Community Service Volunteers?

25 Which city has the busiest heliport in Scotland?

Answers: p228

1 Which suburb of Dundee was once known as 'the richest square mile in Europe'?

2 What and where is Scurdie Ness?

3 Where is the Speyside Cooperage?

4 Which island is known as 'the Jewel of the Hebrides'?

5 How many arches are there on the Dunkeld Bridge?

6 Which distillery is the oldest in Scotland?

7 Where did David I have a vision of a stag with a cross?

8 What is the name of Scotland's oldest continuously inhabited house?

9 What is the highest village in Scotland?

10 The grounds of which Scottish castle boast the world's longest herbaceous border?

11 In which BBC production based on a historical novel by Sir Walter Scott did Craigmillar Castle feature?

12 Which abbey has been called 'the Iona of the East'?

13 Which town in Scotland was the first to use a power loom?

14 Which town is the former centre for justice and government for Fife?

15 Where is the Scottish Seabird Centre?

16 Where is the Armadillo?

17 Which town was once known as 'the Westminster of the North'?

18 Where is the Time Capsule?

19 In which direction would you have to travel to get from Glasgow to Prestwick Airport?

20 What is known by citizens of Glasgow as 'the Clockwork Orange'?

21 Where is Noss National Nature Reserve?

22 Where is the Scottish Vintage Bus Museum?

23 Where were the World Pipe Band Championships 2000 held?

24 What is the name of the twelfth-century church at Leuchars in Fife?

25 What is the name of the fourteenth- to seventeenth-century residence of the Bishops of Moray?

Answers: p228

Scotland & the Media 2

1   When did BBC Scotland come into being?

2   Who was co-founder and first editor of *The Scotsman*?

3   Which former editor of *The Scotsman* died in 1998?

4   Which newspaper group bought the *Daily Record* in 1955?

5   Which minister launched the Gaelic Television Fund?

6   Name the Gaelic news programme which faced the axe following an announcement in November 2000.

7   When was the Gaelic Television Fund launched?

8   Where are STV's headquarters?

9   Which group owns STV?

10 For which radio programme is Kathleen Garscadden remembered?

11 Who were the McFlannels?

12 In which year did Radio Borders start broadcasting?

13 From where does Radio nan Eilean operate?

14 What is the name of the radio station based in Dumfries?

15 When did Radio Free Caledonia make an unwelcome entrance onto Scotland's airwaves?

16 Where is the home of the *West Highland Free Press*?

17 In which century was *The Oban Times* founded?

18 Which company owns the Dundee *Evening Telegraph*?

19 Which company owns the Aberdeen *Evening Express*?

20 In which century was the publication entitled *Diurnal Occurrences touching the Dailie Proceedings in Parliament* first printed?

21 Which Scottish newspaper has the largest circulation?

22 What was the name of the first Scottish newspaper printed in Scotland?

23 In which decade did the *Sunday Standard* make a brief appearance on the news-stands?

24 Which group owns *The Scotsman*?

25 Who publishes the *Edinburgh Gazette*?

Answers: p229

Castles 2

1　Which castle was owned by the Mackenzies of Seaforth?
2　Which castle is said to be the most haunted in Scotland?
3　What is the name of the castle, near Lochgilphead, that was once the home of the first Protestant Bishop of the Isles, John Carswell?
4　Where is Claypotts Castle?
5　Which castle, in Sutherland and Caithness, was bought by HM Queen Elizabeth the Queen Mother, in 1952?
6　In which castle was Cardinal Beaton murdered in 1546?
7　Where did Dunty Porteous, miller, starve to death?
8　What is the name of the fortress that stands overlooking the Forth, east of Bo'ness?
9　Which regiment has its museum in Stirling Castle?
10　Which castle was the last in Britain to be besieged?
11　Which castle in the north-east of Scotland was built around a hawthorn tree?
12　Duart Castle on the Isle of Mull is the family seat of which clan?
13　What was stolen from Scone Palace in 1296?
14　Into which grim fortress in the borders were children said to have disappeared, never to be seen again?
15　In which castle were the public records of Scotland kept during World War II for safekeeping?
16　Inverary Castle is the seat of which family?
17　Which Borders castle is the seat of the Duke of Roxburghe?
18　Who 'dinged doun' Tantallon Castle?
19　Deep beneath Urquhart Castle there is rumoured to be an enormous watery cave. What is supposed to frequent this underground lair?
20　On which river is Hailes Castle situated?
21　What is the ghost that is supposed to haunt the ramparts of Edinburgh Castle?
22　What kind of fortification is Duffus Castle?
23　In which part of Scotland is Newark Castle?
24　Which castle in Fife has a mine (from the outside) and a counter-mine (from the inside)?
25　Which castle was once known as 'Castle Gloom'?

Answers: p229

1   Where is the largest refinery for North Sea Oil in Scotland?
2   Which university did former Secretary of State for Scotland, Michael Forsyth attend?
3   North of which island is the island of South Rona?
4   Which was the first river in Europe to have a passenger turbine steamer service?
5   In which year was Scottish Enterprise formed?
6   In 1995, which region in Scotland had the highest unemployment?
7   Where was Sir Malcolm Rifkind born?
8   Where is the East Lothian home of the Earl of Wemyss and March?
9   What is the name of the oilfield where the first major oil find was made in the North Sea?
10 The first edition of which reference book was edited by Andrew Findlater?
11 In which year did the *Braer* tanker break up off the coast of Shetland?
12 Which trade founded the first Co-operative Society in Britain in 1769, and where?
13 Which Scot was official war artist in 1916 and again in 1939?
14 What was the name given to the fighting flag of the craftspeople of Edinburgh?
15 Which Scottish university botanic garden was established in 1971?
16 Which American newspaper was started by the Scot James Gordon Bennet in the nineteenth century?
17 Name the longest-serving Communist MP in British history.
18 Of which society was Lady Isobella Bishop the first lady fellow?
19 Which train won the Race to the North from London to Aberdeen in 1895?
20 Where was sculptor David Mach born?
21 Who took part in a 'Right to Work' demonstration in 1972?
22 Who was Labour's chief whip at the time of the 1997 landslide election victory?
23 Name the author of *Rodney Stone*, published in 1896.
24 Who painted *The Cottar's Saturday Night* in 1854?
25 What military invention was devised by Patrick Ferguson in the eighteenth century?

Answers: p230

1   Name the two league-topping football teams most closely associated with Glasgow.
2   In which decade was Glasgow Underground electrified?
3   What does the name Glasgow (*glas-cau*) mean?
4   Which two new towns were designed to take overspill from the overcrowded city?
5   What is the name of the park in Glasgow that is also the oldest public park in Britain?
6   Which king granted Glasgow the right to hold an annual fair?
7   Where did the North British Locomotive Company make its manufacturing base?
8   By what other name is St Enoch known?
9   In which year was Glasgow Cathedral ransacked?
10 In which century was work begun on Port Glasgow?
11 What prompted the Shawfield Riot of 1725?
12 With which Glasgow industry is the name of James Monteith associated?
13 Who wrote *No Mean City*?
14 Which theatre was known as 'the Graveyard of English Comedians'?
15 What was the full title of the GEAR project?
16 Who designed the Egyptian Halls?
17 Who moved from Queen's Park to Hampden Park?
18 When did construction begin on the Clyde Tunnel?
19 In which year did the 'Glasgow's Glasgow' exhibition take place?
20 Where will you find a monument to the Queen of the Gypsies?
21 Which building was nicknamed 'the Lally Palais'?
22 Where is the main site of Glasgow University?
23 A monument to which historical figure stands at Robroyston?
24 Where did 'Tennant's Stalk' once stand and what was it?
25 What is the name of the street formerly known as George Place?

Answers: p230

Rugby 2

1   Who captained the Scots against Samoa in November 2000?
2   Of which Edinburgh school are the Hastings brothers former pupils?
3   Which position does Gordon Bulloch play?
4   What position did Andy Irvine play?
5   Who was captain of the British Lions and Scotland in 1989?
6   Which club team did former captain David Sole play for?
7   In which decade was undersoil heating introduced at Murrayfield stadium?
8   With which local club is Gordon Bulloch associated?
9   In which season did Scott Hastings retire from the game?
10 In which year was the SFU formed?
11 How many times did Andy Irvine tour with the British Lions?
12 Which two positions did Ian McGeechan play as a Scottish International?
13 In which year did John Jeffrey first play for Scotland?
14 What part did the grouse play in the Calcutta Cup, 2000?
15 Who was Scotland's head coach at the 1995 World Cup?
16 Who was the Scotland coach for the 1990 Grand Slam victory?
17 When did the first Rugby World Cup take place?
18 Who captained Scotland against Ireland in the 2000 Six Nations Championship?
19 What award was given to Gregor Townsend in the 1999 Queen's Birthday Honours List?
20 In which year did John Leslie make his international debut for Scotland?
21 Who scored all of Scotland's points in the 2000 Calcutta Cup win?
22 What position does Budge Poutney play?
23 What was *The Green Book* and in which century was it written?
24 Where was the first international match played?
25 Which club is Duncan Hodge associated with?

Answers: p231

1 What was the name of the Scot who founded the colony of Nova Scotia in Canada?

2 Which Scot was the first European to find the Victoria Falls on the River Zambezi?

3 Where did Andrew Carnegie make his fortune?

4 Which Scot is remembered as 'the Father of Australia'?

5 Where did Eric Liddell carry out his mission for the church?

6 Who was appointed Governor-General of India in 1847?

7 What is named after explorer Alexander Mackenzie?

8 What was the name of the explorer who wrote *Travels to Discover the Sources of the Nile*?

9 Who was known as 'Great Mother' in Nigeria, where she worked?

10 Where in Scotland was the great Canadian statesman Sir John Macdonald born?

11 Who was the explorer who wrote *To the Central African Lakes and Back* in 1881?

12 Which Scottish financier became Comptrolleur-Général of finance in France in 1720?

13 What was the name of the Scots missionary who helped to found the University of Calcutta?

14 Where did Allan Pinkerton set up his detective agency?

15 Alexander Gordon Laing discovered the source of which river?

16 Who was the scientist in charge of the *Challenger* round-the-world expedition in the 1870s?

17 Name the eighteenth-century Scottish-born sailor who served in the American navy during the American Revolution and then in the Russian navy during the Russo-Turkish War.

18 Name the Scottish explorer who wrote *Travels in the Interior of Africa* in 1799.

19 Which Scot was made Lord Chancellor in 1987?

20 What was the name of the Scot who was surgeon at St George's Hospital in London and surgeon-extraordinary to King George III?

21 David Douglas, the famous botanist and plant-collector, was killed in Hawaii. How did he meet his death?

22 Where in Scotland was explorer Hugh Clapperton born?

23 Which famous Scot died at Old Chitambo?

24 On which island was Alexander Selacraig marooned?

25 Who was Labour Prime Minister of New Zealand from 1940 to 1949?

Answers: p231

General Knowledge 29

1 Which organizations were responsible for maintaining many of the roads in southern Scotland in the nineteenth century?
2 In which city were the Camperdown Works situated?
3 In which decade did the first Cranston's Tearoom open?
4 Against which English King did James IV declare war in 1513?
5 From which document does the following extract come? 'It is not for glory or riches or honour that we fight, but only for liberty . . .'
6 Where is the Archeolink Prehistory Park?
7 Where was the *Cutty Sark* built?
8 Which football club from the west of Scotland was founded in 1868?
9 Which castle in East Lothian has a distinctive round tower?
10 In which Scott novel will you encounter the Laird of Dumbiedykes?
11 What was manufactured by J. & P. Coats?
12 What kind of agricultural machine was invented by Patrick Bell?
13 Which Scottish king was killed at the Battle of Alnwick?
14 Name the photographer who published a set of lithographs entitled *Sketches of Scenery in Perthshire* in 1821.
15 What was the real name of the woman who wrote *Meg Dod's Cookery*?
16 What was the profession of James Keir?
17 Name the Scots nobleman who was involved in the murder of Rizzio, kidnapped James VI, and was finally beheaded at Stirling.
18 Name the Scots philosopher who wrote about the death of David Hume.
19 Which party did Jim Sillars represent as an MP?
20 Which Scottish footballer and manager published an autobiography entitled *No Half Measures*?
21 Who built the *Charlotte Dundas*?
22 Who collaborated with Charles Rennie Mackintosh on his designs for the Cranston Tearooms?
23 Where was the sculptor George Wyllie born?
24 In which year did the North British Railway open between Edinburgh and Berwick-upon-Tweed?
25 In which month is St Serf's day?

Answers: p232

1   Travelling along the coast road from Elie to Anstruther, what is the name of the first village you pass through?

2   On which firth is Bo'ness situated?

3   Which town on the Solway Firth is a haven for painters and craftspeople?

4   What is the name of the bay upon which Creetown is situated?

5   Which fishing port lies just south-east of St Abb's?

6   Which major seaside town lies just to the south of Prestwick?

7   Which island is more northerly: Eigg or Muck?

8   Name the loch upon which Ullapool is situated.

9   What is the name of the bay upon which the fishing town of Buckie is situated?

10   Travelling from Oban to Colonsay by car ferry, where would you land?

11   Which famous lighthouse lies off the east coast, south-east of the town of Arbroath?

12   What is the name of the stretch of water between the islands of Skye and Raasay?

13   On which firth is the town of Oban situated?

14   Where on the Lothian Coast is Eagle Rock?

15   Which town south of Mallaig is famed for its beautiful sandy beaches?

16   Which coastal town is situated at the mouth of the River South Esk?

17   Which island in the Firth of Clyde provided a source of granite for curling stones?

18   Name the burgh in Lothian which stands below the two Forth Bridges.

19   What is the name of the castle, once the seat of the Black Douglas family, which lies to the east of North Berwick?

20   Where, on the east coast, did artist Joan Eardley find inspiration for many landscape paintings?

21   What do St Abb's Head and the Bass Rock have in common?

22   In which castle on the south-west coast did Robert the Bruce live as a child?

23   Which east coast bay, a short walk from Gullane, is an important nature reserve?

24   In which town in the south-west did the artist Jessie M. King live?

25   What is the name of the volcanic hill at North Berwick?

Answers: p232

Law & Order 2

1   Who is regarded as the father of Scots Law?

2   Since when has it been possible to obtain a divorce in Scotland on the grounds of irretrievable breakdown of marriage?

3   In which year was the Scottish Law Commission established?

4   Name the Scots judge who, as an advocate, defended Madeleine Smith in 1857.

5   Who was made Lord Advocate for Scotland in 1979?

6   In which year were the heritable jurisdictions of the clan chiefs abolished?

7   Which Scots Law professor wrote *Principles of the Law of Scotland (1754) and Institutes of the Law of Scotland (1773)*?

8   Name the Scot who was the first British judge to be appointed to the Court of Justice of the European Communities.

9   Who was made King's Advocate in 1677?

10 With what was Patrick Meehan charged in 1969?

11 Which king founded the College of Justice in 1532?

12 Under Scots Law, what share of a dead person's moveable estate is the spouse entitled to, if there are no children?

13 In which decade was the Scottish Legal Aid Board established?

14 Which Scots university was the first to establish the teaching of law?

15 What was the name of the author of *Commentaries on the Law of Scotland Respecting the Description and Punishment of Crimes*, published in 1797?

16 In which year was the Consumer Protection Act passed?

17 Who was the first person to be tried for war crimes on British soil, and where was he tried?

18 In which Scottish prison was John Maclean held during the First World War?

19 Who published *The European Communities and the Rule of Law* in 1977?

20 In which decade was the Special Unit set up in Barlinnie Prison?

21 After how many years of separation may a divorce be granted on the grounds of irretrievable breakdown of marriage, if there is consent to the divorce?

22 What did Mrs May Donohue find in her bottle of ginger beer, which started a case that made legal history in Scotland?

23 Which eighteenth-century judge's memoirs were published posthumously in *Circuit Journeys*?

24 Who appoints the members of the Scottish Law Commission?

25 How many people sit on a jury in the High Court?

QUESTIONS

Answers: p233

QUESTIONS

1 What is the name of the radio station based in Inverness?

2 Which English writer described Inverness as the 'capital of the Highlands?'

3 Which building is the oldest in the city?

4 What is the name of the cathedral in Inverness?

5 In which century was the cathedral built?

6 During the reign of which king did Inverness become a royal burgh?

7 What is the name of Inverness's theatre?

8 In which century did the railway reach Inverness?

9 Whose troops attacked Inverness in 1645?

10 What is the name of the airport for Inverness?

11 Where is the Art Gallery and Museum?

12 What is the *Clach-na-Cudainn*?

13 From which century does the present castle date?

14 What is the name of the fifth-century BC hill-fort by Inverness?

15 Which architect designed the cathedral?

16 From which century does Dunbar's Hospital date?

17 Which order of monks once had a monastery in the town?

18 In which street is the Mercat Cross?

19 From which century does Abertarff House date?

20 Where is the High Church situated?

21 From which century does the old Court House date?

22 Where in Inverness did Lloyd George and Winston Churchill meet in 1921?

23 What is the name of the Bronze Age burial site close to the city?

24 Near which battle site is the Bronze Age burial site to be found?

25 In which decade was the seventeenth-century stone bridge over the River Ness destroyed by flood?

Answers: p233

Poetry 4

1 Who published a collection of poetry entitled *Weirds and Vanities*?
2 Name the seventeenth-century poet who wrote *Poems, Amorous, Funereall, Divine, Pastorall in Sonnets, Songs, Sextains, Madrigals*.
3 Which Scottish poet became Bishop of Dunkeld in 1515?
4 Which poet wrote under the pseudonym of R.G. Sutherland?
5 Who supplied a headstone for the grave of poet Robert Fergusson?
6 Name the Gaelic poet and Nationalist, son of novelist John MacDougall Hay.
7 How did the poet John Davidson die?
8 A posthumous edition of which poet's work was published as *More Poetic Gems* in 1962?
9 Which poet published a collection of poetry called *Voice-Over* in 1988?
10 Name the poet who wrote *Up.in the Morning Early*
11 Poet William Hamilton, contributor to *Tea-table Miscellany*, came from which part of Scotland?
12 Who wrote 'The Twa Dogs'?
13 Which poet wrote 'Ninth Elegy for the Dead in Cyrenaica' in 1948?
14 In which year was the poet Robert Fergusson born?
15 Who wrote 'Dr Faust in Rose Street'?
16 Which poet lived for some years at Brownsbank Cottage, Biggar?
17 Which Gaelic poet produced a collection of work entitled *Reothairt is Contraigh* in 1977?
18 By which other name was seventeenth-century poet Ian Lom known?
19 In which decade did Hugh MacDiarmid publish *The Kind of Poetry I Want*?
20 Who published a verse collection entitled *The Lays of Ancient Rome* in 1842?
21 Which Scottish poet wrote *To the Principal and Professors of the University of St Andrews, on their superb treat to Dr. Samuel Johnson*?
22 Which poet opened the first circulating library in Scotland?
23 What was the title of Edwin Muir's final collection of poetry?
24 Which Scots poet became Professor of English at Glasgow University in 1975?
25 In which century was the poet Gavin Douglas born?

Answers: p234

1   In which decade was the Dunning Report on the Scottish examination system produced?

2   What date is Tailie Day?

3   Who was named Scot of the Year in the 1999 Spirit of Scotland awards?

4   Which company bought the Royal Yacht *Britannia*?

5   How many ships does the National Lighthouse Board of Scotland own?

6   Where were the public records of Scotland stored during World War II?

7   For what medical purpose was birch-leaf tea drunk in the Highlands in olden days?

8   What was the primary function served by Blackness Castle in the sixteenth century?

9   What is the name of the outpost of the Edinburgh Royal Botanic Garden that is situated at Dunoon?

10 Where does the Earl of Aberdour live?

11 Where was the explorer William Balfour Baikie born?

12 Which Scot invented 'noctovision'?

13 Which oil-related industry is associated with Nigg Bay?

14 Who was the eighteenth-century leader of the Society of the Friends of the People in Scotland, campaigning for a parliament chosen by the people?

15 With which 'school' of Scottish fiction was the writer John Watson associated?

16 From which country did intense competition arise to Scotland's jute industry?

17 By what other name is Icolmkill more commonly known?

18 Name the well-known Dundee grocer who started a chain of shops throughout Scotland.

19 At the head of which loch does the village of Killin stand?

20 Which former Conservative MP (now deceased) lived at Fordell Castle?

21 From which part of Scotland does the Gordon clan come?

22 Which Banffshire town has 'Mare Mater' as its motto?

23 Which order of nuns lives at Nunraw Abbey?

24 What were Kingshouses?

25 What was/is a makar?

Answers: p234

1   In which town can you visit the Stuart Strathearn crystal factory?
2   From which century does Clackmannan Tower date?
3   What does the name Dunkeld mean?
4   Which river flows through the Sma' Glen?
5   What kind of ancient tree has Fortingall churchyard become famous for?
6   Where is the island of Inchtalla?
7   Which king held parliament in Forfar in the eleventh century?
8   What is the family name of the Earls of Gowrie?
9   Which famous bard has been said to be buried in the Sma' Glen?
10 Where is the oldest bowling green in Scotland?
11 Which novel by Sir Walter Scott is set around Strathyre?
12 What is the name of the Roman fort near Murthly?
13 With which clan is Struan associated?
14 Which sport is associated with Grandtully?
15 Where is Dalnagar Castle?
16 Which Scots ballad writer was born at Gask?
17 Which town is home to United Glass?
18 Where are the Falls of Bruar?
19 Which industry is celebrated in the museum at Broughty Castle?
20 Where was the rail ferry terminal which served Dundee in the nineteenth century?
21 What large piece of lost property was found in Arbroath Abbey in the 1950s?
22 Near which town is the village of Weem?
23 Who destroyed the castle that once stood at Montrose?
24 Near which town is Hospitalfield House?
25 Which famous company set up its ironworks at Falkirk?

QUESTIONS

Answers: p235

Otherwise Known As . . .

QUESTIONS

1   By which name did Christopher Murray Grieve become famous?
2   What is Lulu's real name?
3   Who was Robert Burns's 'Highland Mary'?
4   Who was known as the Scottish Samurai?
5   Which town was known in fiction as Thrums?
6   Which town in Fife is known as the Auld Grey Toun?
7   Who was the Wisest Fool in Christendom?
8   Who was the Red Fox?
9   Who was known as the Strathspey King?
10 Who was Jinglin' Geordie?
11 Which town in Grampian is also known as Gamrie?
12 Which king of Scotland was known as the Maiden?
13 By which name was Malcolm III known?
14 Which Fife town has been called the Lang Toun?
15 Which footballer was known as Slim Jim?
16 Which Scottish town is known as the Honest Toun?
17 Which king was known as the Lion?
18 Who was known an Toom Tabard?
19 Which writer was known as the Wizard of the North?
20 Who were the Famous Five?
21 Who is the Voice of Scottish Rugby?
22 Who was the Hammer of the Scots?
23 What was the Thin Red Line?
24 Who was known as Bell-the-Cat?
25 Who was Bluidy Mackenzie?

Answers: p235

1 Which Second World War commando hero was described by Winston Churchill as 'the handsomest man who ever cut a throat'?

2 Who was called 'the father of Scotland's Parliament'?

3 Where was Alexander III crowned?

4 In which year did Mary, Queen of Scots marry Darnley?

5 Who was the first heretic to be burned in Scotland?

6 When was the Treaty of Perth between Norway and Scotland?

7 When was the Battle of Harlaw?

8 In which year was the Marquis of Montrose executed?

9 Who became king after the death of David II?

10 Who was burned at St Andrews in 1546?

11 In which year was the Kilbrandon Report published?

12 Which king founded the Court of Session?

13 In which year was the First Book of Discipline drawn up?

14 Which king of Scotland died at Jedburgh in 1165?

15 Who was declared king of Scotland by the Award of Berwick?

16 Which Sottish king was captured by the English at Neville's Cross and held to ransom?

17 In which century did Shetland come under Scottish rule?

18 In which year was the Stone of Destiny finally (officially) returned to Scotland?

19 Who was the last of the Celtic kings of Scotland?

20 Which historical battle anniversary was marked in April, 1996?

21 Between which two kings was the Treaty of Abernethy drawn up in 1072?

22 Which punitive act was passed by the English Parliament in 1705 to force Scotland's acceptance of the Treaty of Union?

23 Who was defeated at the Battle of Annan in 1332?

24 What grisly portent of doom was placed on the table at the Black Dinner at Edinburgh Castle in 1440?

25 In which year was Edinburgh Castle taken by Covenanters?

Answers: p236

QUESTIONS

1   Which Scots actor teamed up with Rangers tycoon David Murray to plan for the creation of a major film studio near Edinburgh?

2   In the year 2000, two letters from Robert Louis Stevenson to Henry Ryder Haggard went on sale amidst much publicity. Where?

3   Name the aristocratic Scot who was married to Diana Rigg.

4   Where was the Stone of Destiny taken after it was stolen from Westminster Abbey?

5   Where is the Cockburn Society based?

6   Susan Brown became the first woman in Britain to take charge of a cathedral. Which cathedral?

7   Where can you visit Granny Shaw's Sweet Factory?

8   What is the name of the walk that runs parallel to the town wall in Stirling?

9   What is the only town in Angus in which witches were executed?

10 What is the longest rail bridge in Britain?

11 Which whisky distillery was established in 1824 by George Smith?

12 What was the name of the first tinned soup produced by Baxter's?

13 Which Hebridean island was once owned by the Redesdale family?

14 Where can you find the tallest tree in Britain?

15 Where is Scotland's largest shingle beach?

16 Which monarch built Falkland Palace?

17 How many stations are there on the Glasgow Underground?

18 In which year was the Museum of Scotland opened in Edinburgh?

19 In which month does the Philips Tour of Mull take place?

20 What is the Monarch of the Highland Skies?

21 In which direction would you travel to get from Perth to Aberfeldy?

22 Who founded Madras College in St Andrews?

23 Which order of monks founded Melrose Abbey?

24 What was the name of the treaty by which the marriage was arranged between Margaret of Norway and the son of Edward I?

25 What is the name of the home of the Duke of Roxburgh?

Answers: p236

1 In which book by Robert Louis Stevenson does the Hawes Inn at South Queensferry feature?

2 In which century were the iron works at Cramond established?

3 Where was Thistle Ware originally produced?

4 From where did train ferries once operate to Burntisland?

5 Where in East Lothian did some 200 whales become stranded in 1950?

6 What was the function of the Forth ship *Gardyloo*?

7 What is the name of the BP tanker terminal offshore from Dalmeny?

8 From which century does the conservatory in the grounds of Dalkeith House date?

9 In which Lothian village is the former home of the painter William Gillies?

10 After whom was the Lady Victoria Colliery named?

11 Where is St Joseph's Hospital?

12 Which school incorporates Pinkie House into its buildings?

13 What was the unexpected site of a siege in East Lothian from 1694 to 1697?

14 For which whisky baron was Vogrie House built?

15 In which decade was the Glenesk railway viaduct closed?

16 In which town is there a monument to French prisoners who died while incarcerated during the Napoleonic Wars?

17 From which period do the fort remains at Traprain Law date?

18 What was produced at Kinleith Mill, Currie?

19 What is the highest point in the Pentland Hills?

20 Where were the Valleyfield Mills?

21 Which town in West Lothian was once a centre for car and truck manufacturing?

22 In which century was Linlithgow Palace destroyed by fire?

23 Who planned the village of Ormiston in the eighteenth century?

24 Where is the source of the North Esk?

25 In which book by Sir Walter Scott does the Goblin Ha' feature?

Answers: p237

QUESTIONS

Sport 4

QUESTIONS

1   To the nearest 10 lb, what is the weight of a curling stone?
2   Which side was victorious when the Scottish rugby team met Samoa in November 2000?
3   With which sport is Graeme Obree associated?
4   In which sport did Andrew Lindsay win a gold medal in the 2000 Olympics?
5   What is the former SFU now known as?
6   Which Scot won sailing gold medals in two successive Olympics in 1968 and 1972?
7   In which year did the Scottish Curling team win a gold medal at Chamonix?
8   What is Paul Lawrie's native town?
9   At which sport did Euan McKenzie excel in the 1980s?
10   In which sport would you have a slippy leg and a grippy foot?
11   Who succeeded Jock Stein as manager of Celtic?
12   Which Glasgow team was founded in 1872?
13   What is the name of Jackie Stewart's son and business partner?
14   Where was the 1991 Walker Cup played?
15   Where was the Alfred Dunhill Links Championship played in 2000?
16   With which sport are the Ayr Eagles associated?
17   Scotland bid to host which major golf tournament in 2009?
18   What is the former Musselburgh Racecourse now known as?
19   Whom did Jackie Paterson defeat to win his world boxing title?
20   Which curling society drew up the rules of the sport?
21   Who was the winning jockey in the 1950 Scottish Grand National?
22   What age was boxer Benny Lynch when he died?
23   What is the Gaelic name for a shinty stick?
24   What is a shinty ball made from?
25   What was the score in the first international football match between Scotland and England?

Answers: p237

Scottish Regiments

1   From which two regiments was the regiment of The Queen's Own Highlanders formed?

2   What is the tartan worn by the Scots Guards?

3   Which regimental pipe band had a number-one hit with 'Amazing Grace'?

4   What is the name of the oldest surviving Highland regiment?

5   In what year did The Cameronians disband?

6   The Royal Highland Fusiliers and The Highland Light Infantry were amalgamated in 1959. What did they become?

7   Where is the Regimental museum of The Royal Scots?

8   Which regiment has its origins in the Edinburgh Regiment, raised in 1689 to defend the capital?

9   With which part of Scotland are the Gordon Highlanders associated?

10 What is the other name for the Black Watch tartan?

11 In which year were the Gordon Highlanders raised?

12 Which regiment has the motto 'Cuidich 'n Righ'?

13 With which regiment did the Royal Scots Greys amalgamate to become the Royal Scots Dragoon Guards?

14 Where is the regimental museum of the Queen's Own Highlanders?

15 Which regiment is affiliated with the 10th Princess Mary's Own Gurkha Rifles?

16 Which regiment has 'The Campbells Are Coming' as a regimental march?

17 Which regiment has Edinburgh Castle on its badge?

18 For what purpose were the companies raised that were ultimately to become the Black Watch?

19 Which tartans are worn by the men of the Argyll and Sutherland Highlanders?

20 Which regiment is sometimes referred to as 'The Greys'?

21 Which regiment is the oldest infantry regiment in the British army?

22 Who raised the Scots Greys in 1681?

23 Where is the museum of the Black Watch regiment?

24 Where is the museum of the Cameronians Scottish Rifles?

25 Which Scottish regiment carries out guard duties at Buckingham Palace?

Answers: p238

QUESTIONS

1. Where can you see the death mask of Mary, Queen of Scots?
2. Which Borders river flows into St Mary's loch?
3. To which British monarch was the Scot David Maclagan surgeon?
4. Which site in Edinburgh becomes a Winter Wonderland at Christmas?
5. With which historical event was James Loch, an MP for Wick in the eighteenth century, connected?
6. Name the Scot who foiled an assassination attempt on President Lincoln in 1861.
7. What was the first railway station in Britain to be lit by electric light?
8. In which century was the Journal of the Royal College of Surgeons founded?
9. Where did the Glendale Martyrs come from?
10. When was the Wheatley Commission on local government first set up?
11. Who founded Highland Airways limited?
12. Who was the first President of the Institute of Civil Engineers?
13. In which decade was the Ballachulish Bridge built?
14. What were Lochaber stones used all over Scotland for?
15. What is the best example of an eighteenth-century fort in Europe?
16. What flower was the emblem of the '45 Jacobites?
17. Which Scottish builder was known as 'Concrete Bob'?
18. What famous ship was launched by Cunard in 1935?
19. In which year was the Empire Exhibition held in Bellahouston Park in Glasgow?
20. In which year was the Central Scottish Electricity Grid built?
21. Who led the engineers' strike at Beardmore's in 1916?
22. Where was the base of Argyll Motors Limited?
23. Where was the Grand Fleet based during World War II?
24. Which bank merged with the Bank of Scotland in 1955?
25. Which road is the second highest in the British Isles?

Answers: p238

Heroes & Villains 2

1   Sir Patrick Manson carried out pioneering research on the cause of malaria and was one of the founders of the London School of Tropical Medicine—what was his nickname?

2   Who was the Scot appointed as the first Director of the United Nations Food and Agriculture Organisation in 1945?

3   He was a thieving cabinet-maker from Edinburgh, executed for his crimes. What was his name?

4   What is the name of the former manager of Celtic football club who died in 1985?

5   What nickname was given to the mystery triple killer who struck fear into the area around the Barrowlands in Glasgow in the 1960s?

6   Name the Scots climber who founded the Glencoe Mountain Rescue Team.

7   How did Captain Porteous die?

8   Who was the first European to cross the Rockies to the Pacific Ocean?

9   Which one of the evil partnership of Burke and Hare escaped the hangman's noose?

10 Name the sailor who was put ashore in a faraway place by William Dampier.

11 Who was killed at Kirk o' Field?

12 Which Scottish saint is thought to have been the teacher of St Kentigern?

13 Who starved Alexander Ramsay of Dalhousie to death in the dungeon of Hermitage Castle?

14 Where is Robert the Bruce believed to have spent his time in exile from 1306 to 1307?

15 What was the profession of explorer Mungo Park?

16 Which religious leader was responsible for the deaths of Patrick Hamilton and George Wishart?

17 Name the explorer who discovered Mount Erebus.

18 This Tayside man's notoriety stemmed not from his sins but from his poetry. What was his name?

19 By which other name was Alexander Selacraig known?

20 With which events in Scottish history is the name of Patrick Sellar associated?

21 What was the name of the founder of the Boy's Brigade?

22 Name the judge, notorious for his harsh sentencing, who presided over the trial of Deacon Brodie.

23 For what is Sir Robert Alexander Watson-Watt remembered?

24 Who killed the sheriff of Lanark in 1297?

25 Who was the first man to cycle from Dumfries to Glasgow?

Answers: p239

QUESTIONS

1   In which Fife town are the Silver Sands?
2   Which eighteenth-century naval hero was born in Inverkeithing?
3   In which Fife town was the first performance of *Ane Satyre of the Three Estaitis* staged in 1535?
4   What does Auchtermuchty mean?
5   In which decade was work begun on the new town of Glenrothes?
6   Whom does the Martyrs' Memorial at the west end of the Scores in St Andrews commemorate?
7   What is the name of the coastguard station near Crail?
8   What was made by Robert Heron and Sons of Kirkcaldy?
9   The Well Cave, the Court Cave and Jonathon's Cave are all part of which group of caves in Fife?
10   Which order of monks lived at the original priory of Dunfermline?
11   Where can you visit the *North Carr* lightship?
12   Name the industrialist who donated the art gallery to Kirkcaldy.
13   For what purpose was the windmill at St Monans used?
14   What does Pittenweem mean?
15   What is the name of the secondary school for the East Neuk of Fife?
16   Where in Fife can you find the first post-Reformation church built in Scotland?
17   For what purpose were the lands around the former Donibristle House used during the Second World War?
18   What is the name of the larger of the two beaches at St Andrews?
19   In which decade did the Wellesley pit in Fife close?
20   What is the largest fishing port in Fife?
21   Name the seventeenth-century minister at Crail who went on to become Archbishop of St Andrews.
22   Which famous nineteenth-century theologian was born in Anstruther?
23   From which century does Leslie House date?
24   In which Fife town did the General Assembly of the Church of Scotland take place in 1601?
25   What nationality of people designed the harbour at Crail?

Answers: p239

Great Scots 4

1   Which Scottish intellect of the nineteenth century married Jane Baillie Welsh?
2   Which historian wrote *De origine, moribus, et rebus gestis Scotorum*?
3   What was the name of the sixteenth-century prodigy, dubbed 'admirable', whose life was cut short when he was stabbed by his pupil?
4   What was the name of the man who wrote *The Handy Book of Meteorology*?
5   What was the name of the Scottish anthropologist who wrote *The Golden Bough: A Study in Comparative Religion*?
6   Which Scottish scholar, astronomer and occultist was made court astrologer by Frederick the Great?
7   What was the name of the publication which Francis, Lord Jeffrey co-founded?
8   At which European University was theologian Andrew Melville a professor before he took up the chair of Principal at Glasgow University in 1574?
9   The subtitle of the work is 'An Attempt to Introduce the Experimental Method of Reasoning into Moral Subjects'. What is the title of the work and who wrote it?
10 Which eminent scholar, teacher and theologian was made moderator of the General Assembly in 1567?
11 What was the name of the first Astronomer Royal for Scotland?
12 Which branch of science is generally regarded as having been founded by James Hutton?
13 Which Scottish king, a great intellectual himself, founded the University of Aberdeen?
14 What is the name of the eighteenth-century philosopher, Professor of Philosphy at Edinburgh for several years, who wrote *The History of the Progress and Termination of the Roman Republic*?
15 John Anderson, who died in 1796, made provision in his will for the founding of which educational institution?
16 What was the name of the founder of the 'Madras System' of education?
17 On which Scottish island was Lachlan Macquarie born?
18 With which city is the name of William Elphinstone associated?
19 Name the Scottish minister's wife and writer who published *Essays on the Superstitions of the Highlands* in the early ninenteenth century.
20 Why was the 'Wolf of Badenoch' excommunicated?
21 Which famous Scottish writer of a children's classic worked for the Bank of England in the early years of the twentieth century?
22 Which well-known Scottish legal figure had his home at Craigcrook Castle in Edinburgh?
23 Who was declared King Henry of Scotland although never crowned?
24 Which famous Scottish writer wrote in 'Synthetic Scots'?
25 Who was the leader of the 'Common Sense' school of Scottish philosophers?

Answers: p240

141

1   For what purpose would a mort house be used?
2   In which town is the annual Angus show held?
3   Which bank was founded in 1727?
4   In which year was the Scottish Development Agency formed?
5   What is the name of the last mine to produce coal for generating electricity in Scotland?
6   What was the profession of Walter Chapman and Andrew Millar of Edinburgh?
7   Where can you visit the Verdant Works?
8   How many steps are there on the Wallace Monument (answer to the nearest 10)?
9   Where is the Strathisla Distillery?
10   Which island in the Hebrides is Pillar Island?
11   Where in Scotland can you visit the Beatrix Potter garden?
12   What were the names of the founder members of the Baxter food company?
13   Where can you visit the Lochnell Mine?
14   In which town in Fife is St Fillan's Cave?
15   How high is Goat Fell (answer to the nearest 10 metres)?
16   In which direction would you have to travel to get to Braemar from Glenshee?
17   What are Bunkle, Billie and Blanerne?
18   For what reason was George Sprott of Eyemouth tortured and hanged in 1608?
19   Where is Scottish Women's Aid based?
20   Where was Osgood Mackenzie born?
21   What was quarried on Seil Island?
22   What part of Scotland features in Sir Walter Scott's *The Pirate*?
23   What is the name of the peninsula on which Portmahomack is situated?
24   What was the name of the celebrated piper to Queen Victoria?
25   In which year did the Clydeside engineers at G. & J. Weir strike for a wage rise of 2d. an hour?

Answers: p240

The Islands of Scotland 2

1   Which island is known as 'the Misty Isle'?
2   On which island is the ferry port of Brodick?
3   On which island is the RSPB Reserve at Loch Gruinart?
4   Which tiny volcanic island is known as Paddy's Milestone?
5   On which island did Bonnie Prince Charlie first land in Scotland?
6   Where is the Bunnahabhain distillery?
7   What is the name of the famous haunted cave on the Island of Mull?
8   What is the island featured in *Kidnapped*?
9   Fladda, Lunga and the Dutchman's Cap are all part of which group of islands?
10 Which island is Deer Island?
11 If you were travelling from Lochmaddy to Uig by ferry, from which island to which island would you be going?
12 Put the following Islay towns in order, north to south: Port Ellen, Port Askaig, Bowmore.
13 On which island is Loch Roag?
14 What kind of creature can be seen in significant numbers on Eilan nan Ron?
15 In which decade did the first steamboat to and from Skye operate?
16 In which century was the priory of Oronsay built?
17 What is the name of the small hill by Iona Abbey?
18 On which island is Breacacha Castle?
19 On which island is the Old Man of Storr?
20 What is the name of the stretch of water to the south-east of Mull?
21 Which Norwegian port lies due east of the Shetland Isles?
22 What stretch of water separates Thurso on the mainland from the Orkney Isles?
23 Which four islands are known collectively as the Small Isles?
24 Where is Scalpay harbour?
25 Which island was once known as the Granary of the Isles?

Answers: p241

1   Which Scottish actress co-starred with Ian McShane in *Lovejoy*?
2   Which role did Gordon Jackson play in *Upstairs Downstairs*?
3   Who played Anna in *This Life*?
4   Which Scots actor played a leading role in the TV serialization of Anna Karenina?
5   In which TV soap did Joe McFadden start his career?
6   Who played Inspector Taggart in the TV series *Taggart*?
7   What is the name of the character played by James Macpherson in *Taggart*?
8   Who was the Scottish producer of *The World at War* and *A Sense of Freedom*?
9   Which Scots actor played Cowley in *The Professionals*?
10 Who presented *The Midnight Hour*?
11 For how many years did Magnus Magnusson present *Mastermind*?
12 Which sport did television star Mark McManus compete in professionally before he took up acting?
13 Who played Private Fraser in *Dad's Army*?
14 What town was used as the setting for the second Dr Finlay series?
15 Which Scottish female comedian starred in her own sitcom *Rhona*, in 2000?
16 Which member of the team in the Scots comedy show *Absolutely* went on to host his own chat-show?
17 Of which television show was Jim McColl one of the original presenters?
18 Who is the Scottish presenter of *Watercolour Challenge*?
19 What is the name of the BBC Gaelic children's programme presented by Donny Macleod?
20 He built a whole comedy cult around the mysteries of the Glasgow dialect and starred in his own television series in the 1970s. What is this comedian's name?
21 With which news programme is the name of Mary Marquis associated?
22 What was the name of the character played by Fulton Mackay in *Porridge*?
23 Which Scots comedy programme featured sketches set in a lighthouse called Aanoch Mor?
24 Where is the Beechgrove Garden?
25 Which Scots presenter co-hosted the first National Lottery show with Anthea Turner?

Answers: p241

Football 2

1   Who was manager of Rangers from 1978 to 1983?
2   How many times was Bill Shankly capped as a player for Scotland?
3   What is the name of the Scot who became head of the English Football Association in 1999?
4   In which year did Jock Stein leave Celtic?
5   Which team won the 1982 Scottish Cup?
6   How many goals did Scotland score in the 1986 World Cup finals?
7   In which year did Gordon Strachan win his first Scottish cap?
8   With which two English teams did Matt Busby play?
9   In which year did Gordon Strachan take over as manager of Coventry City?
10 Name the hero of Scottish football who was born in Burnbank, Lanarkshire in 1922.
11 In which year did Scotland first appear in the World Cup finals?
12 Who was manager of Scotland in the 1974 World Cup?
13 Where is the home town of Caledonian Thistle?
14 When was the Scottish Women's Football Association founded?
15 Which Dundee team plays in blue and white?
16 In which year did Graeme Souness take over from Kenny Dalglish at Liverpool?
17 What was the name of the Italian club Graeme Souness played for?
18 In which year was the Scottish Premier Division formed?
19 How many teams did Bill Shankly manage before Liverpool?
20 What was the score in the Scotland v. Peru game in the 1978 World Cup?
21 In which year was Andy Beattie manager of the Scotland World Cup team?
22 In which year did Arbroath notch up their record score of 360 against Bon Accord in the Scottish Cup?
23 During which decade was Billy Bremner a captain of Scotland?
24 Where is Ross County based?
25 What was the first Scottish (and British) team to compete in the European Cup?

Answers: p242

1 What was the name of the ship, carrying soldiers back to Lewis after the War in 1918, which sank, costing the lives of more than 200 men?

2 Who owns Neidpath Castle?

3 Who wrote *The African Colony: Studies in the Reconstruction*?

4 Put the following rivers in order of length, starting with the longest: Tweed, Spey, Clyde, Tay.

5 What is Scotland's largest seabird?

6 Who wrote *Vestrarum Scoticum*?

7 What kind of building is reviled in 'The Jeely Piece Song'?

8 Which leading media figure from Scotland said the following: 'I do not pretend to give the public what it wants . . . '?

9 Which Scottish monarch travelled among his people disguised as The Gude Man o' Ballengeich?

10 Which king gave Ettrick Forest to his bride?

11 Where is Bear Ale Draught made?

12 By what name is the place once known as Coldburgh Head now known?

13 Which main road connects Haddington and Berwick-upon-Tweed?

14 Where could you take a trip on the SS *Walter Scott*?

15 Where were the 2000 World Curling Championships held in Scotland?

16 Edzell Castle is associated with which family?

17 Where is Talisker whisky made?

18 What are the defining qualities of Harris Tweed?

19 In which town is the Meffan Gallery and Museum?

20 Where is the annual Scottish Transport Extravaganza held?

21 What Motherwell iron works switched to steel production in 1871?

22 Near which town is the Arduaine Garden?

23 In which year did the Elibank Plot take place?

24 On which Hebridean Island can you visit Calgary Bay?

25 In which year was Glasgow Underground opened?

Answers: p242

Clans

1   From which common ancestor are the MacNeills of Barra and the MacNeills of Gigha thought to have been descended?

2   What does the name 'Macpherson' mean?

3   What part of Scotland does the Gordon clan originally come from?

4   Where is the home of the chief of the MacLeod clan?

5   'Cruachan!' is the slogan, or battle-cry, for which clan?

6   Eilean Donan Castle was the stronghold of which clan?

7   Which Campbell was responsible for the massacre at Glencoe?

8   Which clan chiefs were Lords of the Isles before the Stewarts took the title?

9   'Stand Fast Craigellachie' is the motto of which clan?

10 Which clan was a confederation of clans including Mackintosh, Farquharson, Macpherson, Macintyre and Cattanach among others?

11 Where did the Forbes clan have its origins?

12 What does 'Mackenzie' mean?

13 The battle-cry of the clan MacDougall is 'Buaidh no bas!' What does it mean?

14 Which clan is descended from Conn of the Hundred Battles?

15 Which part of Scotland does the MacDuff clan come from?

16 The motto of the clan MacGregor is 'Is Rioghail mo dhream'. What does it mean?

17 In which area of Scotland does the Scott clan have its origins?

18 Complete the following appellation: 'The Haughty . . .'

19 'Duke o' . . . - king in Man,
    An' greatest man in a' Scotlan'.'
    What is the missing name?

20 Which clan had ivy as its clan badge?

21 From which king are the MacGregors descended?

22 In which century did the last of the MacCrimmonds die out?

23 To which clan did the Gentle Lochiel belong?

24 Robertson is a family name of which clan?

25 Of which clan was Somerled of the Isles an ancestor?

Answers: p243

1   Where is St Margaret's Cave?

2   Where can you visit the Tall Ship *Glenlee*?

3   What kind of artwork can be seen at the Wemyss Caves?

4   What do Benromach, Edradour and Caol Ila have in common?

5   Where do the Earl and Countess of Mansfield live?

6   Where is Scotland's first island passenger railway?

7   What is the name of the woman, burnt at the stake in 1657, whose memorial can be found at Dunning?

8   Put the following places in order, West to East: Portknockie, Buckie, Findochty.

9   What does the Star Pyramid in Stirling commemorate?

10   Where can you visit Polarama?

11   What is the name of the nineteenth-century meal mill near Carnoustie?

12   What is the longest Angus glen?

13   What is the name of the only whisky distillery pioneered by a woman?

14   What was previously known as Strathearn Hydropathic?

15   Is St Cyrus to the south or to the north of Stonehaven?

16   Where is the Loch Fad fishery?

17   What are the Bullers of Buchan?

18   In which blockbuster film did Dunottar Castle feature?

19   What is the name of the gallery, housed in the former Glasgow Herald Building, which is Scotland's Centre for Architecture, Design and the City?

20   Which motorway connects Edinburgh and Linlithgow?

21   In which century was Stobo Castle built?

22   Where is the Eduardo Paolozzi collection housed?

23   From which century does the Round Tower in Brechin date?

24   Whose statue stands outside the Bannockburn Heritage Centre?

25   Who donated the Camera Obscura on Kirriemuir Hill to the town of Kirriemuir?

Answers: p243

Industry 4

1   Who was the first 'whisky lord'?

2   Name the poineer of the linoleum industry.

3   Name the family from Tayside who became famous for their jams and marmalade in the late eighteenth and early nineteenth centuries.

4   Where is the Scottish Mining Museum?

5   Which Scottish bank bought NatWest?

6   Which Scottish industry was badly affected by the 'Banana War' between Europe and the US?

7   Which ominous events linked to the power industry in the north of Scotland in the 1980s became known as 'the Riddle of the Sands'?

8   Which Scottish city is home to a new branch of Harvey Nichols?

9   The Scottish Executive imposed severe restrictions on scallop fishing in Scottish waters in the 1990s because of an alleged risk of ASP. What is ASP?

10 Who established the St Rollox Works?

11 What was John Rennie's profession?

12 In which city did printer William Smellie practise his trade?

13 What was the name of the nineteenth-century Scot who revolutionized methods of road construction?

14 Which shipbuilding company built the Queen Mary?

15 Who was president of the Federation of British Industries from 1930 to 1932? What was his business?

16 What did Andrew Meikle devise to help farmers?

17 Name the former Scottish footballer who founded a chain of stationers and confectioners, under his own name, when he retired from the game.

18 Whose building company was awarded the contract to build Wembley Stadium?

19 Who, along with his brother William, set up the Banque Générale in Paris in 1718?

20 Where did Sir Thomas Lipton first set up shop?

21 Which famous Scottish engineering works announced it was to be closed down in November, 2000?

22 In which year was the Carron Company formed?

23 What industrial change was responsible for a dramatic rise in Glasgow's population in the nineteenth century.

24 When did the Blantyre colliery disaster take place?

25 What type of fishing emerged in the late nineteenth century off Scotland's shores?

Answers: p244

QUESTIONS

1   Which famous Scottish merchant had a series of yachts in which he raced, mostly unsuccessfully?

2   In which decade was the Harris Tweed Association formed?

3   During which year were tanks and troops brought to Glasgow in case of trouble during the '40-Hour Strike'?

4   What is brochan?

5   Who founded the thirteenth-century abbey on Iona?

6   Where is the Dalhousie Arch?

7   Ambitious swimmers taking part in the Ne'erday Dook from Broughty Ferry try to swim to where?

8   Where can you see the skull of Moby?

9   Which nineteenth-century engineer designed Leith Docks?

10 Who was the owner of the Parkhead Forge?

11 Which Scottish artist joined the navy and painted images of naval dockyards during World War II?

12 Who invented the recipe for Baxter's Royal Game Soup?

13 What are the real names of The Krankies?

14 In which city is there a memorial to the soldiers who died in the Quintshill rail crash?

15 In which decade was the Glenfinnan Viaduct opened?

16 What is RSAMD?

17 With which sport is the name of W.W. Naismith associated?

18 Which family became Earls of Orkney in the late fourteenth century?

19 Which landmark in Ireland is similar in geology to the island of Staffa?

20 What was the writer Neil Gunn's occupation?

21 What is the English musical term for *puirt a beul*?

22 What is the name of the former hostess on *Wheel of Fortune* who became the presenter of *Changing Rooms*?

23 What is the name for the Scottish school founded and run on the principles of Kurt Hahn?

24 What was the Christian name of the Scottish father of philosopher John Stuart Mill?

25 Which village near Inverary gets its name from the iron smelting industry that once thrived in the area?

Answers: p244

Art 2

1   In which decade did Sir John Lavery die?

2   Name the Scottish sculptor who has created monumental works using car tyres and bricks, among other things.

3   What was the title of the statue of Christ, completed by sculptor Kenny Hunter in 2000, that was commissioned by Glasgow City Council?

4   Which Scottish artist made an oil sketch of his dead fourteen-month old child?

5   Who were the Group of Four?

6   Which sculptor made the statue of John Knox in St Giles Cathedral in Edinburgh?

7   Of which literary figure did Alexander Nasmyth paint a portrait, which hangs in the Scottish National Gallery?

8   What was the name of the man under whom William McTaggart, George Paul Chalmers and George Reid studied art in Edinburgh?

9   Which Scottish bird painter's work was used for the 1937 edition of the Observer's Book of British Birds?

10   David Scott, the nineteenth-century Scottish painter, had a brother, also an artist. What was his name?

11   Where was Anne Redpath born?

12   Name the Scot who was president of the RSA from 1973 to1983.

13   From which king did Sir Henry Raeburn receive his knighthood?

14   With which medium does Alison Kinnaird work?

15   In which century did the portraitist William Aikman live?

16   Which Scottish female artist exhibited a series of paintings entitled *Shift* in 2000?

17   Which nineteenth-century history painter painted *The Murder of Rizzio* and *Slave Market, Constantinople*?

18   Where was the artist James Cowie born?

19   Which eighteenth-century artist made illustrations to *The Gentle Shepherd*?

20   Which famous twentieth-century painter was born in Port Seton?

21   Which nineteenth-century painter became well-known for the Jacobite themes of many of his paintings, such as *Prince Charles's Entry into Edinburgh after Prestonpans*?

22   In which decade did Samuel Peploe die?

23   In which city was Henry Raeburn's studio?

24   Where did artist Stanley Cursiter train?

25   Which Scottish artist painted *The Quarrel of Oberon and Titania* in 1846?

Answers: p245

QUESTIONS

1 Of which political party was Robert McLennan a co-founder?
2 Who was Secretary of State for Scotland from 1976 to 1979?
3 Which position was George Robertson selected for in Tony Blair's cabinet of 1997?
4 Who became the youngest ever Secretary of State for Scotland in 1986?
5 What constituency did John Smith, former leader of the Labour Party, represent?
6 Which leading Scottish politician was instrumental in encouraging the merger of the SDP and the Liberal Party in 1989?
7 Who founded the Scottish Convention and organized the twentieth-century Scottish Covenant?
8 Of which political party was Hugh MacDiarmid a founder member?
9 Who was Prime Minister after Ramsay MacDonald?
10 In which year did Scottish politician Arthur James Balfour make the Balfour Declaration in favour of a Jewish homeland in Palestine?
11 In which year was Highlands and Islands Enterprise formed?
12 In what year was the Scotland Bill published to set up the new Parliament in Scotland?
13 Which seat was won from the Conservatives by Roseanna Cunningham in 1995?
14 Which seat did Jim Sillars win from Labour for the SNP in 1988?
15 Who won the Monklands East by-election in 1994 and for which party?
16 Where was William Whitelaw born?
17 Which party did Sir Henry Campbell-Bannerman lead as Prime Minister?
18 Who was the first Scottish Labour Prime Minister?
19 In which year was the document *Scotland's Parliament, Scotland's Right* published?
20 In which year was the Kilbrandon Commission set up?
21 Who was appointed as Communities Minister in the new Scottish Executive of 1999?
22 Which Scot was leader of the Labour Party from 1911 to 1914?
23 Which Scottish Prime Minister of Great Britain, when elected, was the third youngest person to hold the position?
24 In what year were the rights of the Scottish church asserted in the First Claim of Right?
25 Who became Secretary of State for Scotland in 1995?

Answers: p245

Strathclyde 2

1   After which king are the King's Caves on the Island of Arran so called?
2   Who holds the title of Duke of Rothesay?
3   In which loch is Davaar Island?
4   Name the steam pioneer who was provost of Helensburgh in the early nineteenth century.
5   Of which clan was Dunollie Castle a stronghold?
6   With which saint is Kiel Point on the Mull of Kintyre associated?
7   Which saint is associated with the village of Luss?
8   By which loch is Barcaldine Castle situated?
9   In which loch is the island of Lismore?
10 On which river is Barrhead situated?
11 Where does the Forth and Clyde canal enter the River Clyde?
12 Where is the ancient coronation site of the kingdom of Dalraida?
13 In which decade was the old Kirkintilloch–Monkland railway opened?
14 Where can you visit Souter Johnnie's cottage?
15 With which town was Wishaw amalgamated?
16 For which food product did Dunlop become famous?
17 Where is the island of Inchmurrin?
18 What kind of boats were once built at Fairlie?
19 The father of which famous eighteenth-century literary figure took the title of Lord Auchinleck?
20 What kind of vessel is associated with Holy Loch?
21 In which month is Lanimer Day celebrated?
22 In which century was the town of New Lanark built?
23 What is the name of the tributary of the Clyde upon which the settlement which grew to become the city of Glasgow was founded?
24 Where can you get a ferry across the Clyde to Dunoon?
25 What is the main road connecting Ayr to Stranraer?

Answers: p246

1   What kind of dog is the black dog which features on Black and White whisky bottles?

2   What record did Miss Ballantine set on the River Tay in 1922?

3   What disaster was triggered by MacIan's tardy arrival in Inverary to sign an oath of loyalty?

4   What is the name of the highest mountain in Scotland?

5   From which century is the Book of Deer thought to date?

6   With which American city opera company did Scots singer Mary Garden become chief soprano and director?

7   Name the famous left-wing politician who once ran a newsagents shop in Hamilton.

8   How many articles were proposed by King James VI to the General Assembly at Perth in 1618?

9   Which organization ran the Scottish railway system before it was denationalized?

10   How many Declarations of Indulgence were made altogether?

11   For what crime was the Englishman Thomas Green hanged at Leith in 1705?

12   What is the RSGS?

13   By which name are the islands sometimes called the Seven Hunters more commonly known?

14   In which part of Scotland did the Levellers' Revolt take place?

15   Which Scottish soprano singer had a chart hit in 1969 with 'The Holy City'?

16   What kind of rock is associated with Portsoy?

17   By which other name is Glen Fruin sometimes called?

18   What is the name of the society founded in 1936 for the preservation and promotion of Scottish culture and excellence?

19   What was the profession of Archibald Geikie?

20   What was the name of the famous nephew of the Ballantyne publisher brothers, and what made him famous?

21   What was the name of the Scot who made the first successful balloon descent in Britain in 1784?

22   By what name is Graham's Dyke officially known?

23   What motorway connects Glasgow to Carlisle?

24   Who was lead singer with the band Deacon Blue?

25   In the work of which author can we read about the Gorbals Die-hards?

Answers: p246

Music 4

1   What is the name of the annual competition in Gaelic singing, music and dancing?
2   In which city was the Scottish singer Jean Redpath born?
3   Name the popular Gaelic rock band that comes from Skye.
4   Who wrote the opera *The Cataline Conspiracy*?
5   What kind of voice did Joseph Hislop have - tenor, bass or treble?
6   Which band did Derek Longmuir belong to?
7   Who composed the overture *Aus Dem Schottischen Hochlande*?
8   Which Scottish singer was married to Maurice Gibb?
9   Which one of Neil Gow's sons wrote the reel *Mrs Dundas of Arniston*?
10 Who composed the opera *Mary, Queen of Scots*?
11 Where is the new site of the Army School of Bagpipe Music and Highland Drumming, opened in 2000?
12 Who wrote songs under the pseudonym Mrs Bogan of Bogan?
13 Name the fiddler who composed 'The Bonnie Lass o' Bon Accord'.
14 Who composed the opera *The Black Spider*?
15 Which Scottish musician has published an autobiography entitled *Good Vibrations*?
16 Who was the first professor of music in Scotland?
17 In which century was the Carver Choirbook written?
18 Where was the Panopticon Music Hall?
19 In which year did Scottish Opera first perform at the Edinburgh Festival?
20 Which famous Scots singer published *The Songs of the Hebrides*?
21 Which Scottish composer wrote *Land of the Mountain and the Flood*?
22 Who wrote the overture *Tam o' Shanter*?
23 Which Scottish composer was principal of the Royal Academy of Music in London from 1888 to 1924?
24 Which composer founded the Active Society for the Propagation of Contemporary Music in 1929?
25 In which century did composer James Oswald live?

QUESTIONS

Answers: p247

155

The Borders 2

QUESTIONS

1 What main road connects Peebles and Galashiels?
2 By what name was Cockburnspath formerly known?
3 What is said to lie beneath or around the ruins of Fast Castle?
4 In which Borders abbey was Waldeve an abbot in the twelfth century?
5 Where is the headquarters and crowning place of the Border gypsies?
6 What does the Redeswire Stane commemorate?
7 What was the name of the cannon that killed James II at Roxburgh?
8 In which century was Kelso Abbey destroyed?
9 What is distinctive about the spiral staircases in Queen Mary's House, Jedburgh?
10 Which two Borders rivers join at the Junction Pool?
11 With which Borders castle is the name of De Soulis associated?
12 Where do 'Teries' come from?
13 What are Talla and Megget?
14 Where is Greenmantle Ale produced?
15 What is the only remaining part of the old church of St Andrews in Peebles?
16 By which name did Sir Walter Scott immortalize Davy Ritchie from Manor Valley?
17 What colour is the flag carried by the Hawick Cornet at the Common Riding celebrations?
18 Which Borders town used to be a site for the Royal Highland Show?
19 Where in the Borders can you see Rob Roy's gun?
20 What was the name of the railway that ran from Galashiels to Peebles?
21 To whom was Muckle Mou'ed Meg betrothed at Elibank Tower?
22 Where can you see Robert Smail's printing works?
23 What are the 'Steekit Yetts'?
24 Where is the Scottish Academy of Falconry?
25 Which Borders family name is associated with Bedrule?

Answers: p247

156

Literature 4

1 Who wrote *Katie Stewart* in 1853?

2 What was Robert Ballantyne's most famous children's book?

3 In which city was novelist Nigel Tranter born?

4 Who wrote *Moral Fables* in the sixteenth century?

5 In which decade did Robert Ballantyne write *Martin Rattler*?

6 Where is the home town of fiction's Inspector Rebus?

7 Who was the hero of *The Thirty-Nine Steps*?

8 Who wrote a book of short stories entitled *The Acid House*?

9 Which Scottish author won the James Tait Black Memorial Prize for *Highland River*, in 1937?

10 Who wrote *The Stickit Minister*?

11 Who wrote *The House of Elrig*?

12 Which work by A.J. Cronin criticized the practises of doctors in Harley Street?

13 What was the title of Robert Garioch's account of his experiences in POW camps in the Second World War?

14 Which book by a Scottish writer features Jim Hawkins?

15 Who wrote *Janine*?

16 Name the writer of *Sartor Resartus*.

17 Where was Scots writer and journalist Allan Massie born?

18 Who wrote an autobiographical work entitled *The Company I've Kept*?

19 Who was the author of *Gallipoli Memories*?

20 Which contemporary writer is author of *The Lights Below*?

21 Who was James Boswell's father?

22 In which year did Iain Banks publish *A Song of Stone*?

23 Which Scottish writer and statesman was MP for the Scottish Universities from 1927 to 1935?

24 Who wrote *Just Duffy*?

25 Name the author of *Gillespie*.

Answers: p248

QUESTIONS

1   In what year was the Stone of Destiny removed from Scone?
2   What sort of object is the Monymusk Reliquary?
3   In which forest park is Glentrool?
4   Which famous Scottish accordionist died in December 2000?
5   What old New Year tradition is celebrated in the town of Burghead?
6   In which part of Scotland is the waterfall of Eas Coul Aulin?
7   In which village did Rudolf Hess land when he came to Scotland?
8   Which Scot was world professional darts champion in the 1980s?
9   How old was Robert Burns when he died?
10 Which hotel in Edinburgh was originally called The North British Railway Hotel?
11 During which war were the Lovat Scouts raised?
12 In which part of Scotland was Dunmore Ware once made?
13 In which year was Dundee Contemporary Arts opened?
14 What is the main food of the osprey?
15 What are the two towns at each end of the West Highland Way?
16 What was the original trade of William Collins, publisher?
17 Which town in Fife is home to the exhibition and performance venue, the Crawford Centre?
18 In which Scottish glen can be found a cairn dedicated to Edward Adrian Wilson and Robert Falcon Scott?
19 What was the profession of Marjory Kennedy-Fraser?
20 What kind of disaster struck Auchengeich in 1959?
21 Which illustrious body forms the Queen's ceremonial bodyguard in Scotland?
22 Through which parent could Robert the Bruce claim royal descent?
23 What is the name of the character played by Eileen Macallum in *High Road*?
24 Which fishing town in the Borders has 'Herring Queen Week'?
25 UK Pet Slimmer of the Year, 2000, was Scottish. What kind of pet was he?

Answers: p248

Travel

1 In what year did the Tay Bridge disaster take place?

2 Of which main road is the 'Lang Whang' a part?

3 Which company runs most of the ferry services from the mainland to the Western Isles?

4 How long did it take to build the Caledonian Canal?
a) 5 years b) 18 years c) 15 years

5 What is the name of the canal that was built between 1818 and 1828 to link Edinburgh with the Forth and Clyde Canal at Falkirk?

6 What was the name of the station at the west end of Edinburgh's city centre, beside the Caledonian Hotel, which closed in 1965?

7 How many locks are there on the Caledonian Canal?

8 What was the name of the waterway opened in 1790 to forge a link for shipping between the Atlantic and the North Sea?

9 In which year was the Forth Rail Bridge opened?

10 What is the most southerly station in Scotland at which the train stops on the east coast railway line from Edinburgh to London?

11 What kind of bridge is the Erskine Bridge?

12 When were Glasgow and Edinburgh linked by railway?

13 What is the nearest railway station to St Andrews in Fife?

14 From which airport in Scotland can you fly direct to the USA?

15 Where is Sumburgh airport?

16 When and where did the last tram run in Scotland?

17 Which road in Scotland is most frequently blocked by snow in winter?

18 Where does the Crinan Canal run?

19 Which road crosses the border into England at Gretna Green?

20 In which part of Scotland is Electric Brae?

21 Where was the hairpin bend now replaced by a safer, straighter road known as The Devil's Elbow?

22 From where can you take a ferry across the River Almond to the Rosebery Estate on the banks of the Forth?

23 Before the Forth Road Bridge was built, what was the most easterly road bridge across the Forth?

24 Where is the northerly terminus of the A9?

25 In which decade was Glasgow Central railway station opened?

Answers: p249

Scottish Women

1   What was Mary Slessor's job before she became a missionary?
2   For which constituency did Katharine, Duchess of Atholl become MP in 1923?
3   Which Scottish soprano became director of the Chicago Grand Opera?
4   Which Scottish writer wrote the autobiographical work *Curriculum Vitae*?
5   Who founded the Scottish Women's Suffragette Federation?
6   In which race did Liz McColgan win a silver medal at the Olympic games in Seoul?
7   How did Miranda Barry achieve her ambition to train as a surgeon?
8   What profession did Liz Lochhead follow before she became a writer?
9   When was Winnie Ewing first elected to the European Parliament?
10 What parliamentary position did Helen Liddell hold at the time of the 2001 general election?
11 Which Scottish actress starred in the 1970s TV comedy *My Wife Next Door*?
12 Alison Ramsay received an MBE in 2001 for her sporting achievements for Scotland and Great Britain. At which sport did she achieve excellence?
13 Name the Scottish woman who was composer-in-residence at the RSAM from 1988 to 1991.
14 How many husbands did Mary, Queen of Scots have?
15 Whom did Scots singer Annie Lennox partner in the Eurythmics?
16 Name the woman whose face became famous in TV adverts for her family's soup.
17 Where was barrister Helena Kennedy born?
18 Which Scottish woman started a riot in 1637?
19 Which Scottish painter was the first woman to become a full member of both the RSA and the RA?
20 In which year was Evelyn Glennie born?
21 Which woman ran an inn in the Borders with famous literary connections?
22 Which famous Scottish songwriter wrote a collection of songs that were published after her death as *Lays of Strathearn*?
23 Which Scottish actress starred in the film *From Here to Eternity*?
24 In which century was St Margaret canonized?
25 Name the woman who attempted to ski to the North Pole unsupported in 1969.

Answers: p249

Science, Engineering, Invention & Innovation

1   What was the name of George Stephenson's famous locomotive?
2   In which year was the telephone invented by Alexander Graham Bell?
3   Who was the Scot who designed the Bell Rock Lighthouse?
4   What was invented by Robert William Thomson?
5   Who invented the first duplicating machine?
6   Which father and son were responsible for the design and construction of London Bridge?
7   When was Thomas Telford born?
8   Which Scot first produced pneumatic tyres commercially?
9   Who patented the double engine?
10 With which invention is Sir David Brewster associated?
11 Who invented the oscillating engine?
12 Who built the first pedal bicycle?
13 Which invention is attributed both to Charles Tennant and Charles Macintosh?
14 What was the measurement chosen by George Stephenson, still in use, for the distance between rails?
15 Who pioneered the manufacturing of paraffin in Scotland?
16 Who invented the rotary press?
17 Where was Dolly, the first cloned sheep, born?
18 Who proposed the absolute temperature scale (named after him)?
19 What was the *Charlotte Dundas*?
20 Who discovered the magneto-optic effect?
21 Who was the leader of the team which cloned Dolly, the sheep?
22 Why was Frostie the calf so named?
23 In which year did John Logie Baird give the first demonstration of television?
24 What invention by Ian Donald did much to improve antenatal care for women and their babies?
25 Who invented the patent still?

Answers: p250

QUESTIONS

1   Which famous Scot died during a Wales v. Scotland football match in 1985?

2   What was the name of the Scot who was the second Governor of New South Wales?

3   For what invention is James Nasmyth remembered?

4   How many times has the Fairy Flag of Dunvegan been unfurled in battle?

5   In which country did the eighteenth-century Scots missionary Donald Mitchell carry out his work?

6   What food product is believed to have been named after the village of Findon?

7   In which sea loch did German U-Boats surrender to the British in 1945?

8   Who is Baron of Renfrew?

9   Name the Russian composer who set 'Comin' Thro' the Rye' to music.

10 Which castle is the largest in Scotland?

11 Where is Ravenscraig Castle?

12 In which group of islands is the island of Whalsay?

13 What was manufactured by the firm of Lobnitz and Co.?

14 Which explorer from Dumfriesshire died in Sokoto?

15 Chatelherault is a former hunting-lodge of which dukes?

16 Where in East Lothian did the monks from the Isle of May start a tradition of brewing that continues today?

17 How many times has Scots actor Sean Connery been married?

18 Put the following towns in order north to south: Kingussie, Aviemore, Pitlochry.

19 Which king of Scotland boasted that he governed Scotland with his pen?

20 In which month of the year was the Battle of Culloden fought?

21 What is the 'great chieftain o' the puddin' race'?

22 In which year did actor Fulton Mackay die?

23 Statues of which two great Scots stand at the entrance to Edinburgh Castle?

24 Where did Charles Macintosh set up his factory for the production of waterproof clothing?

25 Which country lies east of Edinburgh across the North Sea?

Answers: p250

Where Were They Born?

1   Robert Adam, architect
2   Alexander Selkirk, sailor
3   Neil Munro, novelist
4   John Knox, Protestant reformer
5   Robert the Bruce, king
6   Mary, Queen of Scots
7   John Buchan, novelist
8   Kenny Dalglish, footballer
9   James Ramsay MacDonald, Prime Minister
10 St Kentigern
11 Adam Smith, economist
12 Alexander Graham Bell, inventor
13 Flora Macdonald, Jacobite heroine
14 Lord Francis Jeffrey, judge
15 David Livingstone, missionary and explorer
16 James Young Simpson, obstetrician
17 Sir Walter Scott, writer
18 Thomas Hamilton, architect
19 Charles Rennie Mackintosh, architect
20 J.M. Barrie, novelist
21 William Gillies, painter
22 James VI
23 James Boswell, writer
24 Hugh MacDiarmid, poet
25 Andrew Carnegie, millionaire philanthropist

QUESTIONS

Answers: p251

QUESTIONS

1 Which suburb of the city boasts a beautifully preserved sixteenth-century round dovecot?

2 Where did the stone come from for building the New Town?

3 What is the name of Edinburgh's airport?

4 What are the names of the three universities of the city?

5 Where is St Bernard's Well?

6 Who designed Ramsay Garden?

7 Where is the Merchants' Hall?

8 Where is the Melville monument?

9 Which body is responsible for maintaining Lauriston Castle?

10 Where is the faculty of Divinity of Edinburgh University housed?

11 Where is the new site of the Royal Infirmary of Edinburgh?

12 In which year did the new extension of the Royal Museum of Scotland open?

13 What occasion was Clermiston Tower on Corstorphine Hill built to commemorate?

14 Which river runs through Colinton Dell?

15 Where, in Edinburgh, is the poet Robert Fergusson buried?

16 Which Edinburgh school was formerly known as 'The Institution'?

17 Between which two village suburbs of Edinburgh does Currie lie?

18 Which Edinburgh theatre suffered extensive fire damage in 1993?

19 Where is the Royal College of Physicians?

20 In which century was the Thistle Chapel built?

21 What is housed in the former John Watson's Hospital?

22 Which architect designed Anne Street?

23 What was the trade of Andrew Usher, who donated money to build the Usher hall?

24 What industry did the buildings in the Dean Village grow up around?

25 What is the name of Adam Ferguson's former home in Edinburgh?

Answers: p251

Medicine in Scotland

1   Name the Scot who discovered penicillin.

2   Who was the founder of the Royal Infirmary of Edinburgh?

3   Who were the brothers from Glasgow who became eminent surgeons in the eighteenth century?

4   In which branch of medicine did James Young Simpson specialize?

5   Which university in Scotland was the first to have a chair in medicine?

6   Who identified the bacterium which causes brucellosis?

7   Who discovered a vaccine for typhoid?

8   Who, along with Sir Ronald Ross, pioneered research into malaria and discovered the connection between the mosquito and the malaria parasite?

9   Which city was the first to have an X-ray unit in a hospital?

10 In what year was the first operation performed under antiseptic conditions in Scotland by Joseph Lister?

11 Name the Scot who, along with Sir Frederick Barting and Charles Best, discovered insulin.

12 Name the electrical engineer who was one of the first to research the potential applications of radiography in medicine.

13 With which branch of medicine is the name of David Ferrier associated?

14 In what sphere of orthopaedic work was Sir William MacEwen a pioneer?

15 With which branch of medicine is the name of Andrew Duncan associated?

16 Which Scottish town was the first to introduce a special training scheme for psychiatric nurses?

17 What kind of hospital is Rottenrow?

18 Name the maternity hospital founded in Edinburgh, now closed, that was originally staffed entirely by women.

19 Name a former Edinburgh hospital in the south side of the city specializing in the treatment of women.

20 Which naval doctor wrote *A Treatise of the Scurvy* in 1753?

21 In which decade did Miranda/James Barry die?

22 Nora Wattie worked tirelessly as a pioneer of medical and social welfare in Glasgow. In which decade did she die?

23 Which prominent Scots obstetrician, professor of midwifery in Aberdeen from 1937 to 1965, was a campaigner for family planning and for reform of the Abortion Act?

24 What was the name of the surgeon who was the first to perform an operation in public with the use of general anaesthesia?

25 Who was the first practising doctor to be made a baronet?

Answers: p252

QUESTIONS

General Knowledge 39

1   Between which two islands is the Cuillin Sound?
2   What is the name of the main road running through Islay and Jura?
3   In which year was Kenny Dalglish born?
4   What does 'sonsie' mean?
5   Who co-starred with Sean Connery in *The Man Who Would Be King*?
6   How long (to the nearest 10 miles) is Loch Maree?
7   Who wrote *The Old Man of Lochnagar*?
8   In which group of mountains is Sgurr Alasdair?
9   In which Highland town was Janet Horne burned for witchcraft in 1722?
10 Which one of the western Isles has its own breed of pony?
11 In 2000, why did some Scottish schools fall foul of the Lord Lyon?
12 Who created the kingdom of Alba?
13 Which organization owns Threave Gardens?
14 In which part of Edinburgh was actor Sean Connery born?
15 Whom did Henry VIII seek out to marry his son Edward in The Rough Wooing?
16 With which band did TV presenter Dougie Vipond once play?
17 What do Traprain Law, the Bass Rock and Edinburgh Castle Rock have in common?
18 Which poetic figure 'is come out of the west'?
19 Which festival is known as *Nollaig* in Gaelic?
20 In which town was Andrew Cruikshank, of *Dr Finlay* fame, born?
21 In which decade did Edinburgh Zco open?
22 Which king did The Lion kill?
23 Which regent for the infant James VI was shot in Linlithgow?
24 Which firm took over Govan Shipbuilders in the 1980s?
25 Which town in the north-east shares its name with a port of Hong Kong?

Answers: p252

Mountains & Hills

1   Which loch does Ben Slioch in Ross and Cromarty overlook?
2   What is a Munro?
3   What is the second highest mountain in the Cairngorms?
4   Where are the Five Sisters?
5   Which mountain overlooks the town of Callander?
6   What is the name of the mountain overlooking Spittal of Glen Muick?
7   What is the name of the mountain range between Aviemore and Braemar?
8   Where is Beinn Nuis?
9   Which mountain is haunted by 'The Big Grey Man'?
10 What range of hills lies to the north of Glasgow?
11 What is the most northerly Munro?
12 There is one Ben Vorlich overlooking Loch Sloy, close to Tarbet. Where is the other one?
13 What does Ben More mean?
14 Which loch stands in the shadow of Ben Lawers?
15 Which mountain is sometimes called The Sugar Loaf?
16 Which mountain range contains four out of five of Britain's tallest mountains?
17 What is the name of the mountain system of which the Cairngorms are a part?
18 What is the name of the second-highest mountain in Scotland?
19 What is the name of the highest peak in the Black Cuillins?
20 What separates the North West Highlands and the Grampians?
21 Which mountain in Scotland has a feature called Sgriob na Cailleach (Old Woman's Furrow)?
22 Where are the Sow of Atholl and the Boar of Badenoch?
23 Where is Liatach?
24 In which part of Scotland is Ben Wyvis?
25 What does Buchaille Etive Mor mean?

Answers: p253

1 From which century does the first written evidence of whisky distillation date?

2 In which year was the Whisky Association founded?

3 In 1942, the Whisky Association was replaced by another organization to protect the whisky trade in Scotland. What was the new organization called?

4 What is the name of the instrument which measures the proof of the spirit?

5 In which century was the patent still invented?

6 Once germination of the barley to be used has reached the right stage for the next part of the distillation process, how is the germination checked?

7 What kind of still is used to produce malt whisky?

8 Which island is particularly well known for its malt whiskies?

9 Where does Highland Park whisky come from?

10 What is the name for the container in which the ground barley is mixed with boiling water to dissolve the starch?

11 Where is the Glenfiddich distillery?

12 In which decade was Distillers Company Limited formed?

13 What event overseas contributed to a slump in the whisky trade in the 1920s?

14 What is a blended whisky?

15 Where is Laphroaig distilled?

16 In the pot-still distilling process, what is the name of the liquid that is drawn off after the sugar from the barley has been dissolved in it?

17 What name is associated with Red Label and Black Label?

18 Which whisky was recommended 'Afore ye go'?

19 In which part of Scotland is Glenkinchie Distillery?

20 In which part of Scotland is the Macallan Distillery?

21 Can Scotch whisky be made outside Scotland?

22 When was Scottish Malt Distillers Ltd formed?

23 What were DCL's patent-still distilleries used for during the First World War?

24 In 1999, a bottle of 50-year-old malt whisky was sold at auction at Christie's for more than £9,000. What was the name of the whisky?

25 Approximately how many bottles of Scotch are consumed worldwide every year?
a) 3 billion b) 20 million c)1 billion

Answers: p253

Dundee 2

1   Who wrote in 1844 that Dundee was 'a sink of atrocity which no moral flushing seems capable of cleansing'?
2   What is the oldest part of St Mary's Parish Church?
3   Where is the Geddes Quadrangle?
4   'With your numerous arches and pillars in so grand array.' To what was the poet McGonagall referring?
5   From which century does Dudhope Castle date?
6   Where is the Wishart Arch?
7   Who owns the Courier Building?
8   Who bought out the Keiller business?
9   In which decade was the Harris Academy built?
10 Who was the first inhabitant of Nethergate House?
11 What is the nickname that was given to the Glasite Chapel?
12 What shape is the Glasite Chapel?
13 When was the Caird Hall completed?
14 How many guns did the *Unicorn* have?
15 In which decade did Dundee's 'Water Wars' begin?
16 Where was the old Palais de Dance?
17 Where is Gardyne's House?
18 Where is the faculty of medicine for Dundee University located?
19 Who was the first chancellor of the University of Dundee?
20 In which decade was Mains Castle in Caird Park restored?
21 In which decade was the Caird Hall built?
22 In which year did the Dundee-Arbroath railway line open?
23 To the nearest 100 feet, how high is Dundee Law?
24 From which century does the Theatre Royal building date?
25 In which year was *Discovery* returned to Dundee?

Answers: p254

The Life & Works of Robert Burns

1   'Sae rantingly, sae wantonly,
    Sae dantonly gaed he:
    He play'd a spring and danced it round,
    Below the gallows-tree.'
    About whom did Robert Burns write these words?
2   What was the name of Burns's father?
3   Where was Highland Mary born?
4   How old was Jean Armour when she married Robert Burns?
5   Who was 'Bonie Lesley'?
6   What was the name of Robert Burns's father's farm?
7   Who was 'Souter Johnnie'?
8   What was the name of the farm occupied by Robert Burns and his family after his marriage?
9   In which year did Robert Burns die?
10 In which year did Burns's father die?
11 What relation was Mrs John Begg to Robert Burns?
12 Which of Burns's legitimate children survived the longest?
13 Who was 'Holy Willie'?
14 To whom did Burns dedicate 'The Cottar's Saturday Night'?
15 Who was 'The Bonie Lass of Albanie'?
16 Where was the first Burns Club to be formally constituted?
17 Which poet scathingly referred to 'Burnomania' in a satirical poem, written in 1811?
18 What was the name of Robert Burns's mother?
19 Where did Burns nearly emigrate to in 1786?
20 As what did Burns find employment in Dumfries?
21 Who was the mother of Burns's first illegitimate child?
22 In which year did Burns move to Dumfries?
23 When did Burns make his Highland tour?
24 What was the name of the collection of songs and music which Burns edited?
25 Where was the farm leased by Burns and his brother after the death of their father?

Answers: p254

1   At which event did Yvonne Murray win a medal in the 1994 Commonwealth Games?
2   How many Academy Awards were won by the film *Chariots of Fire*?
3   From which century does the Order of the Thistle date?
4   What part did a 'howdie' play in people's lives in early times?
5   Where are the Machrie Moor stone circles?
6   What is the longest burgh name in Scotland?
7   Who wrote the poem 'Fisher Jamie'?
8   In which year did Robert the Bruce become Guardian of Scotland?
9   Of which sporting organization is Princess Anne the patron?
10 What is the name of the (now forested) former sandy desert near Nairn?
11 Where did James Hepburn, 4th Earl of Bothwell, die?
12 On which loch are the Falls of Foyers?
13 Which three areas were chosen as sites for Scotland's first National Parks?
14 On which bank of the Clyde is Partick?
15 Who was the famous grandson of George Gordon of Gight?
16 What was the name of the fictional town in which Dr Finlay lived?
17 What was the name of the first of Andrew Lang's 'fairy books'?
18 What was the cause of the Shawfield Riot of 1725?
19 Which famous Scots politician married Margaret Ethel Gladstone?
20 What sport is associated with the Lecht?
21 On which day do the people of Foula celebrate Christmas?
22 In which Angus bay is Red Castle?
23 Where in Scotland was the first golfers' hotel built by a railway company?
24 Who owned Hospitalfield House near Arbroath in the nineteenth century?
25 In which year was the *SS Discovery* launched?

Answers: p255

ANSWERS

ANSWERS

General Knowledge 1

1   Loch Tummel
2   45
3   The nineteenth century
4   Slains Castl
5   Wanlockhead
6   Engineering
7   Skye
8   Glamis
9   Fortingall
10 Near Inver
11 Aberdeen
12 The Strathspey Railway
13 Comrie lies on the Highland Boundary Fault
14 Elgin Cathedral
15 Durness
16 Kilmuir, Skye
17 Evelyn Glennie
18 The Church of St Mary, Haddington
19 *The Name of the Rose*
20 *Comet*
21 Sir Henry Raeburn
22 Dalbeattie
23 Sir Walter Scott
24 Skibo Castle
25 Newark

Industry 1

1   Linen
2   Aberdeen and Dundee
3   Glasgow
4   Cotton
5   Speyside
6   The Carse of Gowrie
7   Kilmarnock
8   Perth
9   Bell and Dewar
10 Thomas Lipton
11 Taynuilt
12 Tennents
13 Textiles
14 Fochabers
15 A jute mill
16 Clydebank
17 1961
18 Fife
19 Coal mining and salt-panning
20 West Lothian
21 1992
22 1963
23 Guinness
24 Chemical works
25 Dundee

	Sport 1		Television Trivia 1
1	David Wilkie	1	Luss, Loch Lomondside
2	Jackie Stewart	2	*Chewin' the Fat*
3	Alan Wells	3	Nick Nairn
4	2000	4	Richard Wilson
5	Jim Clark	5	The Reverend I.M. Jolly
6	Golf	6	BBC 1
7	St Andrews	7	Ally McCoist
8	Boxing	8	Kirsty Wark
9	September	9	John Leslie
10	Stephen Hendry	10	Sheena Macdonald
11	Colin MacRae	11	*Reporting Scotland*
12	American football	12	Gail Porter
13	Sandy Lyle	13	Sport
14	Willie Carson	14	Andy Stewart
15	Paul Lawrie	15	Plockton
16	Shirley Robertson	16	Edinburgh
17	Liz McColgan	17	Robbie Coltrane
18	Long jump	18	*Porridge*
19	Warrender	19	Glen Michael
20	1999	20	Maggie Bell
21	Gavin Hastings	21	Lulu
22	Stephen Hendry	22	Dr Cameron
23	East Stirling	23	John Byrne
24	She was born in Irvine.	24	Joe McFadden
25	1985	25	Russell Hunter

General Knowledge 2

1 Devorgilla, wife of John Balliol and father of King John Balliol
2 HRH The Duke of Edinburgh
3 Fossil hunting
4 David Wilkie
5 A statue of an otter
6 Mauchline
7 Andrew Carnegie
8 Rab C. Nesbitt
9 Perth
10 Montrose
11 Irvine
12 Prestonpans
13 The Eildon Hills
14 St Mary's Loch
15 The Coats family
16 Humbie
17 The Cathedral of the Isles, Millport
18 The 1960s
19 The Society in Scotland for the Propagation of Christian Knowledge
20 James IV
21 Scapa Flow
22 Grampian
23 95 miles
24 There is a hydro in each of these towns.
25 The Brahan Seer

Poetry 1

1 John Barbour
2 William Dunbar
3 Glasgow
4 Edwin Muir
5 George Mackay Brown
6 Liz Lochead
7 *Poems, Chiefly in the Scottish Dialect*
8 *Wallace*
9 John Davidson
10 Sorley Maclean
11 Robert Fergusson
12 Robert Garioch
13 James Graham, Marquis of Montrose
14 Hugh MacDiarmid
15 Agnes Maclehose
16 William Edmonstoune Aytoun
17 Edinburgh
18 James I
19 Robert Louis Stevenson
20 Robert Burns
21 Ettrick
22 Hamish Henderson
23 Hugh MacDiarmid
24 Norman MacCaig
25 *The Vision of Cathkin Braes*

Wildlife 1

1   *Cirsium vulgare*
2   'Horse of the woods'
3   Heather shoots
4   Mink
5   Red Deer
6   Juniper
7   Goose (in particular, the barnacle goose and the Greenland white-fronted goose)
8   A stretch of low-lying land by the shore, often a haven for wild flowers
9   Japan
10 Loch Garten
11 The 1950s
12 The grey squirrel is larger
13 The Tay and the Spey
14 When the hare is losing its white winter coat and remaining white hairs mingle with the brown hairs of its summer coat, its fur can take on a bluish tinge.
15 In the western Highlands
16 A butterfly
17 Loch Lomond
18 The National Nature Reserve of Beinn Eighe
19 Birch
20 *Pinus sylvestris*
21 The eighteenth century
22 St Kilda
23 The Scottish crossbill
24 The Moray Firth
25 The polecat

The Life & Works of Sir Walter Scott

1   The High School
2   Paralysis of his right leg
3   1803
4   Robert, John, Daniel and Tom
5   Robert Burns
6   Effie Dean
7   Sandy Knowe
8   12
9   The Duchess of Wellington
10 The sixteenth century
11 Ashestiel
12 1814
13 'Old Mortality'
14 The coronation of George IV
15 Jonathan Oldbuck
16 Mons Meg
17 *St Ronan's Well*
18 1797
19 Charlotte Charpentier
20 *Götz von Berlichingen*
21 *The Siege of Malta*
22 *The Fair Maid of Perth*
23 Jane Jobson
24 Two
25 James and John Ballantyne

General Knowledge 3

1 His brother Henry, Cardinal of York
2 It is a museum.
3 St Oran
4 1507
5 MacDonald
6 Old Jock Gray
7 Allan Pinkerton
8 The Dean Gallery
9 1637, St Giles Cathedral, Edinburgh
10 George Buchanan
11 Prestwick
12 He drowned before it was completed.
13 He trained as a goldsmith and jeweller.
14 The Kingdom of Dalriada
15 Greenock
16 The Marquis of Montrose
17 Sir George Mackenzie
18 Preston Mill, East Lothian
19 Ettrick
20 Ayr
21 Duns
22 Edinburgh
23 Edinburgh
24 Scottish Qualifications Authority
25 Michael Kelly

Around & About in Scotland 1

1 Glencoe
2 Buchan Ness
3 Dundee
4 St Machar's Cathedral, Aberdeen
5 St Kilda
6 In the North Sea (they are oilfields).
7 Shetland
8 Achnacarry
9 Stirling
10 Near Pitlochry
11 Blackford Hill, Edinburgh
12 By Stirling castle
13 A waterfall
14 Tobermory Bay, the Isle of Mull
15 Pitlochry
16 New Lanark
17 Cromarty
18 Drumelzier
19 Dundee
20 The Lake of Menteith, Perthshire
21 Murrayfield, Edinburgh
22 Croick Church
23 Wanlockhead
24 Dumfries and Galloway (Kirkcudbrightshire)
25 Rannoch Moor

Music 1

1. The Communards
2. 'Pick Up the Pieces'
3. Frankie Miller
4. Japan
5. Simple Minds
6. Punk rock
7. Glasgow
8. Jim Kerr
9. Lonnie Donegan
10. Lulu
11. Elgin
12. Travis
13. The Poets
14. Annie Lennox
15. *Benny and Joon*
16. Lena Zavaroni
17. 'Ally's Tartan Army'
18. Baker Street
19. Maggie Bell
20. Edinburgh
21. The Sensational Alex Harvey Band
22. Ultravox
23. Jim Diamond
24. Fish
25. 1975

Holy People & Places 1

1. St Margaret
2. St Mungo
3. The twelfth century
4. St Aidan
5. St Giles Cathedral
6. November 30
7. John Knox
8. St Mirren
9. Fife
10. Rosslyn Chapel
11. Culross, Fife
12. St Andrews
13. Eskdalemuir
14. Thomas Chalmers
15. David I
16. St Magnus
17. Cistercian
18. Archbishop Kennedy
19. Iona
20. The Borders
21. John Ogilvie
22. Glasgow Cathedral
23. The thirteenth century
24. Cambuskenneth Abbey
25. The Bass Rock

ANSWERS

ANSWERS

General Knowledge 4

1 Edinburgh
2 Edwin Morgan
3 Keir Hardie
4 a) 1965
5 The Lordship of the Isles
6 The Earl of Mar
7 The National Party of Scotland
8 c) 1969
9 John Reid
10 It was carried from place to place by runners to call clansmen to battle.
11 1746
12 *Doutelle*
13 They were all friends or sweethearts of Robert Burns.
14 c) 1832
15 Eigg
16 1964
17 Durness
18 The pine marten
19 Between Jura and Scarba
20 During the reign of Kenneth McAlpin
21 1297
22 Shinty
23 Chris Guthrie
24 William Blackwood, William Chambers, William Collins
25 John Maclean

History 1

1 1320
2 1951
3 Glenfinnan
4 1567
5 The Ninth Legion
6 James VII
7 1788
8 1460
9 Macbeth
10 Duncan I
11 Macbeth
12 1296
13 Carisbrooke Castle
14 Margaret, Queen of Scotland
15 Fotheringay
16 Viscount John Graham of Claverhouse (Bonny Dundee)
17 1542
18 The fifteenth century
19 1328
20 William Wallace
21 1698
22 The Great Michael
23 Sir John Stewart of Menteith
24 James VI
25 30

Literature 1

1   The *Vital Spark*
2   Compton Mackenzie
3   William Robertson Nicoll
4   Sherlock Holmes
5   Thomas Carlyle
6   Sir Walter Scott
7   James Kelman
8   *How Late It Was How Late*
9   *The Man on My Back, A Year of Space* and *Fanfare for a Tin Hat*
10 Andrew Lang
11 *Dancing in the Streets*
12 'The Author of Waverley'
13 Iain Banks
14 George Douglas Brown
15 *Trainspotting*
16 Alasdair Gray
17 David Hume
18 The eighteenth century
19 Naomi Mitchison
20 *A Scots Quair*
21 John Buchan
22 Ian Rankin
23 Janice Galloway
24 *So Gaily Sings the Lark*
25 Kailyard fiction

Myth & Mystery, Magic & Superstition 1

1   The rowan
2   Morag
3   A devilish creature, associated with water
4   Tomnahurich
5   The Brahan Seer
6   A piece of silver
7   Aleister Crowley
8   To protect the dead person from evil spirits until he or she was given a Christian burial
9   Flannan Isle
10 Thomas the Rhymer
11 It was once believed that witches used eggshells as boats.
12 Black Donald the Devil
13 Findhorn
14 William Graham of Claverhouse, 'Bonnie Dundee'
15 Curing consumption
16 Tam Dalyell
17 Saint Columba
18 A yellow monkey
19 Nine of diamonds
20 Green
21 The Lady of Lawers
22 A selkie (seal) could change itself into human form.
23 When the fairy flag is unfurled in battle, the enemies of the Macleod clan will see twice as many Macleods as there are in reality and the Macleods will not be defeated. (The fairy flag, however, can only be used three times and has been used twice already.)
24 Iona
25 Brownies

General Knowledge 5

1 Peter Irvine
2 Reporting Scotland
3 Mike Russell
4 Sean Connery
5 1947
6 b) The 1920s
7 2001
8 Lochdubh
9 Secretary-General of NATO
10 Edinburgh
11 The Netherlands
12 *Sunset Song, Cloud Howe* and *Grey Granite*
13 Queen Margaret Drive, Glasgow
14 David Murray
15 The Liberal Democrats
16 The 1970s
17 Perth
18 Jimmy Somerville
19 1545
20 John Paul Jones
21 1989
22 William Smellie
23 Earl Haig
24 Jim Wallace
25 Sir Walter Scott

The Life & Works of John Buchan

1 Minister
2 Violet
3 From Pathhead
4 A fractured skull
5 Hutcheson's Grammar
6 His grandfather, John Masterton
7 *Chambers's Journal*
8 Lord Milner, High Commissioner for South Africa
9 *Blackwood's Magazine*
10 *The Thirty-Nine Steps*
11 24
12 Huntingtower
13 1935
14 *The Runagates Club* and *The Thirty-Nine Steps*
15 *Memory Hold-the-Door*
16 Four
17 *Prester John*
18 *Sick Heart River*
19 Alfred Hitchcock
20 'The Pilgrim Fathers'
21 Lord Tweedsmuir of Elsfield
22 *Sir Quixote of the Moors*
23 1916
24 Susan Grosvenor
25 1911

Aberdeen 1

1 Her Majesty's Opera House
2 Union Terrace
3 1963
4 John Smith
5 Rubislaw Quarry
6 Castle Hill, Gallowhill and St Catherine's Hill
7 1593
8 William Elphinstone, Bishop of Aberdeen
9 1983
10 Byron
11 St Machar's Cathedral
12 The Aultoun Lily
13 The eighteenth century
14 *The Aberdeen Journal*
15 The Gordon Highlanders Regimental Museum
16 The Castlegate
17 Aberdeen Joint Station
18 Queen Victoria (statue)
19 'Bon Accord'
20 Dr Fenton Wyness
21 Hazlehead Park
22 Alexander Keith
23 His Majesty's Theatre
24 Harry Gordon, entertainer
25 The Gallowgate

Heroes & Villains 1

1 John Muir
2 1305
3 Dunbar Castle
4 He was killed at the battle of Killiecrankie.
5 Sir Archibald David Stirling
6 He was hanged in London.
7 Thomas Guthrie
8 Dennis Nilsen
9 Matt Busby
10 Sawney Bean
11 David Dale
12 Robert the Bruce
13 Major Thomas Weir of Edinburgh (executed in 1670)
14 Founding Quarrier's children's homes
15 Peter Manuel
16 Robert Knox
17 Madeleine Smith
18 Michael Scott
19 Keir Hardie
20 He poisoned them.
21 Aberdeen (Her family moved to Dundee when she was young.)
22 Eric Liddell
23 John Smith
24 Pringle
25 Elsie Inglis

ANSWERS

1   Oban
2   Loch Lochy, Loch Oich and Loch Shiel
3   Keathbank Mill, near Blairgowrie
4   1783
5   Devorgilla
6   Galloway
7   Glasgow (Buccleuch Street)
8   Wanlockhead
9   Barbara Mullen
10 Edinburgh
11 b) the 1690s
12 David Livingstone
13 Cumbernauld
14 Molly Weir
15 The opening of the new Scottish Parliament
16 Billy Bremner
17 Ceres
18 James Bruce
19 Alexander Naysmith
20 James VII and II
21 The Earl of Morton
22 Deep Sea World, North Queensferry
23 Duns
24 Shipowner
25 Sighting of the Loch Ness Monster

1   Kirkcaldy
2   September
3   A Viking longship
4   The Lammas Fair
5   August
6   The birthday of Robert Burns
7   At Hallowe'en
8   Fort William
9   September
10 Peebles
11 The Borders
12 St Andrews
13 January 11 (the old New Year)
14 April 1
15 The first Monday of the New Year
16 Lanark
17 Glasgow
18 St Columba
19 By climbing Arthur's seat to wash their faces in the morning dew
20 November 30
21 Fastern's E'en
22 Glasgow's Mayfest
23 South Ronaldsay
24 Falkland
25 South Queensferry

Great Scots 1

1 A.S. Neill
2 Nigeria
3 Russia
4 The thirteenth century
5 Hugh Miller
6 Saint Margaret
7 David Hume
8 John Knox
9 Sir Henry Raeburn
10 Bonnie Prince Charlie
11 Katharine, Duchess of Atholl
12 Glasgow University
13 Allan Macdonald of Kingsburgh
14 Edwin Morgan
15 John Comyn of Badenoch
16 John Buchan
17 Alexander Graham Bell
18 George Buchanan
19 David I
20 William Thomson, Lord Kelvin
21 Lord Monboddo
22 Lewis Grassic Gibbon
23 Douglas
24 James Hutton
25 John Maclean

Food & Drink 1

1 Smoked haddock
2 A soft, white curd cheese
3 A sheep's stomach
4 The Arbroath smokie, a smoked haddock
5 Forfar
6 Neeps (turnips) and chappit tatties (mashed potatoes)
7 Barley
8 Beef (shin bone)
9 A loaf baked with dried fruit
10 Hogmanay/New Year
11 Traquair Ale
12 The peat in the water
13 A measure of alcohol (about one pint)
14 The brewery
15 Herring
16 Oatmeal, honey, water and whisky
17 A kind of toffee, made with sugar, butter and treacle
18 Water of life (whisky)
19 A sweet a blob of dark mint toffee, made in Jedburgh
20 A mixture of potatoes and onions cooked slowly in a pan with meat scraps
21 Crab
22 Cranachan
23 Ayrshire
24 Aberdeen Angus
25 Salt

ANSWERS

ANSWERS

General Knowledge 7

1   Dornach
2   The Solway Harvester
3   James MacMillan
4   Belinda Robertson
5   Ailsa Craig
6   Jack McConnel
7   Lord Balmerino
8   Lingerbay, Harris
9   The Royal Observatory
10 15 years old
11 b) 1727
12 The sixteenth century
13 Gavin Hastings
14 Sheena Easton
15 J.M. Barrie
16 Sarah Macauley
17 Topher
18 Magnus Magnusson
19 1937
20 Taransay
21 Psychos
22 The Palace of Holyroodhouse
23 Fair Isle
24 E Coli outbreak
25 Finlay Quaye

Law & Order 1

1   Assault of a person in his or her own home
2   Not Proven
3   1965
4   The Court of Session
5   1996
6   Housebreaking and vandalism
7   Three years
8   The Children's Panel
9   Henry John Burnett
10 Madeleine Smith
11 Saughton
12 Robbery with violence
13 Poisoning his wife
14 The Lord Justice-General
15 They were strangled and burnt.
16 Carstairs
17 Advocate
18 Edinburgh
19 Barlinnie
20 The age at which marriage was legal without parental consent was lower in Scotland (16) than it was in England.
21 Kilmarnock
22 Lord Braxfield
23 (James Burnett) Lord Monboddo
24 Glasgow
25 Dean of Faculty

1   Andrew Neil
2   D.C. Thomson Ltd.
3   *The Glasgow Herald* (and before that, *The Glasgow Advertiser*)
4   The *Daily Record*
5   The 1970s
6   Sally
7   *The Scots Magazine*
8   *The Scotsman*
9   The eighteenth century
10 John Reith (Lord Reith)
11 *The Daily Record*
12 *The Sunday Express*
13 *The Sunday Post*
14 The eighteenth century
15 The Gaelic Broadcasting Committee
16 Television Limited
17 The 1930s
18 Glasgow
19 Glasgow
20 Aberdeen
21 Wark Clements Productions
22 Hazel Irvine
23 Gail Porter
24 Radio Clyde
25 1962

1   John Jeffrey
2   1993
3   Three (1925, 1984, 1990)
4   David Sole
5   1871
6   1879
7   1925
8   George Heriot's FP
9   The Milne brothers (Ian, David and Kenneth)
10 Melrose
11 20
12 Hawick
13 1995
14 G.P.S. Macpherson
15 Inverleith
16 Most-capped player for Scotland
17 Melrose
18 1883
19 Ireland
20 10 times
21 Ian McGeechan
22 Three
23 65
24 Tuberculosis
25 Rob Wainwright

ANSWERS

ANSWERS

General Knowledge 8

1   Richard Holloway
2   The Happy Gang
3   Judge George Mackenzie
4   Angus MacKay
5   For playing his pipes while under fire during the Normandy landings
6   Dr William Hunter
7   Collessie
8   An Teallach
9   The mystery of Bible John
10 Celtic
11 Westray and Papa Westray
12 *Scotland on Sunday*
13 Glen Shira
14 Warmer winter temperatures caused by global warming
15 *The Scotsman*
16 1959
17 *Cracker*
18 Enric Miralles
19 Edinburgh
20 The red kite
21 Gruinard
22 Hely Hutchison Almond
23 Aly Bain
24 Donnie McLeod
25 Sir William Arrol

Architecture 1

1   Charles Rennie Mackintosh
2   William Playfair
3   William Burn
4   Rothesay, Isle of Bute
5   Barry Gasson
6   John Thomas Rochead
7   A windowless one-room thatched cottage
8   William Blackie
9   A prehistoric building, round in shape, with tall sloping sides, probably built as both dwelling and defence for many people
10 David Bryce
11 Robert and James
12 Sir Basil Spence
13 James Craig
14 Donaldson's School (formerly Donaldson's Hospital)
15 William Leiper
16 Scotland Street School
17 A small, two-roomed house
18 William Bruce
19 Sir Robert Lorimer
20 Culzean Castle
21 Queens Cross Church
22 Robert Mylne
23 James Gillespie Graham
24 Thomas Hamilton
25 William Adam

ANSWERS

1   David Steel (Lord Steel)
2   In the despatch box in front of which the prime minister stands to speak
3   2000
4   David McLetchie
5   Winnie Ewing
6   Sam Galbraith
7   53
8   Keir Hardie and R.B. Cunninghame Graham
9   1939
10 1950
11 33 per cent
12 First Minister
13 James (Jimmy) Reid
14 1902-5
15 Sir Alec Douglas-Home
16 Edward Heath
17 John Swinney
18 Mike Russell
19 Iona
20 Transport Minister
21 George Hamilton Gordon, 4th Earl of Aberdeen
22 Andrew Fletcher of Saltoun
23 Jimmy Reid
24 John Maclean
25 Jack McConnel and Henry McLeish

1   The Dundee Repertory Theatre Company
2   Mary Slessor
3   Samuel Bell
4   Camperdown Park
5   Step Row
6   The old Tay Ferry
7   1190
8   Thomas Bouch
9   Queen Victoria
10 The *Terra Nova*
11 The *Unicorn*
12 Mills Observatory
13 June
14 Liz McColgan
15 The Average White Band
16 William the Lion
17 The Arabs
18 1881
19 Mary Shelley's Frankenstein
20 1651
21 The 1830s
22 The Baxters
23 The Coxes
24 The Logie Works
25 Alexander Riddoch

ANSWERS

	General Knowledge 9		Golf 1
1	1971	1	Dale Reid
2	Peterhead	2	William Auchterlonie
3	Glasgow	3	1889
4	Alastair Dunnett	4	St Andrews
5	William Collins	5	St Andrews
6	Scottish country dancing – the Royal Scottish Country Dance Society	6	Loch Lomond
7	Glasgow	7	Muirfield
8	Lighthouse engineer	8	1860
9	Thomas Telford	9	The Royal Burgess Golfing Society
10	The thirteenth century	10	James II
11	Shipping	11	Sandy Lyle
12	The Regent Morton	12	Edinburgh
13	1812	13	Willie Park Senior
14	The Scottish Cooperative Wholesale Society	14	1977
15	Rhododendrons	15	The 17th
16	The National Library of Scotland	16	Muirfield
17	Bishop Wardlaw	17	Dalmahoy
18	James Chalmers	18	Seven (Prestwick, St Andrews, Royal Musselburgh, Muirfield, Troon, Carnoustie, Turnberry)
19	James Francis Stewart, the Old Pretender	19	Gleneagles
20	Greyfriars Churchyard	20	'Young Tom' Morris
21	The first decade of the seventeenth century (1603)	21	'Young Tom' Morris
22	John Drummond	22	1988
23	Leith	23	1931
24	Glasgow	24	The King's
25	12	25	22

Films & Film Stars 1

1 Helen Mirren
2 John Hannah
3 Three
4 Dee Hepburn
5 Danny Boyle
6 Orkney
7 *When Eight Bells Toll*
8 *Comfort and Joy*
9 Knoydart
10 The Forth Rail Bridge
11 Glasgow
12 Bill Forsyth
13 Phyllis Logan
14 The sinking of the SS *Politician*
15 Begbie
16 Gordon Jackson
17 Ewan McGregor
18 William McIlvanney
19 Sean Connery
20 Rob Roy
21 Robbie Coltrane
22 Gavin Maxwell
23 John Gordon Sinclair
24 Miss Jean Brodie
25 *Whisky Galore*

The Borders 1

1 Chambers (William and Robert Chambers were both born in Peebles.)
2 King David I
3 William Adam (eighteenth century and William Playfair (nineteenth century)
4 Melrose
5 The River Tweed and the River Teviot
6 Jedburgh Castle
7 Floors Castle
8 Riverside Park
9 Peebles
10 June
11 A museum
12 Eyemouth
13 Galashiels
14 James Hogg
15 Michael Scott
16 James (Jim) Clark
17 The eleventh century
18 Peebles
19 Five
20 Jedburgh
21 Kelso Abbey
22 Melrose Abbey
23 Innerleithen
24 Dryburgh Abbey
25 Drumelzier

ANSWERS

ANSWERS

General Knowledge 10

1   The 1870s
2   Famine
3   The reign of James II
4   The Black Death
5   For the Glasgow Exhibition of 1901
6   The eighteenth century
7   At a reception in his honour held at Holyrood House
8   The Edinburgh International Conference Centre
9   The 250th anniversary of the Battle of Culloden
10 Kinnaird Head
11 The Marquis of Queensberry (8th)
12 Andrew Wilson
13 Strathclyde University
14 James Mollison
15 Anti-nuclear campaigning
16 The Mull of Kintyre
17 Teaching
18 China
19 Westminster Abbey
20 Twice
21 Harry Lauder
22 Moira Shearer
23 Queen Victoria at Balmoral
24 Keith Schellenberg
25 It was a wartime airfield.

Industry 2

1   Proposals for a gold-mining operation
2   The jewellery industry (silversmiths)
3   1970
4   Sir James Hamilton
5   Publishing
6   The eighteenth century
7   Glasgow
8   Brora
9   Slate
10 Robert Owen
11 1838
12 1897
13 Blantyre
14 Robert Bald
15 Summer (July to September)
16 Drift nets
17 Failures of the potato crops
18 Glass
19 1711
20 1965
21 Mining
22 The 1870s
23 The Bank of Scotland
24 Paisley
25 Glasgow

Royalty 1

1 Prince Charles
2 Robert the Bruce
3 1649
4 Mary of Guise
5 Prince Edward, son of Edward I, future Edward II
6 1452
7 Falkland Palace
8 James IV
9 Anne
10 Malcolm III
11 1561
12 He was killed by an exploding cannon.
13 Margaret Tudor
14 James VI
15 Gruoch
16 1603
17 Charles I
18 1685
19 Son-in-law
20 Margaret Tudor
21 15 years old
22 Anne of Denmark
23 Alexander III
24 Rome
25 James I

The Highlands & Grampian 1

1 The West Highland Museum
2 Eight
3 Lochawe
4 Balquhidder churchyard
5 Loch Linnhe
6 Inverary
7 Scott Skinner
8 Dunrobin Castle
9 Loch Shin
10 It was a spa town
11 Oldmeldrum
12 Loch Moidart
13 Mallaig
14 Fort Augustus
15 Glencoe
16 Dunnet Head
17 Invergordon
18 The Beinn Eighe National Nature Reserve
19 Osgood Mackenzie
20 Pluscarden Abbey
21 The eighteenth century
22 Fyvie Castle
23 King William III
24 Chanonry Point, near Fortrose
25 Loch Quoich

ANSWERS

ANSWERS

	Football 1			General Knowledge 11
1	1975/6 season		1	Vane Farm
2	Rangers		2	The Forests of Caledon
3	Celtic		3	Scottish Site of Special Scientific Interest
4	Sir Matt Busby		4	Eriskay and South Uist
5	102		5	St Kilda
6	There were riots after two drawn games between Celtic and Rangers.		6	Sheep cloned from embryo cells
7	1903/4		7	Cockburnspath
8	25		8	Because of erosion of land by the sea which has destroyed some houses in the past and threatens further destruction
9	1990		9	The Scottish deerhound
10	Manchester United		10	Lulu
11	Partick Thistle		11	1996
12	Hibernian		12	Cranium
13	Kenny Dalglish		13	Wigtown
14	1910		14	David I
15	Jock Stein		15	19 years
16	Clydebank		16	Aberdeen
17	Kenny Dalglish		17	Tommy Sheridan
18	Celtic		18	The comedy character he played, Victor Meldrew, was killed off on television.
19	Alex Ferguson		19	*Scotland on Sunday* and Glenfiddich
20	Blue and white		20	The 1990s
21	Third Lanark		21	Blacksmith
22	The 1940s and 50s		22	The Paddy Meehan case
23	World War II		23	James Thin
24	Hearts		24	King Robert II
25	Falkirk		25	Loch Fyne

ANSWERS

1   Joan Eardley
2   Portraiture
3   Son
4   John Bellany
5   George Wyllie
6   The Scottish Colourists
7   Ian Hamilton Finlay
8   Edinburgh
9   Peter Howson
10 James Drummond
11 Edinburgh College of Art
12 The Glasgow Boys
13 Frances (Fra) Newbery
14 Margaret Macdonald
    Mackintosh
15 Anne Redpath
16 Ken Currie
17 William McTaggart
18 David Wilkie
19 Eduardo Paolozzi
20 In a church in Edinburgh's
    Broughton Street
21 The Glasgow Girls
22 Sir Joseph Noel Paton
23 Dundee
24 A.E. Hornel
25 Emilio Coia

1   Thornhill
2   Greyfriars Monastery, Dumfries
3   New Galloway
4   1988
5   The statue of a ram
6   Langholm
7   Broughton House
8   The twelfth century
9   The cotton industry
10 The River Urr
11 Dundrennan Abbey
12 The River Ken
13 Sanquhar
14 The sixteenth century
15 Whithorn (the Priory Museum)
16 Two
17 Keir
18 Kirkcudbright
19 In the graveyard of the Church
    of St Michael, Dumfries
20 Threave Castle
21 Torthorwald
22 Wanlockhead
23 A hill
24 Stranraer
25 Ecclefechan

ANSWERS

	Plays & Theatres 1		General Knowledge 12
1	Liz Lochhead	1	The 1930s
2	The 7:84 Theatre Company	2	Wetsminster Abbey
3	St Andrews, Fife	3	The 1830s
4	John Byrne	4	Juan Fernandez
5	The Royal Lyceum Theatre, Edinburgh	5	William Armstrong
6	Glasgow	6	The Admirable Crichton
7	Hugh MacLennan	7	The sixteenth century
8	His Majesty's Theatre	8	The eighteenth century
9	Sir David Lindsay	9	The Educational Institute of Scotland
10	Comedy characters created by Rikki Fulton and Jack Milroy	10	Lord Advocate and Solicitor-General for Scotland
11	Russell Hunter	11	The 1940s
12	Hector MacMillan	12	John was William's uncle.
13	Stirling	13	The Nobel Prize for Economics
14	Allan Ramsay	14	Charles Macintosh
15	Tony Roper	15	The Turin Exhibition
16	The Mull Little Theatre	16	India
17	Tom Fleming	17	John was the younger.
18	Will Fyffe	18	Photographer
19	Tom McGrath	19	George Heriot
20	Edinburgh	20	1949
21	Rikki Fulton	21	The Cuillins
22	Edinburgh	22	1977
23	Raindog	23	The Royal Highland Show
24	Sir Kenneth Macmillan	24	Balfour Beatty
25	Sydney Goodsir Smith	25	1291

1 The fiddle

2 Aly Bain, Mike Whelans, Cathal McConnel and Robin Morton

3 Lady Grizel Baillie

4 Cedric Thorpe Davie

5 Thomas Brendan Wilson

6 The Queen's Hall, Edinburgh

7 St Cecilia's Hall, Edinburgh

8 The Scottish Exhibition and Conference Centre

9 1990

10 Alexander Campbell Mackenzie

11 Fiddle

12 Shetland

13 The eighteenth century

14 Glasgow

15 Billy Connolly

16 Edinburgh

17 The Royal Academy of Music, London

18 The Sutherland Brothers

19 'When I'm Dead and Gone'

20 Keyboard

21 Ewan McColl

22 Edinburgh

23 Glasgow

24 Clarinet

25 Kenneth McKellar

1 The Long Island

2 Scalpay

3 The MacNeills

4 1930

5 The Fairy Flag

6 Eigg

7 Kirkwall

8 Craignure

9 Staffa

10 Skye

11 Lochmaddy

12 Golf

13 Oronsay

14 Islay

15 Skye

16 Dervaig

17 Lewis

18 Kisimul Castle

19 Ben Mhor

20 Lighthouse

21 Achamore House Gardens

22 Jura (Barnhill)

23 Brodick Castle

24 North Ronaldsay

25 Sunken German fleet

ANSWERS

Great Scots 2

1   Adam Ferguson
2   Robert Cunninghame Graham
3   Ludovic Kennedy
4   James Hogg
5   Thomas Chalmers
6   Chloroform
7   Sir Thomas Craig of Riccarton
8   Sir David Wilkie
9   *Mind*
10 Engineering
11 William Barclay
12 Jock Stein
13 Jackie Stewart
14 Veterinary surgeon
15 Helena Kennedy
16 Rob Roy MacGregor
17 John Kerr
18 Sir James Murray
19 Science (physics)
20 Chemist
21 The Independant Broadcasting Authority
22 Sir James Young Simpson
23 Hugh MacDiarmid
24 William Ramsay
25 Sir Alexander Fleming

General Knowledge 13

1   St Kilda
2   Charles Marjoribanks, the first MP for Berwickshire
3   Portpatrick
4   Six
5   Stan Laurel
6   Selkirk
7   Cooking oatcakes or small loaves
8   *The Fortunes of Nigel*
9   The 1760s
10 Protection in battle (It is a shield.
11 Coffins
12 A shoemaker
13 Pitt the Elder
14 Colin Campbell of Glenure
15 A Scottish battleship
16 The reign of James III
17 The 1960s
18 By government
19 Edinburgh
20 1567
21 April Fool's day
22 Wallace
23 George Wyllie
24 The nineteenth century
25 Bill Shankly

Strathclyde 1

1 The Cowal Peninsula
2 An aqueduct
3 Cora Linn and Bonnington Linn
4 The Cobbler
5 The Island of Arran
6 Ardrishaig
7 Luss
8 The Younger Botanic Garden
9 Faslane
10 On the Mull of Kintyre
11 Ayr
12 Biggar
13 The falls of Clyde, by New Lanark
14 Glasgow
15 Biggar Gasworks Museum
16 Near Paisley
17 A road (A70) leading from Edinburgh through Carnwath to Lanark
18 The seventeenth century
19 Great Cumbrae
20 Robert II and Robert III
21 Leadhills
22 Kilmarnock
23 Annick Water, the River Irvine and the River Garnock
24 Cumnock
25 Near Bridge of Weir

The Tunes That Made Them Famous

1 Bonnie Prince Charlie and Flora Macdonald
2 Lulu
3 The Corries
4 The Bay City Rollers
5 Robert Burns
6 Harry Lauder
7 Lady Carolina Nairne
8 Andy Stewart
9 Sheena Easton
10 Alexander Ewing
11 Alexander Hume
12 Gerry Rafferty
13 Lonnie Donegan
14 The Battle of Prestonpans
15 The Proclaimers
16 John Grieve
17 Wellies
18 Jarvis
19 Robert Burns
20 Lena Zavaroni
21 'I Belong to Glasgow'
22 'Boom Bang-a-Bang'
23 Jimmy Shand
24 Bonnie Prince Charlie
25 Robert Burns

ANSWERS

ANSWERS

Castles 1

1 Mainland Shetland
2 The Dukes and Earls of Sutherland
3 It is triangular in shape.
4 John Napier
5 Hepburn
6 Kilconquhar
7 The MacDonalds of Clan Ranald
8 As a youth hostel
9 Edinburgh Castle
10 George Heriot
11 Rothesay Castle
12 Niddry Castle
13 Yester Castle
14 Sinclair
15 The ghost of a French maid, burned for witchcraft
16 The Ogilvies
17 The sixteenth century
18 Tantallon Castle
19 Dollar
20 Unst
21 Castlebay, Barra
22 Sir Fitzroy Maclean
23 Threave Castle
24 The Isle of Skye
25 The nineteenth century

General Knowledge 14

1 The Royal Botanic Garden
2 Marjory
3 Lord Reith
4 The 1950s
5 Arthur Henderson
6 Sir David Patrick Maxwell Fyfe
7 Norman Lamont
8 Newark
9 Malcolm III was Duncan I's son.
10 James Mackay of Clashfern
11 The Nobel Prize for Medicine
12 Menzies
13 As a soprano
14 The nineteenth century
15 Tarlair
16 Alexander III
17 David Allan
18 1998
19 2000
20 Gordonstoun
21 Colin McRae
22 David I
23 The seventeenth century
24 Duke of York
25 1918

Literature 2

1   Robert Louis Stevenson
2   Hugh Miller
3   J.M. Barrie
4   John Galt
5   Neil Munro
6   Elgin
7   John Buchan
8   George MacDonald
9   William McIlvanney
10   James Kennaway
11   Ian Rankin
12   Sir Walter Scott
13   Archibald Constable
14   Dr Jekyll and Mr Hyde
15   Sir Walter Scott's unfinished memoir of his early life
16   1767
17   Neil Gunn
18   *Blackwood's Edinburgh Magazine*
19   The 1830s
20   Elgin
21   John Hay Beith
22   Printing (as a compositor)
23   Andrew Lang
24   Maurice Lindsay
25   *1984*

Politics 2

1   Edinburgh Pentlands
2   Dennis Canavan
3   Michael Martin
4   Lady Tweedsmuir
5   David Steel (Lord Steel)
6   Gordon Wilson
7   Secretary of State for Nothern Ireland
8   Islay
9   1987
10   Archibald Primrose, Earl of Rosebery
11   Tommy Sheridan
12   2001
13   Arthur James Balfour
14   Andrew Bonar Law
15   Nine
16   1988
17   One
18   The Scottish Conservative and Unionist Party
19   The Kilbrandon Report
20   Eight
21   1842
22   1989
23   32 (29 mainland, 3 island)
24   1886
25   Scottish Workers Representative Committee

ANSWERS

	Around & About in Scotland 2
1	Forres
2	Cambuskenneth Abbey
3	Oldmeldrum
4	Perth
5	Edinburgh
6	Edinburgh
7	Falkland Palace
8	East Linton
9	Shetland, the Mousa Broch
10	Skye
11	St Andrews
12	Between Loch Etive and Loch Linnhe
13	Paisley
14	A series of locks at Banavie, on the Caledonian Canal
15	Close to Innerpeffray Castle, near Crieff
16	Near Moffat
17	Tain
18	Orkney
19	Gruinard
20	Anstruther, Fife
21	The Shetlands
22	Blantyre
23	Kintail, Wester Ross
24	An ornate summerhouse with a pineapple shaped first floor, Airth, Stirlingshire
25	Glencoe

	General Knowledge 15
1	In the reign of Malcolm IV
2	Newhaven
3	The Battle of Tippermuir
4	The Highlands and Islands Alliance (a political party)
5	Ian Vallance
6	Barlinnie
7	*High Road*
8	Canongate
9	The nineteenth century
10	Lord Gordon of Strathblane
11	Wishaw
12	The Gorbals, Glasgow
13	The Kelvin Hall, Glasgow
14	A record shop (in Edinburgh)
15	The 1790s
16	Edinburgh
17	The weavers
18	Henry Cockburn
19	John Maclean
20	John Buchan
21	Peter Manuel
22	Holy Island, Arran
23	The John Muir Trust
24	Adam Smith
25	1736

	Bonnie Prince Charlie		Fife 1
1	December 31, 1720	1	The fourteenth century
2	1725	2	King Robert the Bruce
3	1735	3	Elie
4	Northern Italy	4	The Lomond Hills
5	1744	5	Leuchars
6	Admiral Roqueville	6	North Queensferry
7	They were the seven men who helped Charles in his period of hiding after Culloden and prior to his escape from Scotland.	7	Pittenweem
		8	St Andrews
		9	Coal mining and salt-panning
8	The Tower of London	10	Culross
9	Lieutenant-General Henry Hawley	11	Glenrothes
		12	Dunfermline
10	Francis Strickland	13	The oil industry
11	Prestonpans	14	The fourteenth century
12	Edinburgh Castle	15	The Scottish Fisheries Museum
13	November	16	Leuchars Junction
14	December	17	The linen industry
15	The capture of Carlisle	18	Falkland
16	1745	19	Near Anstruther
17	Derby	20	St Andrews
18	Five months	21	Lochgelly
19	Six days	22	St Monans
20	1753	23	Alexander III
21	1750	24	Culross
22	Archibald Cameron	25	Earlsferry
23	1760		
24	Princess Louise of Stolberg		
25	Vittorio Alfieri		

ANSWERS

Films & Film Stars 2

1 Sean Connery
2 Edinburgh
3 Robert Carlyle
4 Robbie Coltrane
5 *Four Weddings and a Funeral*
6 Pennan
7 Fulton Mackay
8 Tom Conti
9 Edinburgh
10 Billy Connolly
11 St Andrews (the West Sands)
12 *A Sense of Freedom*
13 Alastair Sim
14 James Robertson-Justice
15 Andrew Macdonald
16 1960
17 Ian Charleson
18 Ewan McGregor
19 Rikki Fulton
20 Will Fyffe
21 1956
22 Stanley Baxter
23 Bill Douglas
24 Richard Hannay in *The Thirty-Nine Steps*
25 John Grierson

General Knowledge 16

1 Lord Reith
2 John Steell
3 Eat it (It is salted gannet.)
4 Soay sheep
5 James I
6 Glasgow
7 Hallowe'en
8 1974
9 The seventeenth century (1690)
10 The Bill of Rights
11 James VII
12 700 years
13 The First Bishops' War
14 The Countess of Mar
15 James III
16 James VII
17 St Kilda
18 Kenmore, Perthshire
19 Glasgow Celtic
20 Madeleine Smith
21 1747
22 Govan
23 The Battle of Solway Moss
24 Robert Fergusson
25 1513

Sport 2

1 Kelso
2 Andrew
3 1987
4 Billy McNeill
5 1973
6 Bowls
7 Kintyre
8 25
9 George Heriot's
10 Prop forward
11 Ayrshire
12 28
13 Sri Lanka
14 1992
15 Bill Shankly
16 1838
17 Stevie Chalmers
18 1928
19 c) 12
20 From Murrayfield to Hampden Park
21 David Jenkins
22 Stewart Grand Prix
23 Cycling (Men's Olympic Sprint)
24 Melrose
25 1935

Around Edinburgh & the Lothians 1

1 John Muir
2 Linlithgow Palace
3 Haddington
4 East Linton
5 The Tyne Water
6 East Fortune
7 The island of Inchcolm
8 Sir William St Clair
9 Newtongrange
10 Penicuik
11 North Berwick
12 The twelfth century
13 Calder house, Mid Calder
14 Livingston
15 The John Muir Country Park
16 Haddington
17 Bothwell Castle
18 Edinburgh
19 Sir Walter Scott
20 The shale oil industry
21 Glencorse
22 South Queensferry
23 The North Esk
24 Musselburgh
25 Mary, Queen of Scots

ANSWERS

1   A toad or frog
2   A crow
3   Spend it: a bodle was a unit of currency.
4   Your throat
5   A short shift
6   False. 'Sic-like' means 'such as'.
7   It means don't worry, don't bother or don't trouble yourself.
8   No. To 'flit' means to move house.
9   Twilight, early evening
10 Idle chatter, gossip
11 Mud, muck, filth
12 Hips
13 Eat it. 'Parritch' is porridge.
14 A slice of cheese
15 False. It is a wasps' nest.
16 Girls and boys
17 No. 'Muckle gab' means big mouth.
18 A mole (blemish)
19 A shoemaker. A 'lapstane' was a stone upon which the leather was beaten to soften it.
20 Yes. 'Couthie' means kind, loving.
21 A broody hen
22 A weave and a rope
23 With a struggle
24 A coin (very small value)
25 Doric

1   James Hogg
2   Rob Donn
3   James Sibbald
4   Robert Louis Stevenson
5   'Sir Patrick Spens'
6   Sir Walter Scott
7   Robert Fergusson
8   William Dunbar
9   Douglas Dunn
10 The fourteenth century
11 Janet
12 A dead knight
13 George Gordon Byron
14 John Barbour's *The Brus*
15 Robert Garioch
16 Tom Leonard
17 The Canongate, Edinburgh
18 Seven years
19 Ian Crichton Smith
20 'Jock o' Hazeldean'
21 William Price Turner
22 Robert Louis Stevenson
23 James Hogg
24 Sir Robert Aytoun
25 'The Gaberlunzie Man'

1   The nineteenth century
2   The eighteenth century
3   Alexander Buchan
4   Newcastle, Berwick, Stirling, Perth
5   Matthew Boulton
6   James Bruce
7   The Scottish Home Rule Association
8   The SAS
9   Kenny Dalglish
10 The Orcs and the Cats
11 The SFA
12 The King's Own Scottish Borderers
13 James V
14 Cockburnspath
15 Commander-in-Chief in Scotland
16 The eighteenth century
17 Berwick Rangers
18 Ayr
19 A riverside plain
20 Perthshire
21 1513
22 Victor and Barrie
23 St Andrews
24 Muriel Gray
25 Queen Street Station and Central Station

1   The Allan Water
2   Loch Katrine
3   Dollar Academy
4   Schiehallion
5   Auchterarder
6   Textiles: jute and flax
7   1297
8   No
9   The River Ardoch and the River Teith
10 Fasque House
11 'The Birks o' Aberfeldy'
12 The National Trust for Scotland
13 Moot Hill
14 The River Tummel
15 The children were eaten by wolves.
16 In Pullar's dyeworks in Perth
17 Ben Lawers
18 St Angus
19 The twelfth century
20 Dunkeld
21 Stirling University
22 Loch Earn
23 William Bruce
24 The eighteenth century
25 The Ochils

ANSWERS

The Life & Career of Sean Connery

1. 1930
2. Joe
3. McLean
4. Thomas
5. He was discharged on medical grounds.
6. 1981
7. Jason
8. Dustin Hoffman and Matthew Broderick
9. 1965
10. Micheline
11. *Medicine Man*
12. King Richard
13. Stephan
14. *From Russia with Love*
15. *South Pacific*
16. *No Road Back*
17. Golf
18. 1962
19. *The Hill*
20. Diane Cilento
21. Malone, a Chicago policeman
22. *Murder on the Orient Express*
23. 1983
24. *Indiana Jones and the Last Crusade*
25. Eight

History 2

1. Viscount Haldane
2. He opposed the British Government's involvement in World War I.
3. Alexander Leslie
4. James VII and II and Anne Hyde
5. 1923
6. 1579
7. She was also accused of plotting against King James VI.
8. James Sharp
9. Queen Anne
10. 1688
11. Mary of Modena
12. Falkirk
13. 1580
14. 1600
15. 1930
16. 1595
17. 1822
18. The Wolf of Badenoch
19. Grantown-on-Spey
20. 1716
21. The police and the tenants of Lord MacDonald
22. 1567
23. 1390
24. Montrose
25. 1503

ANSWERS

1   Jimmy Boyle and Hugh Collins
2   Mairi Hedderwick
3   Red, yellow and black
4   It was beneath the sand and was uncovered after a particularly bad storm blew the sand away.
5   Chairman of the Scottish Tourist Board
6   The 1960s
7   Stagecoach
8   James II
9   A four-pronged spear for catching salmon
10 A breed of sheep
11 Dougal Haston
12 Barbie
13 William Younger and William McEwan
14 The 1970s
15 Mining
16 It was the locomotive salvaged and put back into service after the Tay Bridge disaster.
17 Graeme Souness
18 As a composer
19 Allan Ramsay
20 The 1960s
21 W.Y. McGregor
22 Thomas Telford
23 Edinburgh
24 William of Orange was his son-in-law
25 1842

1   1314
2   The English
3   John Cope
4   1297
5   Cumberland
6   1746
7   John Balliol
8   Bothwell Bridge
9   The Marquis of Montrose
10 The Battle of Killiecrankie
11 Flodden
12 Langside
13 Nechtanesmere
14 Alnwick
15 William Wallace
16 Otterburn
17 The Earl of Mar
18 1263
19 Scots
20 James III
21 1645
22 Drumclog
23 1746
24 1689
25 Rullion Green

ANSWERS

Edinburgh 1

1 Arthur's Seat
2 The twelfth century
3 The Caledonian Hotel
4 The Royal Mile
5 The Flodden Wall
6 Princes Street
7 David Rizzio
8 Mary King's Close
9 The One O'clock Gun, fired from the castle
10 The Edinburgh Military Tattoo
11 On the Royal Mile, in front of Parliament Square
12 Greyfriars Bobby
13 The eighteenth century
14 Portobello
15 The site of Princes Street Gardens
16 A lock-up shop (The Luckenbooths were situated in the Royal Mile, close to St Giles.)
17 The National Gallery of Scotland and the Royal Scottish Academy
18 Every two years
19 The Commonwealth Games, 1970
20 The Fringe
21 Mons Meg
22 At the top of Castle Hill, at the entrance to the castle esplanade
23 'Gardyloo!'
24 Robert Adam
25 The Dean Bridge

Politics 3

1 Edinburgh
2 John Smith
3 1934
4 Henry McLeish
5 1945
6 Foreign Secretary
7 Mining
8 The Duchess of Atholl
9 Holyrood, Edinburgh
10 George Hamilton Gordon, 4th Earl of Aberdeen
11 Alex Salmond
12 56
13 Nine
14 Gordon Brown
15 23 years (1974-97)
16 1938
17 Labour
18 Edinburgh
19 72
20 1997
21 1905
22 John Maclean
23 James Connolly
24 John Buchan
25 Robert Cunninghame Graham

ANSWERS

1 Sir Arthur Conan Doyle	1 Drury Street
2 The Uist Tramping Song	2 1163
3 Matilda	3 1652
4 The vacuum flask	4 'Let Glasgow Flourish'
5 St Andrews	5 Queen Street
6 McTavish	6 Pollok Country Park
7 Sir Alexander Fleming	7 Jail Square
8 Finland	8 1451
9 Three (James V, James VI and James VII)	9 Marilyn Manson and Eminem
	10 George Square
10 Margaret, the Maid of Norway	11 1898
11 Alastair Maclean	12 Glasgow's coat of arms
12 The Cairngorms	13 The Barras
13 The Bay City Rollers	14 Trees, plants and ferns. (The Kibble Palace is a glass pavilion in the Botanic Gardens.)
14 Celtic	
15 Coal and steel (He was chairman first of British Steel and then of the National Coal Board.)	15 Templeton's Carpets
	16 Provand's Lordship
16 Napier University	17 George Square
17 Aberdeen	18 The Museum of Transport, Argyle Street
18 1966	
19 Dundee, Aberdeen, Manchester United and Leeds	19 1988
	20 Kingston Dock, Queen's Dock and Prince's Dock
20 Ardeer	
21 Sir Patrick Geddes	21 Castle Street
22 Montrose	22 The nineteenth century
23 George Forrest	23 Victoria Park
24 Philosophy	24 1990
25 George VI	25 The Citizens Theatre

ANSWERS

Literature 3

1 The Scottish Highlands
2 Scottish customs, traditions and folklore
3 John Scott Haldane
4 William Sharp
5 The Clearances
6 Tobias Smollett
7 Africa
8 *Travels with a Donkey in the Cevennes*
9 John Wilson
10 Dorothy Dunnett
11 Kenneth Grahame's son Alastair
12 Nigel Tranter
13 The Blackwood Group
14 John Galt
15 A teacher
16 Mary and Jane
17 William Drummond of Hawthornden
18 Arthur Conan Doyle
19 *Stained Radiance*
20 Aberdeenshire
21 *The Wind in the Willows*
22 John Stirling
23 Iain Banks
24 *Ivanhoe*
25 Janice Galloway

Rivers, Lochs & Falls

1 The Don and the Dee
2 Loch Lochy, Loch Oich and Loch Ness
3 The eighteenth century
4 Loch Ness
5 Loch Lomond
6 Loch Fyne
7 The Nith
8 The Pentland Hills
9 Loch Achray and Loch Katrine
10 The Almond
11 Loch Ericht
12 Eas Coul Aulin, Sutherland
13 Loch Leven
14 The River Garry
15 The River Devon
16 The Falls of Glomach
17 Dunbar
18 1964
19 The River Spey
20 'On the Bonnie, Bonnie banks of Loch Lomond'
21 Tweed's Well
22 The Lowther Hills
23 65 miles long
24 The River Tay
25 The River Avon

ANSWERS

General Knowledge 20

1   Aberdeer
2   On the Isle of Mull, a tree fossilized by lava
3   Harry Lauder
4   Dumfries and Galloway
5   Glasgow
6   Robert II
7   By Loch Fyne, near Inverary
8   Powan
9   A cache of Roman silver, dating from the fourth century
10 Edinburgh
11 William Collins
12 Andrew Carnegie
13 Edinburgh
14 Douglas Dunn
15 *A Study in Scarlet*
16 St Mirren
17 Andrew Fletcher of Saltoun
18 The Erskine Hospital
19 The Potato Famine
20 Pottery, Kirkcaldy
21 1990
22 Niel Gow
23 Fraserburgh
24 Orkney
25 A racehorse

Great Scots 3

1   David Hume
2   Africa
3   R.D. Laing
4   Saint Columba
5   Dugald Stewart
6   The Douglas fir
7   Alexander Todd (Baron Todd of Trumpington)
8   Mary, Queen of Scots
9   Andrew Melville
10 The 1860s (1868)
11 William Lorimer
12 He was shot by an unknown assailant.
13 John Napier
14 James Watt
15 Japan
16 Bill McLaren
17 James Adam
18 Robert Barclay
19 Law
20 James IV
21 1702
22 Adam Smith
23 1711
24 Hugh Miller
25 William Roughead

ANSWERS

Perth

1   St John's Kirk
2   Catherine Glover
3   The Salutation Hotel
4   Balhousie Castle
5   Sir Walter Scott (statue)
6   The National Trust for Scotland
7   Pullar
8   1814
9   St Johnstone Football Club
10 1992
11 A new bridge over the River Tay
12 Dewar's Rinks (built on the site of the Dewar's building)
13 St John's Kirk (They are bells.)
14 The nineteenth century
15 1559
16 1967
17 The Battle of the Clans
18 James Smeaton
19 63
20 1911
21 Thomas Anderson and Thomas Hay Marshall
22 George Street
23 1623
24 In the River Tay (It is also known as the Abernethy Pearl.)
25 The Kirkgate

Music 3

1   A Gaelic harp
2   *I Don't Want a Lover*
3   Northumbrian pipes are inflated with bellows under the piper's arm. Highland pipes are inflated by mouth.
4   Ravel
5   Scotch Snap
6   Roy Williams
7   The Corries
8   Wordless unaccompanied singing, for dancing
9   Accordion
10 Same home town (Auchtermuchty)
11 Midge Ure
12 Three
13 2/4
14 The Eurythmics
15 Scottish Opera
16 Reels
17 Judith Weir
18 Perthshire, near Dunkeld
19 Kenneth McKellar
20 Piano
21 Wet Wet Wet
22 Andy Stewart
23 Felix Mendelssohn
24 *Scottish Fantasy*
25 The fiddle

1   John Balliol and Robert the Bruce
2   Four
3   Dundee United
4   California
5   The Dee
6   Physician
7   St Johnstone
8   The nineteenth century
9   Dunkeld Cathedral
10 The Clyde Workers Committee
11 David McCallum
12 355 metres
13 Gordon Strachan
14 David Erskine
15 Cliff Hanley
16 Ben Arthur
17 The Edinburgh Commonwealth Games
18 Perth
19 Bartholomew
20 George VI
21 Edinburgh
22 'Via Veritas Vita'
23 Gigha
24 Andrew Carnegie
25 Grangemouth

1   1586
2   Four (one of them twice)
3   The Earl of Moray
4   The Earls of Maitland and Kirkcaldy
5   She was his great-granddaughter.
6   Seton, Beaton, Livingston and Fleming
7   Lord James Stewart, Earl of Moray
8   Archbishop James Hamilton
9   Nôtre Dame
10 1560
11 1548
12 Duke of Albany, King of Scots
13 Glasgow
14 Duke of Orkney
15 The Earl of Moray
16 Lady Jean Gordon
17 Archbishop Hamilton
18 The Earl of Morton
19 Carberry Hill
20 To Edinburgh
21 Langside
22 He was hanged at Stirling.
23 1570
24 1573
25 The Earl of Lennox

ANSWERS

ANSWERS

Stirling

1   Robert the Bruce
2   William Wallace
3   The Wallace Monument
4   The Chapel Royal, Stirling Castle
5   1967
6   The 1750s
7   The fifteenth century
8   The Castle Wynd
9   William Bruce
10 Broad Street
11 The figure of a unicorn on top of the Mercat Cross
12 The 1st Earl of Stirling
13 Gowan Hill
14 Cowanes Hospital
15 James VI
16 The seventeenth century
17 A youth hostel
18 James III
19 The Campanile (bell tower)
20 In the castle cemetery
21 The sixteenth century
22 The eleventh century
23 The Smith Art Gallery
24 The King's Knot
25 St John Street

Holy People & Places 2

1   George MacLeod
2   Blantyre
3   Ellary, Argyll
4   The United Presbyterian Church, St Vincent Street
5   St Salvator's College, St Andrews
6   The sixth century
7   1617
8   St Mirren
9   Eigg
10 St Brendan
11 Greece
12 St Martin of Tours
13 Alan Archibald Campbell Tait
14 St Thenew
15 Bishop Richard Holloway
16 St Cuthbert
17 St Leonard
18 Sir Basil Spence
19 Adamnan
20 Mary Levison
21 The twelfth century
22 Dornoch Cathedral
23 The eighth century
24 Farne Island
25 The 1980s

ANSWERS

Golf 2

1   1973
2   Carnoustie
3   Sam Torrance
4   Loch Lomond
5   2000
6   Colin Montgomerie
7   Lyle Anderson
8   Eight
9   Edinburgh (He emigrated to the US.)
10 The first decade of the twentieth century (1902)
11 Old Troon
12 The 1960s
13 1982
14 Bruntsfield Links (part of The Meadows), Edinburgh
15 Barnton, Edinburgh
16 The Silver Claret Jug
17 The Swilcan Burn
18 Severiano Ballesteros
19 Musselburgh
20 Sam Torrance
21 Mungo Park
22 The old nine-hole Musselburgh course
23 Five
24 The Honourable Company of Edinburgh Golfers
25 Wood

General Knowledge 22

1   Iona
2   Francis, Lord Jeffrey
3   Haakon
4   Railway locomotives
5   The Treaty of London
6   The Clan MacGregor
7   The nineteenth century
8   The Dundee Shipbuilding Company
9   Loch Lomond
10 Edinburgh, Holyrood Park
11 The 1900s
12 c) 67
13 Paper making
14 Publishing, bookselling
15 Oban
16 Near Peterhead
17 Mary Campbell
18 Glasgow
19 Jarlshof
20 1666
21 Thomas Carlyle
22 The 1880s
23 The midge
24 The Royal Army Service Corps and the RAF
25 Three

ANSWERS

	Industry 3
1	Dundee
2	Penicuik
3	Knitted goods
4	Railway locomotives
5	Cotton
6	Paper
7	The eighteenth century
8	The Carron Ironworks
9	Linoleum-making
10	World War II
11	Edinburgh
12	Aberdeen
13	Textiles, woollens
14	George Bennie
15	The Tawse, or strap, once used for corporal punishment
16	The nineteenth century
17	Torness
18	1964
19	Motherwell (Ravenscraig)
20	1986
21	Barr's
22	Petro-chemicals
23	Malt whisky distilling
24	Ayrshire
25	Paisley shawl

	Dumfries & Galloway 2
1	Newton Stewart
2	Rockcliffe
3	The Gem Rock Museum
4	Kirkcudbright
5	Bladnoch
6	Castle Douglas
7	The Logan Botanic Garden
8	Sanquhar
9	James Murray of Broughton
10	Balmaclellan
11	The A712
12	The Border Collie and Shepherd Centre
13	Gavin Maxwell
14	The RSPB
15	Glen Trool
16	Loch Ken
17	Portpatrick
18	Cistercian
19	They are all the sites of Roman forts.
20	Grierson of Lag
21	The National Trust for Scotland
22	Hestan Island
23	The Twelve Apostles
24	The twelfth century
25	Annie Laurie

	Architecture 2		General Knowledge 23
1	Thomas Hamilton	1	Edinburgh
2	Alexander Thomson	2	Coleridge
3	The Thistle Chapel	3	Nigeria
4	1903-4	4	Curling
5	Thomas Tait	5	Saint Mungo and Saint Columba
6	Portraiture	6	Herring fishing
7	Edinburgh College of Art	7	Inverness-shire
8	Four	8	John Stuart Mill
9	Wood	9	James Keir Hardie
10	Edinburgh	10	Juniper and Scots Pine
11	Art Deco	11	Eilean Mor
12	Glasgow	12	Robert the Bruce
13	The seventeenth century	13	The 1960s
14	William Playfair	14	Andrew Carnegie
15	The National Monument on Calton Hill	15	The nineteenth century
16	A copy of the Parthenon in Athens	16	Nancy
17	1909	17	Off the west coast of Mull
18	William Whitfield	18	The eighteenth century
19	Robert Reid	19	Henry
20	Robert Rowand Anderson	20	Grangemouth
21	William Burn	21	By Perth
22	Glasgow	22	Dundas Vale, Glasgow
23	Aberdeen	23	The eighteenth century
24	The Dean Cemetery	24	Glenrothes
25	Aberdeen	25	J.M. Barrie

ANSWERS

Myth & Mystery, Magic & Superstition 2

1   Glamis Castle
2   A poltergeist
3   A dish of salt
4   A healthy, fine-looking stalk and leaves meant a healthy, handsome husband (and a poor-looking one, the opposite). The amount of earth left on the root indicated the wealth her future husband would have.
5   It was believed to cause the child to become a thief.
6   It is inviting death into the house.
7   Thomas the Rhymer
8   Greyfriars Kirkyard, Edinburgh
9   Samson
10 '. . . 'Til May is oot.'
11 If the person was indeed the murderer, it was believed that the corpse would bleed
12 The ghost of a monk
13 '. . . Deil's luck.'
14 Imminent death in the vicinity
15 A mark on a woman's skin which identified her as a witch. (If a pin was plunged into the mark, it would not bleed.)
16 The Battle of Pinkie
17 The sixteenth century
18 Pebbles on the beach
19 To allow the dead person's soul a clear flight
20 It was thought to bring about the early death of the child who was normally the occupant.
21 Mary of Guise
22 Ben Macdui
23 Mary King's Close
24 The ghost of a sailor
25 Glamis Castle

The Highlands & Grampian 2

1   Loch Ness
2   The 1886 Crofters' Act
3   The nineteenth century
4   The fifteenth century
5   The aluminium industry
6   George Washington Wilson
7   Cullen
8   Ben Alder
9   Craig Dhu
10 People hang rags on surrounding trees to make wishes.
11 Inverness
12 Glen Cannich
13 The A82
14 Madonna and Guy Ritchie
15 As an art gallery
16 Oil platform construction
17 Auldearn
18 Herring fishing
19 Red
20 Sandstone
21 The National Trust for Scotland
22 Charles Grant
23 Alexander II
24 Garmouth
25 Banchory

The Life & Works of Robert Louis Stevenson

1 Charles Robinson
2 No
3 *An Inland Voyage*
4 A journey across America
5 *The Black Arrow*
6 America
7 Engineering
8 Law
9 1850
10 *Kidnapped*
11 W.E. Henley
12 Edinburgh
13 Tuberculosis
14 A brain haemorrhage
15 *New Arabian Nights*
16 1885
17 1890
18 Fanny Osborne (née Vandegrift)
19 His stepson, Lloyd Osborne
20 The eighteenth century
21 Thomas
22 *Catriona*
23 Isobel
24 1894
25 Professor Sydney Colvin

General Knowledge 24

1 Alloway
2 Glenrothes
3 The Glasgow Boys
4 The nineteenth century
5 Two (both died in infancy)
6 1989
7 Leith
8 Glasgow
9 Tea
10 The first decade of the twentieth century
11 Historic Scotland
12 Edinburgh
13 Berwick Rangers
14 Augustinian
15 The seventh century
16 Ayrshire
17 David Napier
18 St Monans
19 Four
20 Benedictine
21 Charles I
22 Galashiels
23 The National Trust for Scotland
24 James V
25 He committed suicide.

ANSWERS

	Sport 3		Poetry 3
1	Granite	1	'To a Haggis'
2	St Andrews	2	James Hogg
3	Twelve	3	Robert Louis Stevenson
4	1889	4	Lewis
5	Lanark Racecourse	5	Sydney Goodsir Smith
6	Ice hockey	6	Hugh MacDiarmid
7	Motorcycle racing	7	Sorley Maclean
8	Jackie Stewart	8	Robert Burns
9	Ally McCoist	9	Orkney
10	1968	10	Sir Walter Scott
11	Benny Lynch	11	Leadhills, Dumfriesshire
12	1983	12	John Gibson Lockhart
13	Liz McColgan	13	1920
14	Three	14	Hugh MacDiarmid
15	Stephen Hendry	15	Thomas Campbell
16	St Andrews Rowing Club	16	Edwin Muir
17	Jim McLean	17	Andrew Young
18	Hillend, Edinburgh	18	'Tam o' Shanter'
19	Braemar	19	Liz Lochhead
20	Willie Carson	20	Robert Louis Stevenson
21	Camanachd	21	James MacPherson
22	McLaren-Mercedes	22	Teacher
23	30	23	Hugh MacDiarmid
24	The Royal and Ancient, St Andrews	24	James Hogg
25	Yacht races	25	William Miller

Wildlife 2

1. The adder
2. The pine marten
3. Giant hogweed
4. St Kilda
5. The wildcat
6. Balranald
7. The Bass Rock
8. The Flow Country, Caithness and Sutherland
9. St Kilda
10. The Highlands, particularly in pine forest
11. Purple (with a yellow eye)
12. Caithness, Orkney and Shetland
13. The second decade of the twentieth century
14. The sea eagle
15. The white-tailed eagle
16. The great black-backed gull
17. The tenth century
18. The puffin
19. The gannet
20. Near Stonehaven
21. St Kilda
22. The Sands of Forvie
23. A great skua
24. Beinn Eighe
25. The grey seal

General Knowledge 25

1. Lichen, used for dyeing material
2. The sea eagle
3. Off Shetland
4. A small hamlet
5. Brown and white
6. Katherine Grainger, Olympic rowing silver medallist
7. The Master of Ballantrae
8. Field Marshall Lord Kitchener
9. Hamilton
10. Loch Fyne
11. John Brown
12. The Mull of Kintyre
13. Sir Cameron Mackintosh
14. The National Trust for Scotland
15. Robert Kirk
16. 1970
17. Abbotsinch
18. Three
19. Robin Oig
20. Sir James Horlicks
21. Bruce
22. 1773
23. Celtic
24. Aberlour
25. Lord Braxfield

ANSWERS

ANSWERS

#	Scottish Towns & Villages	#	Royalty 2
1	St Andrews	1	1566
2	Portree, Skye	2	Malcolm and Donald Ban
3	Strontian (strontianite, strontium)	3	Charles II
4	Dundee	4	Kenneth II
5	Ballater	5	James II
6	Macpherson	6	French
7	Glen Lyon	7	Edgar, his brother
8	The River Earn	8	Henrietta Maria
9	Ayr	9	James VI
10	Inverness	10	Lulach was Macbeth's stepson.
11	James Ramsay MacDonald	11	Princess Madeleine, daughter of Francis I
12	Lerwick	12	Annabella
13	Pitlochry	13	Malcolm III
14	Birnam	14	They were brothers.
15	Edinburgh	15	Kenneth MacAlpin
16	Saltcoats	16	Once
17	The Moray Firth	17	51
18	Fort William	18	1612
19	Peterhead	19	They were brothers.
20	North Berwick	20	Charles I
21	Peebles	21	France
22	Gifford (Yester House estate)	22	Alexander II
23	Helmsdale	23	The tenth century
24	Bridge of Allan	24	William I
25	East Kilbride	25	Ermengarde de Beaumont

Plays & Theatres 2

1 Andy Stewart
2 John Home
3 Sir David Lindsay
4 James Bridie
5 Sir Alexander Gibson
6 A butler
7 The Usher Hall, Edinburgh
8 43
9 Edinburgh
10 Tom Taylor
11 As an art teacher
12 *A Wee Touch of Class*
13 Rikki Fulton
14 Tom Fleming
15 The Traverse
16 Glasgow Repertory
17 The Gateway
18 The Edinburgh Civic Theatre Company
19 John McGrath
20 1977
21 Roddy Macmillan
22 The Empire Theatre
23 Hugh Corcoran
24 The Empire Theatre
25 The Apollo

History 3

1 James VI
2 The Darien Scheme
3 1305
4 1941
5 1941
6 Mungo Park
7 Typhoid
8 Skye
9 1582
10 1651 (Charles II)
11 Malcolm I
12 1822
13 Edinburgh
14 1639
15 Robert Campbell of Glenlyon
16 1306
17 David Leslie
18 Katharine, Duchess of Atholl
19 1586
20 1782
21 c) 1729
22 74 per cent of those who voted
23 12
24 1988
25 Aberdeen

ANSWERS

ANSWERS

	General Knowledge 26		Aberdeen 2
1	Arthur Anderson	1	The Maritime Museum
2	Ayr	2	An Aberdeen tea clipper
3	The second Friday in July	3	The nineteenth century
4	Stranraer-Larne	4	Robert the Bruce
5	Kenneth McAlpin	5	Hexagonal
6	Hamilton	6	Aberdeen Grammar
7	Devorgilla	7	King Street
8	The Queen	8	The nineteenth century
9	A statue of the Virgin and Child	9	Robert Stevenson
10	Montrose	10	The Old Tolbooth
11	A prison	11	1644
12	Cairngorm	12	The land for Duthie Park
13	1919	13	The sixteenth century
14	1850	14	The 1920s
15	Islay	15	The Wallace Tower
16	Samuel Greig	16	Webster and Macdonald
17	The 1820s	17	Torry
18	Janet Dalrymple	18	Black
19	1611	19	St Nicholas
20	Berwick	20	Crombie Hall
21	Dutch	21	The nineteenth century
22	Near Lauder	22	Bon Accord Terrace
23	Borrowstounness	23	St Nicholas's
24	40 miles	24	The 500th anniversary of Bishop Elphinstone's birth
25	Barr's Irn Bru	25	Thomas Telford

1 'Some ha'e meat and canna eat
   And some wad eat that want it.
   But we ha'e meat and we can
   eat
   And sae the Lord be thankit.'
2 An oatcake
3 Yellow (It is smoked, filleted
   haddock.)
4 Soft fruit, in particular,
   raspberries
5 Flour, butter and sugar
6 A fruit very like a raspberry
7 Oatmeal
8 Meal made from scorched oat
   grains
9 A flat stone upon which an oat
   bannock would be baked
10 A smoked haddock, smoked in
   the fishing village of Crail in
   Fife
11 Nick Nairn
12 Scotland on Sunday
13 A spherical, striped
   mint-flavoured sweet
14 Irn Bru
15 A Michelin Star
16 Shortbread
17 Brewing
18 1985
19 The Belhaven Brewery
20 Tennent's
21 Nick Nairn
22 Chips
23 Cheese
24 White Horse
25 A variety of potato

1 Cramond, Edinburgh
2 The Forth and the Clyde
3 The second century AD
4 Dere Street
5 Trimontium
6 Circa AD 80
7 19
8 North of the River Tay
9 Agricola
10 Caledonia
11 Septimus Severus
12 Quintus Lollius Urbicus
13 Banffshire
14 Ardoch
15 AD 84
16 Constantius
17 Hadrian's Wall
18 The Royal Museum of Scotland,
   Edinburgh
19 Circa AD140
20 Tacitus
21 AD 84
22 Near Falkirk
23 The A68
24 Vespasian
25 Constantine

ANSWERS

ANSWERS

General Knowledge 27

1   Alexander Melville Bell, father of Alexander Graham Bell
2   David Balfour
3   David Mach
4   1962
5   Miss Anne Cruickshank
6   Borthwick Castle
7   The rules of boxing
8   Birch
9   The 1930s
10   Railway locomotives
11   Burns Cottage
12   Melrose Abbey
13   Lady of the Most Ancient and Most Noble Order of the Thistle
14   St Andrews
15   Ronald Frame
16   James VI
17   Flyweight
18   1999
19   Liz Lochhead
20   Deacon Brodie
21   The Average White Band
22   Aberdeen Granite
23   The Marquis of Bute
24   Alec Dickson
25   Aberdeen

Around & About in Scotland 3

1   Broughty Ferry
2   A lighthouse near Montrose
3   Craigellachie
4   Islay
5   Seven
6   Glenturret
7   The site of Holyrood Abbey
8   Traquair
9   Wanlockhead
10   Dirleton Castle
11   *Ivanhoe*
12   Inchcolm Abbey
13   Kirkcaldy
14   Cupar
15   North Berwick
16   Glasgow
17   Dunfermline
18   Coatbridge
19   South-west
20   The Glasgow Underground
21   Shetland
22   Lathalmond, by Dunfermline
23   Glasgow Green
24   The Church of St Athernase
25   Spynie Palace

1	1942	1	Brahan Castle
2	Charles McLaren	2	Glamis Castle
3	Alastair Dunnett	3	Carnasserie Castle
4	The Mirror Group	4	By Broughty Ferry
5	Michael Forsyth	5	The Castle of Mey
6	*Telfios*	6	St Andrews Castle
7	1992	7	Spedlins Tower
8	Cowcaddens, Glasgow	8	Blackness Castle
9	The Scottish Media Group	9	The Argyll and Sutherland Highlanders
10	*Children's Hour*	10	Blair Castle
11	Characters in a radio soap	11	Cawdor Castle
12	1990	12	The Macleans of Duart
13	Stornoway	13	The Stone of Scone, or the Stone of Destiny
14	Radio Solway	14	Hermitage Castle
15	During World War II	15	Borthwick Castle
16	Skye	16	The Campbells
17	The nineteenth century	17	Floors Castle
18	D.C. Thomson Ltd.	18	Cromwell
19	Aberdeen Journals	19	The Loch Ness Monster
20	The seventeenth century	20	The River Tyne
21	*The Sunday Post*	21	A headless drummer
22	*Mercurius Scoticus*	22	A motte and bailey castle
23	The 1980s	23	Fife
24	Thomson Regional Newspapers	24	St Andrews
25	HMSO	25	Castle Campbell

ANSWERS

ANSWERS

	General Knowledge 28		Glasgow 2
1	Grangemouth	1	Rangers and Celtic
2	St Andrews University	2	The 1930s
3	Raasay	3	Green Hollows
4	The Clyde	4	East Kilbride and Cumbernauld
5	1989	5	Glasgow Green
6	Fife	6	William I
7	Edinburgh	7	Springburn
8	Gosford House, by Aberlady	8	St Thenew
9	The Forties Field	9	1560
10	The Chambers Encyclopaedia	10	The seventeenth century
11	1993	11	An increase in malt tax (and subsequent increase in the price of beer)
12	Weavers, at Fenwick, Ayrshire	12	The cotton industry
13	David Muirhead Bone	13	Alexander McArthur
14	The Blue Blanket	14	The Empire Theatre
15	Dundee	15	The Glasgow Eastern Area Renewal Project
16	*The New York Herald*	16	Alexander Thomson
17	Willie Gallagher	17	Queen's Park Football Club
18	The Royal Geographical Society	18	1964
19	The West Coast train (via Carlisle and Glasgow)	19	1990
20	Methil	20	The Necropolis
21	The Great Upper Clyde Shipbuilders	21	The Royal Concert Hall
22	Donald Dewar	22	Gilmorehill
23	Sir Arthur Conan Doyle	23	William Wallace
24	John Faed	24	St Rollox Chemical Works, Springburn (It was a chimney.)
25	A breech-loading rifle	25	Nelson Mandela Place

Rugby 2

1 Budge Poutney
2 George Watson's
3 Hooker
4 Full-back
5 Finlay Calder
6 Edinburgh Academicals
7 The 1950s (1959)
8 Glasgow Caledonians
9 1999/2000 season
10 1873
11 Three
12 Stand-off and centre
13 1984
14 Sponsor (Famous Grouse Whisky)
15 Douglas Morgan
16 Ian McGeechan
17 1987
18 Bryan Redpath
19 MBE
20 1998
21 Duncan Hodge
22 Flanker
23 A book of rules, the nineteenth century
24 Raeburn Park, Edinburgh
25 Edinburgh Reivers

Scots in England & Overseas

1 Sir William Alexander
2 David Livingstone
3 America
4 Lachlan Macquarie
5 China
6 James Andrew Broun-Ramsay, Marquis of Dalhousie
7 The River Mackenzie, Canada
8 James Bruce
9 Mary Slessor
10 Glasgow
11 Joseph Thomson
12 John Law
13 Alexander Duff
14 Chicago
15 The River Niger
16 Charles Wyville Thomson
17 John Paul Jones
18 Mungo Park
19 Lachlan Macquarie
20 John Hunter
21 He was gored to death by a bull
22 Annan, Dumfriesshire
23 David Livingstone
24 Juan Fernandez
25 Peter Fraser

ANSWERS

ANSWERS

	General Knowledge 29		Scotland's Coastline
1	The Turnpike Trusts	1	St Monans
2	Dundee	2	The Firth of Forth
3	The 1880s	3	Kirkcudbright
4	Henry VIII	4	Wigtown Bay
5	The Declaration of Arbroath	5	Eyemouth
6	Oyne, near Insch	6	Ayr
7	Dumbarton	7	Eigg
8	Partick Thistle	8	Loch Broom
9	Dirleton	9	Spey Bay
10	*Heart of Midlothian*	10	Scalasaig
11	Thread	11	The Bell Rock Lighthouse
12	A reaping machine	12	The Sound of Raasay
13	Malcolm III	13	The Firth of Lorn
14	David Octavius Hill	14	Dalmeny
15	Isobel Johnstone	15	Morar
16	Chemist	16	Montrose
17	William Ruthven, Earl of Gowrie	17	Ailsa Craig
18	Adam Smith	18	South Queensferry
19	The Scottish National Party	19	Tantallon Castle
20	Graeme Souness	20	Catterline
21	William Symington	21	Lighthouses
22	George Walton	22	Turnberry Castle
23	Glasgow	23	Aberlady Bay
24	1846	24	Kirkcudbright
25	July	25	North Berwick Law

1	Viscount Stair		1	Highland Radio
2	1976		2	Dr Johnson
3	1965		3	Abertarff House
4	John Inglis, Lord Glencorse		4	St Andrews Cathedral
5	James Mackay of Clashfern		5	The nineteenth century
6	1747		6	King David I
7	John Erskine		7	The Eden Court theatre
8	Lord Alexander John Mackenzie Stuart		8	The nineteenth century
9	Sir George Mackenzie of Rosehaugh		9	Montrose
10	Murder		10	Dalcross
11	James V		11	Bridge Street
12	Half		12	A stone on which women rested their washing tubs to break the journey carrying water from the river.
13	The 1980s		13	The nineteenth century
14	Glasgow		14	Craig Phadrig
15	David Hume		15	Sir Alexander Ross
16	1987		16	The seventeenth century
17	Antony Gecas, Edinburgh		17	Dominican
18	Peterhead		18	Bridge Street
19	Lord Alexander John Mackenzie Stuart		19	The sixteenth century
20	The 1970s		20	St Michael's Mount
21	Two years		21	The eighteenth century
22	A snail		22	The Town House
23	Henry Thomas, Lord Cockburn		23	Clava Cairns
24	The Lord Advocate		24	Culloden Moor
25	15		25	The 1840s (1849)

ANSWERS

ANSWERS

Poetry 4

1. (James) Lewis Spence
2. William Drummond of Hawthornden
3. Gavin Douglas
4. Robert Garioch
5. Robert Burns
6. George Campbell Hay
7. He committed suicide.
8. William McGonagall
9. Norman MacCaig
10. John Hamilton
11. West Lothian
12. Robert Burns
13. Hamish Henderson
14. 1750
15. Robert Garioch
16. Hugh MacDiarmid
17. Sorley Maclean
18. John MacDonald
19. The 1960s
20. Thomas Babington Macauley
21. Robert Fergusson
22. Allan Ramsay
23. *One Foot in Eden*
24. Edwin Morgan
25. The fifteenth century

General Knowledge 30

1. The 1970s (1977)
2. April 2nd
3. Sharleen Spiteri
4. Forth PLC
5. Two
6. Borthwick Castle
7. As a cure for rheumatism
8. A prison
9. The Younger Botanic Garden
10. Aberdour House
11. Orkney
12. John Logie Baird
13. Oil platform construction
14. Thomas Muir
15. The Kailyard School
16. India
17. Iona
18. William Low
19. Loch Tay
20. Sir Nicholas Fairbairn
21. Berwickshire
22. Buckie
23. Cistercian
24. Inns built on the military roads constructed in Scotland
25. A poet

1   Crieff
2   The fourteenth century
3   Fort of the Celts
4   The River Almond
5   Yew tree
6   The Lake of Menteith
7   Malcolm III
8   Ruthven
9   Ossian
10 Stirling
11 *The Lady of the Lake*
12 Inchtuthil
13 Robertson
14 Canoeing
15 Glenshee
16 Lady Carolina Nairne (née Oliphant)
17 Alloa
18 Near Blair Atholl
19 Whaling
20 Tayport
21 The Stone of Destiny
22 Aberfeldy
23 William Wallace
24 Arbroath
25 The Carron Company

1   Hugh MacDiarmid, poet
2   Marie McDonald McLaughlin Lawrie
3   Mary Campbell
4   Thomas Glover
5   Kirriemuir
6   Dunfermline
7   James VI
8   Colin Campbell
9   James Scott Skinner
10 George Heriot
11 Gardenstown
12 Malcolm IV
13 Canmore
14 Kirkcaldy
15 Jim Baxter
16 Musselburgh
17 William I
18 John Balliol
19 Sir Walter Scott
20 Football players for Hibernian (Gordon Smith, Bobby Johnstone, Lawrie Reilly, Eddie Turnbull, Willie Ormond)
21 Bill McLaren
22 Edward I of England
23 The name given to the 93rd Sutherland Highlanders defending Balaclava
24 Archibald, 5th Earl of Angus
25 George Mackenzie, judge

ANSWERS

ANSWERS

1   Lord Lovat
2   Donald Dewar
3   Scone
4   1565
5   Patrick Hamilton
6   1266
7   1411
8   1650
9   Robert II
10 George Wishart
11 1973
12 James V
13 1560
14 Malcolm IV
15 John Balliol
16 David II
17 The fifteenth century
18 1996
19 Malcolm III
20 The 250th anniversary of the Battle of Culloden
21 Malcolm III and William the Conqueror
22 The Alien Act
23 Edward Balliol
24 A black bull's head
25 1539

1   Sean Connery
2   The USA
3   Archibald Stirling
4   Arbroath Abbey
5   Edinburgh
6   Dornoch Cathedral
7   Dundee
8   Back Walk
9   Forfar
10 The Tay Bridge
11 The Glenlivet Distillery
12 Royal Game Soup
13 Inchkenneth
14 The Hermitage, Dunkeld
15 Garmouth, Moray
16 James V
17 15
18 1998
19 October
20 The Golden Eagle
21 North-west
22 Andrew Bell
23 Cistercian
24 The Treaty of Bingham
25 Floors Castle

Around Edinburgh & the Lothians 2

1   *Kidnapped*
2   The eighteenth century
3   Portobello
4   Granton
5   Thorntonloch
6   Sewage ship
7   Hound Point
8   The nineteenth century
9   Temple
10 The wife of the Marquess of Lothian
11 Rosewell
12 Loretto
13 The Bass Rock
14 Dewar
15 The 1960s
16 Penicuik
17 The Bronze Age
18 Paper
19 Scald Law
20 Penicuik
21 Bathgate
22 The eighteenth century
23 John Cockburn
24 In the Pentland Hills
25 *Marmion*

Sport 4

1   40 lb
2   Scotland
3   Cycling
4   Rowing (eight)
5   The SRU
6   Rodney Pattison
7   1924
8   Aberdeen
9   Mountaineering
10 Curling
11 Billy McNeill
12 Rangers
13 Paul
14 Nairn
15 St Andrews
16 Ice hockey
17 The Ryder Cup
18 The Edinburgh Racecourse
19 Peter Kane
20 The Duddingston Curling Society
21 Ken Oliver
22 33
23 Caman
24 Leather cover over cork
25 0-0

ANSWERS

1 The Seaforth Highlanders and the Queen's Own Cameron Highlanders

2 The Royal Stewart tartan

3 The Royal Scots Dragoon Guards

4 The Black Watch

5 1968

6 The Royal Highland Fusiliers (Princess Margaret's Own Glasgow and Ayrshire Regiment)

7 Edinburgh Castle

8 The King's Own Scottish Borderers

9 The north east of Scotland

10 Government tartan

11 1494

12 The Queen's Own Highlanders

13 The 3rd Carabiniers

14 Fort George

15 The Royal Scots

16 The Argyll and Sutherland Highlanders

17 The King's Own Scottish Borderers

18 Policing the Highlands

19 Cameron of Erracht, Mackenzie of Seaforth

20 Royal Scots Dragoon Guards

21 Royal Scots

22 Thomas Dalyell

23 Perth

24 Hamilton

25 The Scots Guards

1 Queen Mary's House, Jedburgh

2 The Yarrow

3 Queen Victoria

4 Princes Street Gardens

5 The Sutherland Clearances

6 Allan Pinkerton

7 St Enoch Station, Glasgow

8 The twentieth century

9 Skye

10 1966

11 E.E. Fresson

12 Thomas Telford

13 The 1970s

14 Grinding corn

15 Fort George

16 The white rose

17 Robert McAlpine

18 The *Queen Mary*

19 1938

20 1931

21 David Kirkwood

22 Glasgow

23 Scapa Flow

24 The Union Bank of Scotland

25 The Lecht Road

	Heroes & Villains 2		Fife 2
1	'Mosquito'	1	Aberdour
2	John Boyd Orr	2	Samuel Greig
3	Deacon Brodie	3	Cupar
4	Jock Stein	4	The place of the wild boar
5	Bible John	5	The 1940s (1948)
6	Hamish MacInnes	6	The martyrs of the Reformation
7	He was lynched.	7	Fife Ness
8	Sir Alexander Mackenzie	8	Pottery (Wemyss Ware)
9	William Hare	9	The Wemyss Caves
10	Alexander Selkirk	10	Benedictine
11	Lord Darnley	11	Anstruther
12	St Serf	12	John Nairn
13	William Douglas	13	To power the pump bringing sea water into the salt pans
14	Rathlin Island	14	Place of the cave
15	Surgeon	15	Waid Academy
16	Cardinal David Beaton	16	Burntisland
17	Sir James Ross	17	As an RAF fighter base
18	William McGonagall	18	The West Sands
19	Alexander Selkirk	19	The 1960s
20	The Sutherland Clearances	20	Anstruther
21	Sir William Smith	21	James Sharp
22	Robert MacQueen, Lord Braxfield	22	Thomas Chalmers
23	The development of radar	23	The seventeenth century
24	William Wallace	24	Burntisland
25	Kirkpatrick Macmillan	25	Dutch

ANSWERS

Great Scots 4

1 Thomas Carlyle
2 John Leslie
3 James Crichton
4 Alexander Buchan
5 Sir James Frazer
6 Michael Scott
7 *The Edinburgh Review*
8 Geneva
9 *A Treatise of Human Nature*, David Hume
10 George Buchanan
11 Thomas Henderson
12 Geology
13 James IV
14 Adam Ferguson
15 Anderson's College, Glasgow
16 Andrew Bell
17 Ulva
18 Aberdeen
19 Anne Grant of Laggan
20 For burning Elgin Cathedral
21 Kenneth Grahame
22 Francis, Lord Jeffrey
23 Henry Stewart, Lord Darnley
24 Hugh MacDiarmid
25 Thomas Reid

General Knowledge 33

1 To keep the bodies of the dead long enough before burial for them to be sufficiently decomposed as to be no longer useful to body snatchers
2 Brechin
3 The Royal Bank of Scotland
4 1975
5 Longannet
6 Printers
7 Dundee
8 246 (250 to the nearest 10)
9 Keith
10 Staffa
11 Dunkeld
12 George and Margaret Baxter
13 Wanlockhead
14 Pittenweem
15 880 metres
16 North
17 Castles in the Borders
18 Alleged involvement in the Gowrie Conspiracy
19 Edinburgh
20 France
21 Slate
22 Shetland
23 Tarbat Ness
24 Angus Mackay
25 1915

The Islands of Scotland 2	Television Trivia 2
1 Skye	1 Phyllis Logan
2 Arran	2 Hudson
3 Islay	3 Daniella Nardini
4 Ailsa Craig	4 Dougie Henshall
5 Eriskay	5 *High Road*
6 Islay	6 Mark McManus
7 McKinnon's cave	7 Mike Jardine
8 Erraid	8 Sir Jeremy Isaacs
9 The Treshnish Isles	9 Gordon Jackson
10 Jura	10 Andrew Neil
11 North Uist to Skye	11 25
12 Port Askaig, Bowmore, Port Ellen	12 Boxing
	13 John Laurie
13 Lewis	14 Auchtermuchty
14 Atlantic seals	15 Rhona Cameron
15 The 1830s	16 Jack Docherty
16 The fourteenth century	17 *The Beechgrove Garden*
17 Dun I	18 Hannah Gordon
18 Coll	19 *Dotaman*
19 Skye	20 Stanley Baxter
20 The Firth of Lorn	21 *Reporting Scotland*
21 Bergen	22 Mr Mackay
22 The Pentland Firth	23 *Chewin' the Fat*
23 Eigg, Muck, Rum and Canna	24 Aberdeen
24 Harris	25 Gordon Kennedy
25 Tiree	

ANSWERS

ANSWERS

#	Football 2		General Knowledge 34
1	John Greig	1	The *Iolaire*
2	Five	2	The Earls of Wemyss and March
3	Adam Crozier	3	John Buchan
4	1978	4	Tay, Spey, Clyde, Tweed
5	Aberdeen	5	Gannet
6	One	6	The Sobieski-Stuarts
7	1980	7	Multi-storey flats
8	Manchester City, Liverpool	8	Lord Reith
8	1996	9	James V
10	Jock Stein	10	James IV (to Margaret Tudor)
11	1958	11	Traquair House Brewery
12	Willie Ormond	12	St Abb's Head
13	Inverness	13	The A1
14	1972	14	Loch Katrine
15	Dundee FC	15	Braehead, Glasgow
16	1991	16	The Lindsay family
17	Sampdoria	17	Skye
18	1975	18	It must be made from virgin Scottish wool, spun, dyed and hand-woven in the Outer Hebrides.
19	Four	19	Forfar
20	Peru 3, Scotland 1	20	Glamis Castle
21	1958	21	Colville's
22	1885	22	Near Oban
23	1970s	23	1752
24	Dingwall	24	Mull
25	Hibs	25	1896

Clans

1 Niall Og
2 Son of the parson
3 The Borders
4 Dunvegan Castle, Isle of Skye
5 Clan Campbell
6 Mackenzie
7 Campbell of Glenlyon
8 MacDonald
9 Grant
10 Clan Chattan
11 Aberdeenshire
12 Son of Kenneth
13 'Victory or death!'
14 MacDonald
15 Fife
16 'Royal is my race'
17 The Borders
18 Hamiltons
19 Atholl
20 Gordon
21 Kenneth McAlpin
22 The nineteenth century
23 Cameron
24 Clan Donnachie
25 Clan Donald

Around & About in Scotland 4

1 Dunfermline
2 Glasgow Harbour
3 Pictish carvings
4 They are all whisky distilleries
5 Scone Palace
6 The Isle of Mull
7 Maggie Wall
8 Buckie, Findochty, Portknockie
9 Religious martyrs
10 Discovery Point, Dundee
11 Barry Mill
12 Glen Esk
13 Cardhu
14 Crieff Hydro
15 To the south
16 The Isle of Bute
17 Cliffs
18 *Hamlet*
19 The Lighthouse
20 The M9
21 The nineteenth century
22 The Dean Gallery, Edinburgh
23 The eleventh century
24 Robert the Bruce
25 J.M. Barrie

ANSWERS

ANSWERS

Industry 4

1 John Dewar
2 Michael Nairn
3 Keiller
4 The Lady Victoria Colliery, Newtongrange
5 The Royal Bank of Scotland
6 The knitwear industry (cashmere)
7 The discovery of hundreds of radioactive particles on beaches close to Dounreay
8 Edinburgh
9 Amnesiac Shellfish Poisoning
10 Charles Tennant
11 Civil engineer
12 Edinburgh
13 John Loudon McAdam
14 John Brown and Co.
15 Sir James Lithgow, shipbuilder
16 A threshing machine
17 R.S. McColl
18 Robert McAlpine
19 John Law of Lauriston
20 Glasgow
21 John Brown's
22 1760
23 The rise of the textile industry
24 1877
25 Trawling

General Knowledge 35

1 Sir Thomas Lipton
2 The first decade of the twentieth century (1909)
3 1919
4 Oatmeal mixed with boiling water and butter
5 Ragnall, King of the Isles
6 At the entrance to Edzell in Angus
7 Tayport
8 Deep Sea World, North Queensferry
9 Robert Rennie
10 William Beardmore
11 J.D. Fergusson
12 Ethel Baxter
13 Ian and Janette Tough
14 Edinburgh
15 The first decade of the twentieth century (1901)
16 The Royal Scottish Academy of Music and Drama
17 Mountaineering
18 Sinclair
19 The Giant's Causeway
20 Excise officer
21 Mouth music
22 Carol Smillie
23 Gordonstoun
24 James
25 Furnace

Art 2

1   The 1940s
2   David Mach
3   *Man Walks Among Us*
4   Allan Ramsay
5   Charles Rennie Mackintosh,
    Margaret Macdonald, Frances
    Macdonald and Herbert Macnair
6   James MacGillivray
7   Robert Burns
8   Scott Lauder
9   Archibald Thorburn
10 William Bell Scott
11 Galashiels
12 Sir Robin Philipson
13 George IV
14 Glass
15 The eighteenth century
16 Alison Watt
17 Sir William Allan
18 Aberdeen
19 David Allan
20 John Bellany
21 Thomas Duncan
22 The 1930s (1935)
23 Edinburgh
24 Edinburgh College of Art
25 Sir Joseph Noel Paton

Politics 4

1   The Social Democratic Party
2   Bruce Millan
3   Secretary of State for Defence
4   Malcolm Rifkind
5   Monklands East
6   David Steel (Lord Steel)
7   John MacDonald MacCormick
8   The National Party of Scotland
9   Stanley Baldwin
10 1917
11 1989
12 1997
13 Perth and Kinross
14 Govan
15 Helen Liddell, Labour
16 Nairn
17 Liberal
18 James Ramsay MacDonald
19 1995
20 1969
21 Wendy Alexander
22 James Ramsay MacDonald
23 Tony Blair
24 1689
25 Michael Forsyth

ANSWERS

ANSWERS

Strathclyde 2

1. Robert the Bruce
2. Prince Charles
3. Campbeltown Loch
4. Henry Bell
5. MacDougall
6. St Columba (He is said to have landed here.)
7. St Kessog (His effigy is in the parish church.)
8. Loch Creran
9. Loch Linnhe
10. The Levern Water
11. Bowling
12. Dunadd Hill
13. The 1820s
14. Kirkoswald
15. Motherwell
16. Cheese
17. On Loch Lomond
18. Yachts
19. James Boswell
20. Submarine (US)
21. June
22. The eighteenth century
23. The Molendinar Burn
24. Gourock
25. The A77

General Knowledge 36

1. The Scottish terrier
2. She caught the largest salmon ever fished by rod and line in Scotland.
3. The Massacre of Glencoe
4. Ben Nevis
5. The ninth century
6. Chicago
7. Keir Hardie
8. Five
9. Scotrail
10. Four
11. Piracy
12. The Royal Scottish Geographical Society
13. The Flannan Isles
14. Dumfries and Galloway
15. Moira Anderson
16. Serpentine (known as Portsoy Marble)
17. 'The Glen of Sorrow'
18. The Saltire Society
19. Geologist
20. R.M. Ballantyne, writer of children's books
21. James ('Balloon') Tytler
22. The Antonine Wall
23. The M74
24. Ricky Ross
25. John Buchan

Music 4

1. The Mod
2. Edinburgh
3. Runrig
4. Ian Ellis Hamilton
5. Tenor
6. The Bay City Rollers
7. Frederick Lamond
8. Lulu
9. William
10. Thea Musgrave
11. Redford Barracks
12. Lady Carolina Nairne
13. James Scott Skinner
14. Judith Weir
15. Evelyn Glennie
16. John Thomson
17. The sixteenth century
18. Argyle Street, Glasgow
19. 1967
20. Marjory Kennedy-Fraser
21. Hamish MacCunn
22. Learmot Drysdale
23. Sir Alexander Campbell Mackenzie
24. Erik Chisholm
25. The eighteenth century

The Borders 2

1. The A72
2. Coldbrandspaith
3. Hidden treasure
4. Melrose
5. Yetholm
6. The Raid, or Fray of Redeswire, 1575
7. The Lion
8. The sixteenth century
9. They are left-handed.
10. The Teviot and the Tweed
11. Hermitage
12. Hawick
13. Borders reservoirs
14. The Broughton Brewery
15. The St Andrews Tower
16. The Black Dwarf
17. Blue and gold
18. Kelso
19. Abbotsford
20. The Caledonian Railway
21. William Scott of Harden
22. Innerleithen High Street
23. The Bear Gates at Traquair
24. Bonchester Bridge
25. Turnbull

ANSWERS

Literature 4

1. Margaret Oliphant
2. *Coral Island*
3. Glasgow
4. Robert Henryson
5. The 1850s (1859)
6. Edinburgh
7. Richard Hannay
8. Irvine Welsh
9. Neil Gunn
10. Samuel Rutherford Crockett
11. Gavin Maxwell
12. *The Citadel*
13. *Two Men and a Blanket*
14. *Treasure Island*
15. Alasdair Gray
16. Thomas Carlyle
17. Singapore
18. Hugh MacDiarmid
19. Compton Mackenzie
20. Carl MacDougall
21. Lord Auchinleck
22. 1997
23. John Buchan
24. Robin Jenkins
25. John MacDougall Hay

General Knowledge 37

1. 1296
2. A decorated wooden and metal box (dating from the eighth century)
3. Galloway Forest Park
4. Jimmy Shand
5. The Burning of the Clavie
6. Sutherland
7. Eaglesham
8. Jocky Wilson
9. 37
10. The Balmoral
11. The Boer War
12. Stirlingshire (near Airth)
13. 1999
14. Fish
15. Milngavie, Fort William
16. Weaver
17. St Andrews
18. Glen Prosen
19. Singer
20. A mining accident
21. The Royal Company of Archers
22. Through his mother
23. Isobel Blair
24. Eyemouth
25. A cat (called Tommy)

Travel	Scottish Women

#	Travel		Scottish Women
1	1897	1	She worked in a jute mill.
2	The A70	2	Kinross and Perthshire
3	Caledonian MacBrayne	3	Mary Garden
4	b) 18 years	4	Dame Muriel Spark
5	The Union Canal	5	Elsie Inglis
6	Princes Street Station	6	10,000 metres
7	29	7	She disguised herself as a man, and was known throughout her career as James Barry.
8	The Forth and Clyde Canal		
9	1890	8	She was an art teacher.
10	Dunbar	9	1979
11	Suspension	10	Scottish Secretary
12	1842	11	Hannah Gordon
13	Leuchars Junction	12	Hockey
14	Prestwick	13	Judith Weir
15	Shetland (Mainland)	14	Three
16	Glasgow, 1962	15	Dave Stewart
17	Cockbridge to Tomintoul	16	Ena Baxter
18	Across the Kintyre Peninsula, from Ardrishaig to Crinan	17	Glasgow
		18	Jenny Geddes
19	A74	19	Elizabeth Blackadder
20	Ayrshire	20	1965
21	Glenshee	21	Tibbie Shiel
22	Cramond	22	Lary Carolina Nairne
23	The Kincardine Bridge	23	Deborah Kerr
24	John o' Groats	24	The thirteenth century (1251)
25	The 1870s (1879)	25	Myrtle Lillias Simpson

ANSWERS

1 The Rocket
2 1875
3 Robert Stevenson
4 A pneumatic tyre
5 James Watt
6 John Rennie senior and John Rennie junior
7 1757
8 John Dunlop
9 James Watt
10 The kaleidoscope
11 William Murdock
12 Kirkpatrick Macmillan
13 Bleaching powder
14 Four feet eight and a half inches
15 James Young
16 Thomas Nelson
17 The Roslin Institute, Penicuik
18 Lord Kelvin
19 The paddle-steamer built by William Symington
20 John Kerr
21 Professor Ian Wilmut
22 It was created from a frozen calf embryo, defrosted and implanted in a 'surrogate mother' cow.
23 1926
24 The Ultrasound scanning machine
25 Robert Stein

1 Jock Stein
2 John Hunter
3 The steam hammer
4 Twice
5 India
6 The 'finnan haddie'
7 Loch Eriboll
8 Prince Charles
9 Dmitri Shostakovich
10 Edinburgh Castle
11 Near Kirkcaldy in Fife
12 The Shetland Islands
13 Ships (on the Clyde)
14 Hugh Clapperton
15 The Dukes of Hamilton
16 Belhaven
17 Twice
18 Aviemore, Kingussie, Pitlochry
19 James VI
20 April
21 The haggis
22 1987
23 Robert the Bruce and William Wallace
24 Manchester
25 Denmark

Where Were They Born?

1   Kirkcaldy, Fife
2   Largo, Fife
3   Inverary, Argyll
4   Haddington, East Lothian
5   Turberry, Ayrshire
6   Linlithgow Palace
7   Perth
8   Glasgow
9   Lossiemouth, Morayshire
10 Culross, Fife
11 Kirkcaldy, Fife
12 Edinburgh
13 South Uist
14 Edinburgh
15 Blantyre, Lanarkshire
16 Bathgate, West Lothian
17 Edinburgh
18 Glasgow
19 Glasgow
20 Kirriemuir, Angus
21 Haddington, East Lothian
22 Edinburgh Castle
23 Edinburgh
24 Langholm, Dumfriesshire
25 Dunfermline

Edinburgh 2

1   Corstorphine
2   Craigleith Quarry
3   Turnhouse
4   Edinburgh, Heriot-Watt, Napier
5   The Water of Leith, Stockbridge
6   Patrick Geddes
7   Hanover Street
8   St Andrew Square
9   The City of Edinburgh Council
10 New College, the Mound
11 Little France
12 1999
13 The centenary of the birth of Sir Walter Scott
14 The Water of Leith
15 The Canongate Kirkyard
16 Melville College (later merged with Daniel Stewart's College to form Daniel Stewart's and Melville College)
17 Juniper Green and Balerno
18 The Playhouse
19 Queen Street
20 The twentieth century
21 The Scottish National Gallery of Modern Art
22 James Milne
23 Brewer
24 Meal milling
25 Sciennes Hill House

ANSWERS

ANSWERS

	Medicine in Scotland		General Knowledge 39
1	Sir Alexander Fleming	1	Skye and Rhum
2	Provost George Drummond	2	The A846
3	John and William Hunter	3	1951
4	Obstetrics	4	Plump, comely
5	Aberdeen	5	Michael Caine
6	Sir David Bruce	6	10 miles (12)
7	Sir William Boog Leishman	7	Prince Charles
8	Sir Patrick Manson	8	The Cuillins (South Cuillin)
9	Glasgow	9	Dornoch
10	1867	10	Eriskay
11	John James Macleod	11	They had not registered their school badges as coats of arms.
12	Alan Archibald Campbell Swinton	12	Kenneth MacAlpin
13	Neuropathology	13	The National Trust for Scotland
14	Bone grafts	14	Fountainbridge
15	Psychiatry	15	Mary, Queen of Scots
16	Dunfermline	16	Deacon Blue
17	Maternity (The Glasgow Royal Maternity Hospital)	17	They are all formed from volcanic rock.
18	The Elsie Inglis Hospital	18	Young Lochinvar
19	Bruntsfield Hospital	19	Christmas
20	James Lind	20	Aberdeen
21	The 1860s	21	The second decade of the twentieth century (1913)
22	The 1990s	22	James II (The Lion was the name of the cannon that exploded causing his death.)
23	Dugald Baird		
24	Robert Liston	23	James Stewart, Earl of Moray
25	James Young Simpson	24	Kvaerner
		25	Aberdeen

Mountains & Hills

1   Loch Maree
2   A mountain over 3,000 feet in height
3   Ben Macdui
4   Kintail
5   Ben Ledi
6   Lochnagar
7   The Cairngorms
8   Arran
9   Ben MacDuibh
10 The Campsie Fells
11 Ben Hope
12 Beside Loch Earn
13 Big Hill
14 Loch Tay
15 Suilven
16 The Cairngorms
17 The Grampians
18 Ben MacDuibh
19 Sgurr Alasdair
20 The Great Glen
21 Schiehallion
22 Drumochter Pass
23 Torridon
24 Easter Ross
25 The Great Shepherd of Etive

Whisky

1   The fifteenth century
2   1917
3   The Scotch Whisky Association
4   A Sikes Hydrometer
5   The nineteenth century
6   By drying the grains
7   A pot still
8   Islay
9   Orkney
10 A mash tun
11 Dufftown
12 The 1870s
13 American Prohibition
14 A mixture of malt and grain whiskies
15 Islay
16 Wort
17 Johnnie Walker
18 Bell's
19 East Lothian
20 Morayshire (Craigellachie)
21 No. The legal definition of Scotch whisky is whisky distilled in Scotland
22 1914
23 Producing industrial alcohol
24 Macallan
25 c) 1 billion

ANSWERS

ANSWERS

Dundee 2

1. Lord Cockburn
2. The tower
3. Dundee University
4. The first Tay Bridge
5. The sixteenth century
6. The Cowgate
7. D.C. Thomson Ltd.
8. The Okhai brothers
9. The 1920s
10. Alexander Riddoch
11. The Kail Kirk
12. Octagonal
13. 1922
14. 46
15. The 1830s
16. Tay Street
17. High Street
18. Ninewells Hospital
19. HM the Queen Mother
20. The 1980s
21. The 1930s
22. 1839
23. 600 feet
24. The nineteenth century
25. 1986

The Life & Works of Robert Burns

1. James MacPherson, hanged in Banff
2. William Burness
3. Auchamore, by Dunoon
4. 21
5. Mrs Robert Cumming (Lesley Baillie)
6. Lochlea
7. John Davidson
8. Ellisland
9. 1796
10. 1784
11. His sister
12. His son, William
13. William Fisher
14. R. (Robert) Aitken, Esq.
15. Charlotte Stuart, daughter of Bonnie Prince Charlie
16. Greenock
17. William Peebles
18. Agnes Brown
19. Jamaica
20. As an excise officer
21. Elizabeth Paton
22. 1790
23. 17867
24. *Scots Musical Museum*
25. Mossgiel

1 10,000 m
2 Four
3 The first century AD
4 Midwife
5 Arran
6 The United Burghs of Kilrenny, Anstruther Easter and Anstruther Wester
7 John Buchan
8 1299
9 The Scottish Rugby Union
10 The Culbin Sands
11 Norway
12 Loch Ness
13 Loch Lomond, The Trossachs and Cairngorm
14 North
15 George Gordon, Lord Byron
16 Tannochbrae
17 *The Blue Fairy Book*
18 An increase in the malt tax
19 James Ramsay MacDonald
20 Skiing
21 January 6
22 Lunan Bay
23 Troon
24 Patrick Allan-Fraser
25 1901

ANSWERS